Mometrix
TEST PREPARATION

ACE

hemistry

ecrets Study Guide

Dear Future Exam Success Story

First of all, **THANK YOU** for purchasing Mometrix study materials!

Second, congratulations! You are one of the few determined test-takers who are committed to doing whatever it takes to excel on your exam. **You have come to the right place.** We developed these study materials with one goal in mind: to deliver you the information you need in a format that's concise and easy to use.

In addition to optimizing your guide for the content of the test, we've outlined our recommended steps for breaking down the preparation process into small, attainable goals so you can make sure you stay on track.

We've also analyzed the entire test-taking process, identifying the most common pitfalls and showing how you can overcome them and be ready for any curveball the test throws you.

Standardized testing is one of the biggest obstacles on your road to success, which only increases the importance of doing well in the high-pressure, high-stakes environment of test day. Your results on this test could have a significant impact on your future, and this guide provides the information and practical advice to help you achieve your full potential on test day.

Your success is our success

We would love to hear from you! If you would like to share the story of your exam success or if you have any questions or comments in regard to our products, please contact us at **800-673-8175** or **support@mometrix.com**.

Thanks again for your business and we wish you continued success!

Sincerely,
The Mometrix Test Preparation Team

Need more help? Check out our flashcards at:
http://MometrixFlashcards.com/GACE

Written and edited by the Mometrix Exam Secrets Test Prep Team
Printed in the United States of America

TABLE OF CONTENTS

Introduction

Thank you for purchasing this resource! You have made the choice to prepare yourself for a test that could have a huge impact on your future, and this guide is designed to help you be fully ready for test day. Obviously, it's important to have a solid understanding of the test material, but you also need to be prepared for the unique environment and stressors of the test, so that you can perform to the best of your abilities.

For this purpose, the first section that appears in this guide is the **Secret Keys**. We've devoted countless hours to meticulously researching what works and what doesn't, and we've boiled down our findings to the five most impactful steps you can take to improve your performance on the test. We start at the beginning with study planning and move through the preparation process, all the way to the testing strategies that will help you get the most out of what you know when you're finally sitting in front of the test.

We recommend that you start preparing for your test as far in advance as possible. However, if you've bought this guide as a last-minute study resource and only have a few days before your test, we recommend that you skip over the first two Secret Keys since they address a long-term study plan.

If you struggle with **test anxiety**, we strongly encourage you to check out our recommendations for how you can overcome it. Test anxiety is a formidable foe, but it can be beaten, and we want to make sure you have the tools you need to defeat it.

Secret Key #1 – Plan Big, Study Small

There's a lot riding on your performance. If you want to ace this test, you're going to need to keep your skills sharp and the material fresh in your mind. You need a plan that lets you review everything you need to know while still fitting in your schedule. We'll break this strategy down into three categories.

Information Organization

Start with the information you already have: the official test outline. From this, you can make a complete list of all the concepts you need to cover before the test. Organize these concepts into groups that can be studied together, and create a list of any related vocabulary you need to learn so you can brush up on any difficult terms. You'll want to keep this vocabulary list handy once you actually start studying since you may need to add to it along the way.

Time Management

Once you have your set of study concepts, decide how to spread them out over the time you have left before the test. Break your study plan into small, clear goals so you have a manageable task for each day and know exactly what you're doing. Then just focus on one small step at a time. When you manage your time this way, you don't need to spend hours at a time studying. Studying a small block of content for a short period each day helps you retain information better and avoid stressing over how much you have left to do. You can relax knowing that you have a plan to cover everything in time. In order for this strategy to be effective though, you have to start studying early and stick to your schedule. Avoid the exhaustion and futility that comes from last-minute cramming!

Study Environment

The environment you study in has a big impact on your learning. Studying in a coffee shop, while probably more enjoyable, is not likely to be as fruitful as studying in a quiet room. It's important to keep distractions to a minimum. You're only planning to study for a short block of time, so make the most of it. Don't pause to check your phone or get up to find a snack. It's also important to **avoid multitasking**. Research has consistently shown that multitasking will make your studying dramatically less effective. Your study area should also be comfortable and well-lit so you don't have the distraction of straining your eyes or sitting on an uncomfortable chair.

The time of day you study is also important. You want to be rested and alert. Don't wait until just before bedtime. Study when you'll be most likely to comprehend and remember. Even better, if you know what time of day your test will be, set that time aside for study. That way your brain will be used to working on that subject at that specific time and you'll have a better chance of recalling information.

Finally, it can be helpful to team up with others who are studying for the same test. Your actual studying should be done in as isolated an environment as possible, but the work of organizing the information and setting up the study plan can be divided up. In between study sessions, you can discuss with your teammates the concepts that you're all studying and quiz each other on the details. Just be sure that your teammates are as serious about the test as you are. If you find that your study time is being replaced with social time, you might need to find a new team.

Secret Key #2 – Make Your Studying Count

You're devoting a lot of time and effort to preparing for this test, so you want to be absolutely certain it will pay off. This means doing more than just reading the content and hoping you can remember it on test day. It's important to make every minute of study count. There are two main areas you can focus on to make your studying count.

Retention

It doesn't matter how much time you study if you can't remember the material. You need to make sure you are retaining the concepts. To check your retention of the information you're learning, try recalling it at later times with minimal prompting. Try carrying around flashcards and glance at one or two from time to time or ask a friend who's also studying for the test to quiz you.

To enhance your retention, look for ways to put the information into practice so that you can apply it rather than simply recalling it. If you're using the information in practical ways, it will be much easier to remember. Similarly, it helps to solidify a concept in your mind if you're not only reading it to yourself but also explaining it to someone else. Ask a friend to let you teach them about a concept you're a little shaky on (or speak aloud to an imaginary audience if necessary). As you try to summarize, define, give examples, and answer your friend's questions, you'll understand the concepts better and they will stay with you longer. Finally, step back for a big picture view and ask yourself how each piece of information fits with the whole subject. When you link the different concepts together and see them working together as a whole, it's easier to remember the individual components.

Finally, practice showing your work on any multi-step problems, even if you're just studying. Writing out each step you take to solve a problem will help solidify the process in your mind, and you'll be more likely to remember it during the test.

Modality

Modality simply refers to the means or method by which you study. Choosing a study modality that fits your own individual learning style is crucial. No two people learn best in exactly the same way, so it's important to know your strengths and use them to your advantage.

For example, if you learn best by visualization, focus on visualizing a concept in your mind and draw an image or a diagram. Try color-coding your notes, illustrating them, or creating symbols that will trigger your mind to recall a learned concept. If you learn best by hearing or discussing information, find a study partner who learns the same way or read aloud to yourself. Think about how to put the information in your own words. Imagine that you are giving a lecture on the topic and record yourself so you can listen to it later.

For any learning style, flashcards can be helpful. Organize the information so you can take advantage of spare moments to review. Underline key words or phrases. Use different colors for different categories. Mnemonic devices (such as creating a short list in which every item starts with the same letter) can also help with retention. Find what works best for you and use it to store the information in your mind most effectively and easily.

Secret Key #3 – Practice the Right Way

Your success on test day depends not only on how many hours you put into preparing, but also on whether you prepared the right way. It's good to check along the way to see if your studying is paying off. One of the most effective ways to do this is by taking practice tests to evaluate your progress. Practice tests are useful because they show exactly where you need to improve. Every time you take a practice test, pay special attention to these three groups of questions:

- The questions you got wrong
- The questions you had to guess on, even if you guessed right
- The questions you found difficult or slow to work through

This will show you exactly what your weak areas are, and where you need to devote more study time. Ask yourself why each of these questions gave you trouble. Was it because you didn't understand the material? Was it because you didn't remember the vocabulary? Do you need more repetitions on this type of question to build speed and confidence? Dig into those questions and figure out how you can strengthen your weak areas as you go back to review the material.

Additionally, many practice tests have a section explaining the answer choices. It can be tempting to read the explanation and think that you now have a good understanding of the concept. However, an explanation likely only covers part of the question's broader context. Even if the explanation makes perfect sense, **go back and investigate** every concept related to the question until you're positive you have a thorough understanding.

As you go along, keep in mind that the practice test is just that: practice. Memorizing these questions and answers will not be very helpful on the actual test because it is unlikely to have any of the same exact questions. If you only know the right answers to the sample questions, you won't be prepared for the real thing. **Study the concepts** until you understand them fully, and then you'll be able to answer any question that shows up on the test.

It's important to wait on the practice tests until you're ready. If you take a test on your first day of study, you may be overwhelmed by the amount of material covered and how much you need to learn. Work up to it gradually.

On test day, you'll need to be prepared for answering questions, managing your time, and using the test-taking strategies you've learned. It's a lot to balance, like a mental marathon that will have a big impact on your future. Like training for a marathon, you'll need to start slowly and work your way up. When test day arrives, you'll be ready.

Start with the strategies you've read in the first two Secret Keys—plan your course and study in the way that works best for you. If you have time, consider using multiple study resources to get different approaches to the same concepts. It can be helpful to see difficult concepts from more than one angle. Then find a good source for practice tests. Many times, the test website will suggest potential study resources or provide sample tests.

Practice Test Strategy

If you're able to find at least three practice tests, we recommend this strategy:

Untimed and Open-Book Practice

Take the first test with no time constraints and with your notes and study guide handy. Take your time and focus on applying the strategies you've learned.

Timed and Open-Book Practice

Take the second practice test open-book as well, but set a timer and practice pacing yourself to finish in time.

Timed and Closed-Book Practice

Take any other practice tests as if it were test day. Set a timer and put away your study materials. Sit at a table or desk in a quiet room, imagine yourself at the testing center, and answer questions as quickly and accurately as possible.

Keep repeating timed and closed-book tests on a regular basis until you run out of practice tests or it's time for the actual test. Your mind will be ready for the schedule and stress of test day, and you'll be able to focus on recalling the material you've learned.

Secret Key #4 – Pace Yourself

Once you're fully prepared for the material on the test, your biggest challenge on test day will be managing your time. Just knowing that the clock is ticking can make you panic even if you have plenty of time left. Work on pacing yourself so you can build confidence against the time constraints of the exam. Pacing is a difficult skill to master, especially in a high-pressure environment, so **practice is vital**.

Set time expectations for your pace based on how much time is available. For example, if a section has 60 questions and the time limit is 30 minutes, you know you have to average 30 seconds or less per question in order to answer them all. Although 30 seconds is the hard limit, set 25 seconds per question as your goal, so you reserve extra time to spend on harder questions. When you budget extra time for the harder questions, you no longer have any reason to stress when those questions take longer to answer.

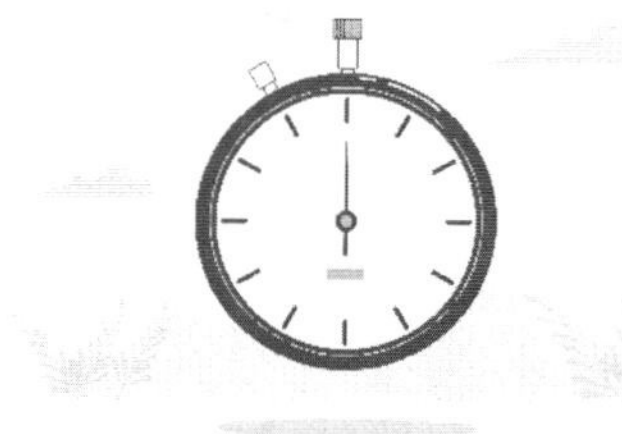

Don't let this time expectation distract you from working through the test at a calm, steady pace, but keep it in mind so you don't spend too much time on any one question. Recognize that taking extra time on one question you don't understand may keep you from answering two that you do understand later in the test. If your time limit for a question is up and you're still not sure of the answer, mark it and move on, and come back to it later if the time and the test format allow. If the testing format doesn't allow you to return to earlier questions, just make an educated guess; then put it out of your mind and move on.

On the easier questions, be careful not to rush. It may seem wise to hurry through them so you have more time for the challenging ones, but it's not worth missing one if you know the concept and just didn't take the time to read the question fully. Work efficiently but make sure you understand the question and have looked at all of the answer choices, since more than one may seem right at first.

Even if you're paying attention to the time, you may find yourself a little behind at some point. You should speed up to get back on track, but do so wisely. Don't panic; just take a few seconds less on each question until you're caught up. Don't guess without thinking, but do look through the answer choices and eliminate any you know are wrong. If you can get down to two choices, it is often worthwhile to guess from those. Once you've chosen an answer, move on and don't dwell on any that you skipped or had to hurry through. If a question was taking too long, chances are it was one of the harder ones, so you weren't as likely to get it right anyway.

On the other hand, if you find yourself getting ahead of schedule, it may be beneficial to slow down a little. The more quickly you work, the more likely you are to make a careless mistake that will affect your score. You've budgeted time for each question, so don't be afraid to spend that time. Practice an efficient but careful pace to get the most out of the time you have.

Secret Key #5 – Have a Plan for Guessing

When you're taking the test, you may find yourself stuck on a question. Some of the answer choices seem better than others, but you don't see the one answer choice that is obviously correct. What do you do?

The scenario described above is very common, yet most test takers have not effectively prepared for it. Developing and practicing a plan for guessing may be one of the single most effective uses of your time as you get ready for the exam.

In developing your plan for guessing, there are three questions to address:

- When should you start the guessing process?
- How should you narrow down the choices?
- Which answer should you choose?

When to Start the Guessing Process

Unless your plan for guessing is to select C every time (which, despite its merits, is not what we recommend), you need to leave yourself enough time to apply your answer elimination strategies. Since you have a limited amount of time for each question, that means that if you're going to give yourself the best shot at guessing correctly, you have to decide quickly whether or not you will guess.

Of course, the best-case scenario is that you don't have to guess at all, so first, see if you can answer the question based on your knowledge of the subject and basic reasoning skills. Focus on the key words in the question and try to jog your memory of related topics. Give yourself a chance to bring the knowledge to mind, but once you realize that you don't have (or you can't access) the knowledge you need to answer the question, it's time to start the guessing process.

It's almost always better to start the guessing process too early than too late. It only takes a few seconds to remember something and answer the question from knowledge. Carefully eliminating wrong answer choices takes longer. Plus, going through the process of eliminating answer choices can actually help jog your memory.

Summary: Start the guessing process as soon as you decide that you can't answer the question based on your knowledge.

How to Narrow Down the Choices

The next chapter in this book (**Test-Taking Strategies**) includes a wide range of strategies for how to approach questions and how to look for answer choices to eliminate. You will definitely want to read those carefully, practice them, and figure out which ones work best for you. Here though, we're going to address a mindset rather than a particular strategy.

Your odds of guessing an answer correctly depend on how many options you are choosing from.

Number of options left	5	4	3	2	1
Odds of guessing correctly	20%	25%	33%	50%	100%

You can see from this chart just how valuable it is to be able to eliminate incorrect answers and make an educated guess, but there are two things that many test takers do that cause them to miss out on the benefits of guessing:

- Accidentally eliminating the correct answer
- Selecting an answer based on an impression

We'll look at the first one here, and the second one in the next section.

To avoid accidentally eliminating the correct answer, we recommend a thought exercise called **the $5 challenge**. In this challenge, you only eliminate an answer choice from contention if you are willing to bet $5 on it being wrong. Why $5? Five dollars is a small but not insignificant amount of money. It's an amount you could afford to lose but wouldn't want to throw away. And while losing $5 once might not hurt too much, doing it twenty times will set you back $100. In the same way, each small decision you make—eliminating a choice here, guessing on a question there—won't by itself impact your score very much, but when you put them all together, they can make a big difference. By holding each answer choice elimination decision to a higher standard, you can reduce the risk of accidentally eliminating the correct answer.

The $5 challenge can also be applied in a positive sense: If you are willing to bet $5 that an answer choice *is* correct, go ahead and mark it as correct.

Summary: Only eliminate an answer choice if you are willing to bet $5 that it is wrong.

Which Answer to Choose

You're taking the test. You've run into a hard question and decided you'll have to guess. You've eliminated all the answer choices you're willing to bet $5 on. Now you have to pick an answer. Why do we even need to talk about this? Why can't you just pick whichever one you feel like when the time comes?

The answer to these questions is that if you don't come into the test with a plan, you'll rely on your impression to select an answer choice, and if you do that, you risk falling into a trap. The test writers know that everyone who takes their test will be guessing on some of the questions, so they intentionally write wrong answer choices to seem plausible. You still have to pick an answer though, and if the wrong answer choices are designed to look right, how can you ever be sure that you're not falling for their trap? The best solution we've found to this dilemma is to take the decision out of your hands entirely. Here is the process we recommend:

Once you've eliminated any choices that you are confident (willing to bet $5) are wrong, select the first remaining choice as your answer.

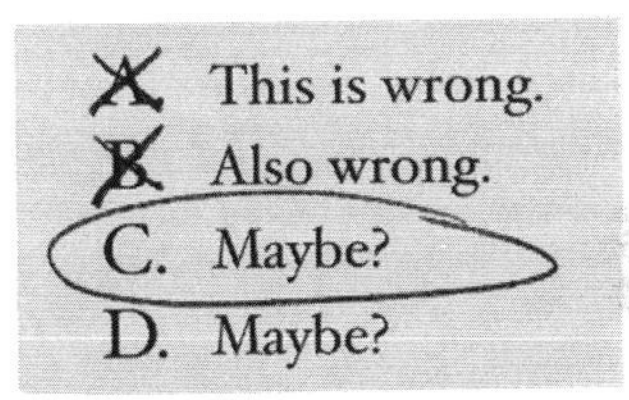

Whether you choose to select the first remaining choice, the second, or the last, the important thing is that you use some preselected standard. Using this approach guarantees that you will not be enticed into selecting an answer choice that looks right, because you are not basing your decision on how the answer choices look.

This is not meant to make you question your knowledge. Instead, it is to help you recognize the difference between your knowledge and your impressions. There's a huge difference between thinking an answer is right because of what you know, and thinking an answer is right because it looks or sounds like it should be right.

Summary: To ensure that your selection is appropriately random, make a predetermined selection from among all answer choices you have not eliminated.

Test-Taking Strategies

This section contains a list of test-taking strategies that you may find helpful as you work through the test. By taking what you know and applying logical thought, you can maximize your chances of answering any question correctly!

It is very important to realize that every question is different and every person is different: no single strategy will work on every question, and no single strategy will work for every person. That's why we've included all of them here, so you can try them out and determine which ones work best for different types of questions and which ones work best for you.

Question Strategies

✓ Read Carefully

Read the question and the answer choices carefully. Don't miss the question because you misread the terms. You have plenty of time to read each question thoroughly and make sure you understand what is being asked. Yet a happy medium must be attained, so don't waste too much time. You must read carefully and efficiently.

✓ Contextual Clues

Look for contextual clues. If the question includes a word you are not familiar with, look at the immediate context for some indication of what the word might mean. Contextual clues can often give you all the information you need to decipher the meaning of an unfamiliar word. Even if you can't determine the meaning, you may be able to narrow down the possibilities enough to make a solid guess at the answer to the question.

✓ Prefixes

If you're having trouble with a word in the question or answer choices, try dissecting it. Take advantage of every clue that the word might include. Prefixes can be a huge help. Usually, they allow you to determine a basic meaning. *Pre-* means before, *post-* means after, *pro-* is positive, *de-* is negative. From prefixes, you can get an idea of the general meaning of the word and try to put it into context.

✓ Hedge Words

Watch out for critical hedge words, such as *likely, may, can, often, almost, mostly, usually, generally, rarely,* and *sometimes.* Question writers insert these hedge phrases to cover every possibility. Often an answer choice will be wrong simply because it leaves no room for exception. Be on guard for answer choices that have definitive words such as *exactly* and *always.*

✓ Switchback Words

Stay alert for *switchbacks.* These are the words and phrases frequently used to alert you to shifts in thought. The most common switchback words are *but, although,* and *however.* Others include *nevertheless, on the other hand, even though, while, in spite of, despite,* and *regardless of.* Switchback words are important to catch because they can change the direction of the question or an answer choice.

☑ FACE VALUE

When in doubt, use common sense. Accept the situation in the problem at face value. Don't read too much into it. These problems will not require you to make wild assumptions. If you have to go beyond creativity and warp time or space in order to have an answer choice fit the question, then you should move on and consider the other answer choices. These are normal problems rooted in reality. The applicable relationship or explanation may not be readily apparent, but it is there for you to figure out. Use your common sense to interpret anything that isn't clear.

Answer Choice Strategies

☑ ANSWER SELECTION

The most thorough way to pick an answer choice is to identify and eliminate wrong answers until only one is left, then confirm it is the correct answer. Sometimes an answer choice may immediately seem right, but be careful. The test writers will usually put more than one reasonable answer choice on each question, so take a second to read all of them and make sure that the other choices are not equally obvious. As long as you have time left, it is better to read every answer choice than to pick the first one that looks right without checking the others.

☑ ANSWER CHOICE FAMILIES

An answer choice family consists of two (in rare cases, three) answer choices that are very similar in construction and cannot all be true at the same time. If you see two answer choices that are direct opposites or parallels, one of them is usually the correct answer. For instance, if one answer choice says that quantity x increases and another either says that quantity x decreases (opposite) or says that quantity y increases (parallel), then those answer choices would fall into the same family. An answer choice that doesn't match the construction of the answer choice family is more likely to be incorrect. Most questions will not have answer choice families, but when they do appear, you should be prepared to recognize them.

☑ ELIMINATE ANSWERS

Eliminate answer choices as soon as you realize they are wrong, but make sure you consider all possibilities. If you are eliminating answer choices and realize that the last one you are left with is also wrong, don't panic. Start over and consider each choice again. There may be something you missed the first time that you will realize on the second pass.

☑ AVOID FACT TRAPS

Don't be distracted by an answer choice that is factually true but doesn't answer the question. You are looking for the choice that answers the question. Stay focused on what the question is asking for so you don't accidentally pick an answer that is true but incorrect. Always go back to the question and make sure the answer choice you've selected actually answers the question and is not merely a true statement.

☑ EXTREME STATEMENTS

In general, you should avoid answers that put forth extreme actions as standard practice or proclaim controversial ideas as established fact. An answer choice that states the "process should be used in certain situations, if…" is much more likely to be correct than one that states the "process should be discontinued completely." The first is a calm rational statement and doesn't even make a definitive, uncompromising stance, using a hedge word *if* to provide wiggle room, whereas the second choice is far more extreme.

✓ Benchmark

As you read through the answer choices and you come across one that seems to answer the question well, mentally select that answer choice. This is not your final answer, but it's the one that will help you evaluate the other answer choices. The one that you selected is your benchmark or standard for judging each of the other answer choices. Every other answer choice must be compared to your benchmark. That choice is correct until proven otherwise by another answer choice beating it. If you find a better answer, then that one becomes your new benchmark. Once you've decided that no other choice answers the question as well as your benchmark, you have your final answer.

✓ Predict the Answer

Before you even start looking at the answer choices, it is often best to try to predict the answer. When you come up with the answer on your own, it is easier to avoid distractions and traps because you will know exactly what to look for. The right answer choice is unlikely to be word-for-word what you came up with, but it should be a close match. Even if you are confident that you have the right answer, you should still take the time to read each option before moving on.

General Strategies

✓ Tough Questions

If you are stumped on a problem or it appears too hard or too difficult, don't waste time. Move on! Remember though, if you can quickly check for obviously incorrect answer choices, your chances of guessing correctly are greatly improved. Before you completely give up, at least try to knock out a couple of possible answers. Eliminate what you can and then guess at the remaining answer choices before moving on.

✓ Check Your Work

Since you will probably not know every term listed and the answer to every question, it is important that you get credit for the ones that you do know. Don't miss any questions through careless mistakes. If at all possible, try to take a second to look back over your answer selection and make sure you've selected the correct answer choice and haven't made a costly careless mistake (such as marking an answer choice that you didn't mean to mark). This quick double check should more than pay for itself in caught mistakes for the time it costs.

✓ Pace Yourself

It's easy to be overwhelmed when you're looking at a page full of questions; your mind is confused and full of random thoughts, and the clock is ticking down faster than you would like. Calm down and maintain the pace that you have set for yourself. Especially as you get down to the last few minutes of the test, don't let the small numbers on the clock make you panic. As long as you are on track by monitoring your pace, you are guaranteed to have time for each question.

✓ Don't Rush

It is very easy to make errors when you are in a hurry. Maintaining a fast pace in answering questions is pointless if it makes you miss questions that you would have gotten right otherwise. Test writers like to include distracting information and wrong answers that seem right. Taking a little extra time to avoid careless mistakes can make all the difference in your test score. Find a pace that allows you to be confident in the answers that you select.

✓ KEEP MOVING

Panicking will not help you pass the test, so do your best to stay calm and keep moving. Taking deep breaths and going through the answer elimination steps you practiced can help to break through a stress barrier and keep your pace.

Final Notes

The combination of a solid foundation of content knowledge and the confidence that comes from practicing your plan for applying that knowledge is the key to maximizing your performance on test day. As your foundation of content knowledge is built up and strengthened, you'll find that the strategies included in this chapter become more and more effective in helping you quickly sift through the distractions and traps of the test to isolate the correct answer.

Now that you're preparing to move forward into the test content chapters of this book, be sure to keep your goal in mind. As you read, think about how you will be able to apply this information on the test. If you've already seen sample questions for the test and you have an idea of the question format and style, try to come up with questions of your own that you can answer based on what you're reading. This will give you valuable practice applying your knowledge in the same ways you can expect to on test day.

Good luck and good studying!

Scientific Inquiry, Processes, Technology, and Society

Safety and Equipment

Laboratory Accidents

Any spills or accidents should be **reported** to the teacher so that the teacher can determine the safest clean-up method. The student should start to wash off a **chemical** spilled on the skin while reporting the incident. Some spills may require removal of contaminated clothing and use of the **safety shower**. Broken glass should be disposed of in a designated container. If someone's clothing catches fire they should walk to the safety shower and use it to extinguish the flames. A fire blanket may be used to smother a **lab fire**. A fire extinguisher, phone, spill neutralizers, and a first aid box are other types of **safety equipment** found in the lab. Students should be familiar with **routes** out of the room and the building in case of fire. Students should use the **eye wash station** if a chemical gets in the eyes.

Safety Procedures

Students should wear a **lab apron** and **safety goggles**. Loose or dangling clothing and jewelry, necklaces, and earrings should not be worn. Those with long hair should tie it back. Care should always be taken not to splash chemicals. Open-toed shoes such as sandals and flip-flops should not be worn, nor should wrist watches. Glasses are preferable to contact lenses since the latter carry a risk of chemicals getting caught between the lens and the eye. Students should always be supervised. The area where the experiment is taking place and the surrounding floor should be free of clutter. Only the lab book and the items necessary for the experiment should be present. Smoking, eating, and chewing gum are not permitted in the lab. Cords should not be allowed to dangle from work stations. There should be no rough-housing in the lab. Hands should be washed after the lab is complete.

Fume Hoods

Because of the potential safety hazards associated with chemistry lab experiments, such as fire from vapors and the inhalation of toxic fumes, a **fume hood** should be used in many instances. A fume hood carries away vapors from reagents or reactions. Equipment or reactions are placed as far back in the hood as practical to help enhance the collection of the fumes. The **glass safety shield** automatically closes to the appropriate height, and it should be low enough to protect the face and body. The safety shield should only be raised to move equipment in and out of the hood. One should not climb inside a hood or stick one's head inside. All spills should be wiped up immediately, and the glass should be cleaned if a splash occurs.

Common Safety Hazards

Some specific safety hazards possible in a chemistry lab include:

- **Fire**: Fire can be caused by volatile solvents such as ether, acetone, or benzene being kept in an open beaker or Erlenmeyer flask. Vapors can creep along the table and ignite if they reach a flame or spark. Solvents should be heated in a hood with a steam bath, not on a hot plate.
- **Explosion**: Heating or creating a reaction in a closed system can cause an explosion, resulting in flying glass and chemical splashes. The system should be vented to prevent this.

- **Chemical and thermal burns**: Many chemicals are corrosive to the skin and eyes.
- **Inhalation of toxic fumes**: Some compounds severely irritate membranes in the eyes, nose, throat, and lungs.
- **Absorption** of toxic chemicals such as dimethyl sulfoxide (DMSO) and nitrobenzene through the skin.
- **Ingestion** of toxic chemicals.

Safety Gloves

There are many types of **gloves** available to help protect the skin from cuts, burns, and chemical splashes. There are many considerations when choosing a glove. For example, gloves that are highly protective may limit dexterity. Some gloves may not offer appropriate protection against a specific chemical. Other considerations include degradation rating, which indicates how effective a glove is when exposed to chemicals; breakthrough time, which indicates how quickly a chemical can break through the surface of the glove; and permeation rate, which indicates how quickly chemicals seep through after the initial breakthrough. Disposable latex, vinyl, or nitrile gloves are usually appropriate for most circumstances, and offer protection from incidental splashes and contact. Other types of gloves include butyl, neoprene, PVC, PVA, Viton, Silver Shield, and natural rubber. Each offers its own type of protection but may have drawbacks as well.

Proper Handling and Storage of Chemicals

Students should take care when **carrying chemicals** from one place to another. Chemicals should never be taken from the room, tasted, or touched with bare hands. **Safety gloves** should be worn when appropriate and glove/chemical interactions and glove deterioration should be considered. Hands should always be **washed** thoroughly after a lab. Potentially hazardous materials intended for use in chemistry, biology, or other science labs should be secured in a safe area where relevant **Safety Data Sheets (SDS)** can be accessed. Chemicals and solutions should be used as directed and labels should be read before handling solutions and chemicals. Extra chemicals should not be returned to their original containers, but should be disposed of as directed by the school district's rules or local ordinances. Local municipalities often have hazardous waste disposal programs. Acids should be stored separately from other chemicals. Flammable liquids should be stored away from acids, bases, and oxidizers.

Bunsen Burners

When using a **Bunsen burner**, loose clothing should be tucked in, long hair should be tied back, and safety goggles and aprons should be worn. Students should know what to do in case of a fire or accident. When lighting the burner, strikers should always be used instead of matches. Do not touch the hot barrel. Tongs (never fingers) should be used to hold the material in the flame. To heat liquid, a flask may be set upon wire gauze on a tripod and secured with an iron ring or clamp on a stand. The flame is extinguished by turning off the gas at the source.

Safety Procedures Related to Animals

Animals to be used for **dissections** should be obtained from a company that provides animals for this purpose. Road kill or decaying animals that a student brings in should not be used. It is possible that such an animal may have a pathogen or a virus, such as rabies, which can be transmitted via the saliva of even a dead animal. Students should use gloves and should not participate if they have open sores or moral objections to dissections. It is generally accepted that biological experiments may be performed on lower-order life forms and invertebrates, but not on mammalian vertebrates and birds. No animals should be harmed physiologically. Experimental animals should be kept, cared for, and handled in a safe manner and with compassion. Pathogenic (anything able to cause a disease) substances should not be used in lab experiments.

Lab Notebooks

A **lab notebook** is a record of all pre-lab work and lab work. It differs from a lab report, which is prepared after lab work is completed. A lab notebook is a formal record of lab preparations and what was done. **Observational recordings** should not be altered, erased, or whited-out to make corrections. Drawing a single line through an entry is sufficient to make changes. Pages should be numbered and should not be torn out. Entries should be made neatly, but don't necessarily have to be complete sentences. **Entries** should provide detailed information and be recorded in such a way that another person could use them to replicate the experiment. **Quantitative data** may be recorded in tabular form, and may include calculations made during an experiment. Lab book entries can also include references and research performed before the experiment. Entries may also consist of information about a lab experiment, including the objective or purpose, the procedures, data collected, and the results.

Lab Reports

A **lab report** is an item developed after an experiment that is intended to present the results of a lab experiment. Generally, it should be prepared using a word processor, not hand-written or recorded in a notebook. A lab report should be formally presented. It is intended to persuade others to accept or reject a hypothesis. It should include a brief but descriptive **title** and an **abstract**. The abstract is a summary of the report. It should include a purpose that states the problem that was explored or the question that was answered. It should also include a **hypothesis** that describes the anticipated results of the experiment. The experiment should include a **control** and one **variable** to ensure that the results can be interpreted correctly. Observations and results can be presented using written narratives, tables, graphs, and illustrations. The report should also include a **summation** or **conclusion** explaining whether the results supported the hypothesis.

Types of Laboratory Glassware

Two types of flasks are Erlenmeyer flasks and volumetric flasks. **Volumetric flasks** are used to accurately prepare a specific volume and concentration of a solution. **Erlenmeyer flasks** can be used for mixing, transporting, and reacting, but are not appropriate for accurate measurements.

A **pipette** can be used to accurately measure small amounts of liquid. Liquid is drawn into the pipette through a bulb. The liquid measurement is read at the **meniscus**. There are also plastic disposable pipettes. A **repipette** is a hand-operated pump that dispenses solutions.

Beakers can be used to measure mass or dissolve a solvent into a solute. They do not measure volume as accurately as a volumetric flask, pipette, graduated cylinder, or burette.

Graduated cylinders are used for precise measurements and are considered more accurate than Erlenmeyer flasks or beakers. To read a graduated cylinder, it should be placed on a flat surface and read at eye level. The surface of a liquid in a graduated cylinder forms a lens-shaped curve. The measurement should be taken from the bottom of the curve. A ring may be placed at the top of tall, narrow cylinders to help avoid breakage if they are tipped over.

A **burette**, or buret, is a piece of lab glassware used to accurately dispense liquid. It looks similar to a narrow graduated cylinder, but it includes a stopcock and tip. It may be filled with a funnel or pipette.

Microscopes

There are different kinds of microscopes, but **optical** or **light microscopes** are the most commonly used in lab settings. Light and lenses are used to magnify and view samples. A specimen or sample is placed on a slide, and the slide is placed on a stage with a hole in it. Light passes through the hole and illuminates the sample. The sample is magnified by lenses and viewed through the eyepiece. A simple microscope has one lens, while a typical compound microscope has three lenses. The light source can be room light redirected by a mirror, or the microscope can have its own independent light source that passes through a condenser. In this case, there are diaphragms and filters to allow light intensity to be controlled. Optical microscopes also have coarse and fine adjustment knobs.

Other types of microscopes include **digital microscopes**, which use a camera and a monitor to allow viewing of the sample. **Scanning electron microscopes (SEMs)** provide greater detail in terms of a sample's surface topography and can produce magnifications much greater than those possible with optical microscopes. The technology of an SEM is quite different from an optical microscope in that it does not rely on lenses to magnify objects, but uses samples placed in a chamber. In one type of SEM, a beam of electrons from an electron gun scans and actually interacts with the sample to produce an image.

Wet mount slides designed for use with a light microscope typically require a thin portion of the specimen to be placed on a standard glass slide. A drop of water is added, and a cover slip or cover glass is placed on top. Air bubbles and fingerprints can make viewing difficult. Placing the cover slip at a 45-degree angle and allowing it to drop into place can help avoid the problem of air bubbles. A **cover slip** should always be used when viewing wet mount slides. The viewer should start with the objective in its lowest position and then fine-focus. The microscope should be carried with two hands and stored with the low-power objective in the down position. **Lenses** should be cleaned with lens paper only. A **graticule slide** is marked with a grid line, and is useful for counting or estimating a quantity.

Balances

Balances such as triple-beam balances, spring balances, and electronic balances measure mass and force. An **electronic balance** is the most accurate, followed by a **triple-beam balance** and then a **spring balance**. One part of a **triple-beam balance** is the plate, which is where the item to be weighed is placed. There are also three beams, which have hash marks indicating amounts and which hold the weights that rest in the notches. The front beam measures weights between 0 and 10 grams, the middle beam measures weights in 100-gram increments, and the far beam measures weights in 10-gram increments. The sum of the weight of each beam is the total weight of the object. A triple beam balance also includes a set screw to calibrate the equipment, as well as a mark indicating that the object and counterweights are in balance.

Chromatography

Chromatography refers to a set of laboratory techniques used to separate or analyze **mixtures**. Mixtures are dissolved in their mobile phases. In the stationary or bonded phase, the desired component is separated from other molecules in the mixture. In chromatography, the analyte is the substance to be separated. **Preparative chromatography** refers to the type of chromatography that involves purifying a substance for further use rather than further analysis. **Analytical chromatography** involves analyzing the isolated substance. Other types of chromatography include column, planar, paper, thin layer, displacement, supercritical fluid, affinity, ion exchange, and size exclusion chromatography. Reversed phase, two-dimensional, simulated moving bed, pyrolysis, fast protein, counter current, and chiral are also types of chromatography. **Gas**

chromatography refers to the separation technique in which the mobile phase of a substance is in gas form.

Review Video: Paper Chromatography
Visit mometrix.com/academy and enter code: 543963

Reagents and Reactants

A **reagent** or **reactant** is a chemical agent for use in chemical reactions. When preparing for a lab, it should be confirmed that glassware and other equipment have been cleaned and/or sterilized. There should be enough materials, reagents, or other solutions needed for the lab for every group of students completing the experiment. Distilled water should be used instead of tap water when performing lab experiments because distilled water has most of its impurities removed. Other needed apparatus such as funnels, filter paper, balances, Bunsen burners, ring stands, and/or microscopes should also be set up. After the lab, it should be confirmed that sinks, workstations, and any equipment used have been cleaned. If chemicals or specimens need to be kept at a certain temperature by refrigerating them or using another storage method, the temperature should be checked periodically to ensure the sample does not spoil.

Diluting Acids

When preparing a solution of **dilute acid**, always add the concentrated acid solution to water, not water to concentrated acid. Start by adding approximately $\frac{2}{3}$ of the total volume of water to the graduated cylinder or volumetric flask. Next, add the concentrated acid to the water. Add additional water to the diluted acid to bring the solution to the final desired volume.

Cleaning After Acid Spills

In the event of an **acid spill**, any clothes that have come into contact with the acid should be removed and any skin contacted with acid must be rinsed with clean water. To the extent a window can be opened or a fume hood can be turned on, do so. Do not try to force air circulation, such as by adding a fan, as acid fumes can be harmful if spread.

Next, pour one of the following over the spill area: sodium bicarbonate, baking soda, soda ash, or cat litter. Start from the outside of the spill and then move towards the center, in order to prevent splashing. When the clumps have thoroughly dried, sweep up the clumps and dispose of them as chemical waste.

Centrifuges

A centrifuge is used to separate the components of a heterogeneous mixture (consisting of two or more compounds) by spinning it. The solid precipitate settles in the bottom of the container, and the liquid component of the solution, called the **centrifugate**, is at the top. A well-known application of this process is using a centrifuge to separate blood cells and plasma. The heavier cells settle on the bottom of the test tube, and the lighter plasma stays on top. Another example is using a salad spinner to help dry lettuce.

Electrophoresis, Calorimetry, and Titration

- **Electrophoresis** is the separation of molecules based on electrical charge. This is possible because particles dispersed in a fluid usually carry electric charges on their surfaces. Molecules are pulled through the fluid toward the positive end if the molecules have a negative charge and are pulled through the fluid toward the negative end if the molecules have a positive charge.
- **Calorimetry** is used to determine the heat released or absorbed in a chemical reaction.
- **Titration** helps determine the precise endpoint of a reaction. With this information, the precise quantity of reactant in the titration flask can be determined. A burette is used to deliver the second reactant to the flask and an indicator or pH meter is used to detect the endpoint of the reaction.

Field Studies and Research Projects

Field studies may facilitate scientific inquiry in a manner similar to indoor lab experiments. Field studies can be interdisciplinary in nature and can help students learn and apply scientific concepts and processes. **Research projects** can be conducted in any number of locations, including school campuses, local parks, national parks, beaches, or mountains. Students can practice the general techniques of observation, data collection, collaborative planning, and analysis of experiments. Field studies give students the chance to learn through hands-on applications of scientific processes, such as map making in geography, observation of stratification in geology, observation of life cycles of plants and animals, and analysis of water quality.

Students should watch out for obvious outdoor **hazards**. These include poisonous flora and fauna such as poison ivy, poison oak, and sumac. Depending on the region of the United States in which the field study is being conducted, hazards may also include rattlesnakes and black widow or brown recluse spiders. Students should also be made aware of potentially hazardous situations specific to **geographic locales** and the possibility of coming into contact with **pathogens**.

Field studies allow for great flexibility in the use of traditional and technological methods for **making observations** and **collecting data**. For example, a nature study could consist of a simple survey of bird species within a given area. Information could be recorded using still photography or a video camera. This type of activity gives students the chance to use technologies other than computers. Computers could still be used to create a slide show of transferred images or a digital lab report. If a quantitative study of birds was being performed, the simple technique of using a pencil and paper to tabulate the number of birds counted in the field could also be used. Other techniques used during field studies could include collecting specimens for lab study, observing coastal ecosystems and tides, and collecting weather data such as temperature, precipitation amounts, and air pressure in a particular locale.

Scientific Concepts Related to Physical Science

Basic Safety Equipment

All labs should contain the following items:

- Bucket of sand for absorption of spills and smothering of alkali fires
- Fire blanket
- First-aid kit, containing bandages and antiseptic
- One GFCI within two feet of all water supplies
- Exit signs
- Emergency shower
- Emergency eyewash station
- Splashproof eye protection for all parties, and a means to sanitize it
- Face shields
- Emergency exhaust fans that vent to the outside of the building
- Fire blanket
- Gloves, both rubber and nitrile
- Master cutoff switches for gas, electricity, and compressed air
- ABC fire extinguisher
- Storage cabinets for flammable items
- Chemical spill-control kit
- Fume hood with a spark-proof motor
- Flame-retardant lab aprons
- Mercury clean-up kit
- Neutralizing agents, including acetic acid and sodium bicarbonate
- Signs drawing attention to potential hazards
- Segregated, clearly labeled containers for storing broken glassware, flammable items, solid chemicals, corrosive items, and waste.

Major Energy Issues

Since the Industrial Revolution, energy for industrialized human needs has come from **fossil fuels**, particularly coal and petroleum, but increased use means that this source of fuel is quickly being depleted, in addition to causing pollution. The search for alternative, safe sources of energy for an increasingly industrialized world population is therefore increasingly important to scientists.

An ideal source of energy would be **efficient, renewable, and sustainable**. Various sources of alternative energy have been proposed, including wind, water, solar, nuclear, geothermal, and biomass, but thus far none have been made practically available on a large scale. Some, such as wind and water, blight the landscape, while the conversion methods for other sources, such as solar and biomass, are still relatively inefficient. The scientific community is still unclear on the best way to harness the power of photosynthesis and biomass for energy needs in a way that would allow a large-scale energy industry to use it. Scientists remain at work studying the long-term solutions to an increasingly urgent problem for humanity.

Effects of Improvements in Scientific and Technological Knowledge

Since the Industrial Revolution, technological **improvements to agricultural production** have made agriculture productive on an industrial scale, while advances in medical knowledge have brought about the **cures for many diseases**. People in many parts of the world live longer and enjoy a higher standard of living than ever before.

However, this progress does not come without a price. The **effects on the environment** of industrialization are almost exclusively negative. Monoculture farming practices resulting from industrialization mean that **farming no longer exists as a closed ecosystem**; the chemical fertilizers that create record crop yields have changed the nutrient environment, and the waste products of industrial agriculture pollute the water rather than fertilizing the soil. Increased travel creates dangerous carbon dioxide emissions and depletes the earth's limited store of fossil fuels. **Water pollution** means limited access to potable water, and **deforestation** has begun to change the makeup of ecosystems and cause the extinction of many species. However, through the increased contact made available by improved technology, humans are collaborating on solutions to these new problems.

Increased Production of Consumer Goods

Electric-based, industrial production of manufactured goods has led to an increase in the standard of living for many, especially those in the industrialized world. Consumer goods are produced more cheaply than ever before, since the means of production is not as dependent on the physical abilities of human beings. Scientific advancements have led to a huge number of new synthetic materials from which goods can be made, including plastics and nylon.

However, this increased production damages the environment. Waste products are now created of which humans can make no use, which constitutes a new phenomenon. Trash created from these new products is buried in landfills, where it has no access to the air, water, and sunlight that are a necessary part of biodegradation; trash made from some synthetic materials does not biodegrade at all. While some waste products can be recycled, many byproducts of industrial manufacturing are hazardous, with no safe way to dispose of them. The long-term sustainability of the environment as a result of massively increased consumer production is an issue of increasing urgency for scientists.

Nuclear Power Controversy

Nuclear fission power, while sustainable, has a host of attendant controversial problems. Among them is the **incredibly dangerous transportation and long-term storage of its radioactive waste** products, for which there is still no safe permanent solution. The effects on environments and creatures that come in contact with nuclear waste are still largely unknown. In addition, nuclear materials can be used in weaponry, and accidents at nuclear power plants like the one at Chernobyl can be devastating for thousands of years.

Scientists continue their study of the process of nuclear fusion, hoping that if humans can learn to harness the energy produced by smashing atoms (nuclear fusion) rather than splitting them (nuclear fission), the attendant problems of nuclear waste storage will be minimized.

Management of Non-Renewable Resources

Non-renewable resources include minerals, which are created naturally over millions of years. The industrialized world extracts minerals for fuel as well as for use in electronic equipment and medicine. Increased human extraction of **non-renewable resources** has endangered their availability, and over-mining has created other ecological problems, including runoff and water pollution. The use of fossil fuels for energy and transportation causes air pollution and is unsustainable. Fossil fuels cannot be replaced once depleted, and they are being depleted at an increasing rate. The need to find a sustainable alternative to the use of non-renewable fossil fuels is imperative.

Management of Renewable Resources

Natural resources can be divided into two types, renewable and non-renewable. **Renewable** resources include plants and animals, along with water, air, and soil.

A **pre-industrial earth** was a self-sustaining system, maintaining a natural balance among plants, animals, and non-living elements in which waste products from one natural process were the fuel for another. Modern humans have intervened in this process in a way that upsets the natural balance of life. Humans have introduced non-native species from one part of the world to another, resulting in the devastation of local populations. Industrial-scale buildings can create disasters for local ecosystems, ruining habitats for animal populations.

Humans remove an increasing amount of the world's resources for industrial use, too quickly for nature to recover from easily. Renewable resources must be carefully managed to maintain a balanced ecosystem; over-harvesting of forests or over-hunting of animal populations can be devastating. Pollution of the air and water with chemical pollutants has far-reaching effects on the ecosystems of the earth, including the depletion of the ozone layer that protects earth life from ultraviolet rays, as does the removal of forests that produce the earth's oxygen.

Social Impacts of Science and Technology

Recent developments in science and technology have had both positive and negative effects on human society. The issue of **sustainable growth** is an increasingly important one, as humans realize that the resources they use are not unlimited. Genetic research into diseases, stem cell research, and cloning technology have created great controversies as they have been introduced, and an increasing number of people reject the morality of scientific practices like animal testing in the pursuit of scientific advancement. In addition, an increasingly technology-based world has produced a new social inequality based on access to computers and Internet technology.

These issues are beginning to be debated at all levels of human government, from city councils to the United Nations. Does science provide the authoritative answer to all human problems, or do ethics carry weight in scientific debates as well? Ultimately, humans must weigh the competing needs of facilitating scientific pursuits and maintaining an ethical society as they face new technological questions.

Recent Applications of Science and Technology

Scientific and technological developments have led to the widespread availability of technologies heretofore unheard of, including cellular phones, satellite-based applications, and a worldwide network of connected computers. Some of the notable recent applications include:

- **Health care:** Antibiotics, genetic screening for diseases, the sequencing of the human genome. Issues include problems with health care distribution on an increasingly industrialized planet.
- **The environment**: Computerized models of climate change and pollution monitoring. Issues include increased pollution of the water, air, and soil, and the over-harvesting of natural resources with mechanized equipment.

- **Agriculture**: Genetic improvements in agricultural practices, including increased output on the same amount of arable land. Issues include unknown environmental effects of hybrid species, cross-pollination with organic species, and pollution caused by synthetic chemical fertilizers.
- **Information technology**: New Internet-based industries, increased worldwide collaboration, and access to information. Issues include the depletion of natural resources for electronics production.

Contributing Individuals to Physics

Archimedes (Ancient Greece)

Archimedes designed the **compound pulley**, articulated the principles of the lever, and made important contributions to engineering and geometry, calculating the area of a sphere and an ellipse and approximating the value of **pi**. Archimedes' Law of the Lever states that when objects are set at distances reciprocally proportional to their respective weights, they are in equilibrium.

Amedeo Avogadro (Italian, 18th Century)

Avogadro established the principles of **molarity**, clarified the relationship between atoms and molecules, and formalized what became known as Avogadro's principle: that equal volumes of gases held at the same pressure and temperature will contain an equal number of molecules, and that their masses will be proportionate to their respective molecular weights. **Avogadro's constant** is the number of particles present in 1 mole of any substance.

Review Video: Avogadro's Hypothesis
Visit mometrix.com/academy and enter code: 968309

Robert Boyle (Irish, 17th Century)

Though regarded as the first modern chemist, Boyle also distinguished himself in physics and contributed to **experimental design**. Boyle's Law is a mathematical expression of the relationship between volume and pressure within an **ideal gas**.

Sir Isaac Newton (English, 17th/18th Century)

Newton, one of the most important scientists of all time, made critical breakthroughs in the understanding of **scientific methods, motion, and optics**. Newton described **universal gravitation**, observed that white light contains the entire spectrum of colors, and discovered the calculus independently of Leibniz (who is credited with it). The three Newtonian laws of motion are:

- An object in motion (or at rest) remains in motion (or at rest) unless acted upon by an external force.
- Force equals mass times acceleration.
- For every action, there is an equal and opposite reaction.

Galileo Galilei (Italian, 17th Century)

Galileo determined that all bodies, regardless of mass, fall at the same rate. He argued that motion is continuous, changed only when an external force is applied to it (later incorporated in Newton's laws of motion). His work in astronomy was important in confirming **Copernicus' heliocentric model of the solar system**. His principle of relativity states that the laws of physics are constant within a constantly moving system, a theory that became central to Einstein's work on relativity.

Marie Curie (Polish/French, 19th Century)

Curie was the foremost pioneer of **radioactivity**. She isolated the radioactive elements polonium and radium, and established that radioactivity was a property of an atom itself rather than of the relationship between multiple molecules.

Michael Faraday (English, 18th/19th Century)

Faraday's most important work was in the fields of **electromagnetism** and **electrochemistry**. His work led directly to some of the most important breakthroughs in electrical technology of the twentieth century. Faraday introduced the concept of fields to the study of magnetism and electricity. He discovered what would become known as the Faraday Effect, the effect of a strong magnetic field on the behavior of light rays. The Farad (the SI unit of capacitance) and the Faraday constant (the amount of charge on one mole of electrons) are both named for him.

Wilhelm Ostwald (Latvian, 19th/20th Century)

One of the founders of classical physical chemistry, Ostwald did important work on the **properties of atomic particles**, and defined a **mole** as the molecular weight, in grams, of a given substance.

Albert Einstein (German, 20th Century)

Einstein, the most famous twentieth-century scientist, was a theoretical physicist **whose special theory of relativity** describes the relationship of **time** and **space**, and **mass** and **gravity**. In it, he declared that gravity is a consequence of the properties of space-time and that the speed of light is constant. He hypothesized that electromagnetic energy can be absorbed or expelled by matter in quanta, and he discovered the photoelectric effect.

Stephen Hawking (English, 20th/21st Century)

Hawking's principal fields of research were theoretical cosmology and quantum gravity. Expanding on Einstein's work, he hypothesized about the physical properties of black holes, described conditions necessary for a singularity, and made important contributions in string theory, in an attempt to generalize Einstein's special theory of relativity.

J. Robert Oppenheimer (American, 20th Century)

Oppenheimer's scientific contributions were in astrophysics, nuclear physics, and quantum field theory. He served as scientific director of the Manhattan Project, which constructed the first atomic bomb.

Linus Pauling (American, 20th Century)

Pauling applied new discoveries in **quantum mechanics** to the field of chemistry, pioneering the study of **molecular medicine**. He researched the biochemical origins of genetic diseases like sickle-cell anemia.

Enrico Fermi (Italian/American, 20th Century)

Fermi discovered the process of making **elements artificially radioactive** by bombarding them with neutrons. He divided elements into the two groups of **fermions** and **bosons**. His work on nuclear reactions led him to participate in the **Manhattan Project**.

Niels Bohr (Danish, 20th Century)

Bohr established that the number of electrons determined the **atom's chemical properties**. He articulated the organization of electrons, in discrete orbits around an atom's nucleus, and that electrons could move orbits, thereby emitting radiation—the **basis for quantum theory**. Bohr worked on the Manhattan Project along with Oppenheimer and Fermi.

Scientific Inquiry and Reasoning

Scientific Inquiry

The concept of **scientific inquiry** refers to the idea of how one thinks and asks questions in a logical way to gain trustworthy information. The underlying motivation of science is to try to understand the natural world. Much of human thought is based on assumptions about how things work that may or may not be true. The goal of scientific inquiry is to test those assumptions to gain a greater understanding of the world with good questions and objective tests, and then re-use what was learned to ask better questions. The more we understand about the natural world, the better the questions we can ask, and that is the general idea behind scientific inquiry. The applied practice of scientific inquiry is to ask questions in a systematic method, called the scientific method.

Scientific Knowledge

Scientific knowledge refers to any topic that is studied **empirically**, meaning that it is based on observation of a **phenomenon** in an objective way. The body of **scientific knowledge** is often broken down into several domains including biology, ecology, Earth science, space science, physics, and chemistry. These each have further subdomains and are overlapping in many ways. For instance, ecology is the study of ecosystems, which are made up of biological factors and geological factors, so it contains elements of both biology and Earth science. Each of these domains is subject to the concepts of scientific inquiry, such as the scientific method, scientific facts, hypotheses, and scientific laws.

Important Terminology

- A **phenomenon** is an event or effect that is observed.
- A **scientific fact** is considered an objective and verifiable observation. Usually, a fact can be repeated or demonstrated to others.
- A **scientific theory** is a proposition explaining why or how something happens and is built on scientific facts and laws. Scientific theories can be tested, but are not fully proven. If new evidence is found that disproves the theory, it is no longer considered true.
- A **hypothesis** is an educated guess that is not yet proven. It is used to predict the outcome of an experiment in an attempt to solve a problem or answer a question.
- A **law** is an explanation of events that always leads to the same outcome. It is a fact that an object falls. The law of gravity explains why an object falls. The theory of relativity, although generally accepted, has been neither proven nor disproved.
- A **model** is used to explain something on a smaller scale or in simpler terms to provide an example. It is a representation of an idea that can be used to explain events or applied to new situations to predict outcomes or determine results.

History of Scientific Knowledge

When one examines the history of **scientific knowledge**, it is clear that it is constantly **evolving**. The body of facts, models, theories, and laws grows and changes over time. In other words, one scientific discovery leads to the next. Some advances in science and technology have important and long-lasting effects on science and society. Some discoveries were so alien to the accepted beliefs of the time that not only were they rejected as wrong, but were also considered outright blasphemy. Today, however, many beliefs once considered incorrect have become an ingrained part of scientific knowledge, and have also been the basis of new advances. Examples of advances include: Copernicus's heliocentric view of the universe, Newton's laws of motion and planetary orbits, relativity, geologic time scale, plate tectonics, atomic theory, nuclear physics, biological evolution, germ theory, industrial revolution, molecular biology, information and communication, quantum theory, galactic universe, and medical and health technology.

Scientific Inquiry and Scientific Method

Scientists use a number of generally accepted techniques collectively known as the **scientific method**. The scientific method generally involves carrying out the following steps:

- Identifying a problem or posing a question
- Formulating a hypothesis or an educated guess
- Conducting experiments or tests that will provide a basis to solve the problem or answer the question
- Observing the results of the test
- Drawing conclusions

An important part of the scientific method is using acceptable experimental techniques. Objectivity is also important if valid results are to be obtained. Another important part of the scientific method is peer review. It is essential that experiments be performed and data be recorded in such a way that experiments can be reproduced to verify results. Historically, the scientific method has been taught with a more linear approach, but it is important to recognize that the scientific method should be a cyclical or **recursive process**. This means that as hypotheses are tested and more is learned, the questions should continue to change to reflect the changing body of knowledge. One cycle of experimentation is not enough.

Review Video: The Scientific Method
Visit mometrix.com/academy and enter code: 191386

Metric and International System of Units

The **metric system** is the accepted standard of measurement in the scientific community. The **International System of Units (SI)** is a set of measurements (including the metric system) that is almost globally accepted. The United States, Liberia, and Myanmar have not accepted this system. **Standardization** is important because it allows the results of experiments to be compared and reproduced without the need to laboriously convert measurements. The SI is based partially on the **meter-kilogram-second (MKS) system** rather than the **centimeter-gram-second (CGS) system**. The MKS system considers meters, kilograms, and seconds to be the basic units of measurement, while the CGS system considers centimeters, grams, and seconds to be the basic units of measurement. Under the MKS system, the length of an object would be expressed as 1 meter instead of 100 centimeters, which is how it would be described under the CGS system.

Review Video: Metric System Conversions
Visit mometrix.com/academy and enter code: 163709

Basic Units of Measurement

Using the **metric system** is generally accepted as the preferred method for taking measurements. Having a **universal standard** allows individuals to interpret measurements more easily, regardless of where they are located. The basic units of measurement are: the **meter**, which measures length; the **liter**, which measures volume; and the **gram**, which measures mass. The metric system starts with a base unit and increases or decreases in units of 10. The prefix and the base unit combined are used to indicate an amount. For example, deka- is 10 times the base unit. A dekameter is 10 meters; a dekaliter is 10 liters; and a dekagram is 10 grams. The prefix hecto- refers to 100 times the base amount; kilo- is 1,000 times the base amount. The prefixes that indicate a fraction of the base unit are deci-, which is $\frac{1}{10}$ of the base unit; centi-, which is $\frac{1}{100}$ of the base unit; and milli-, which is $\frac{1}{1,000}$ of the base unit.

Common Prefixes

The prefixes for multiples are as follows:

Deka	(da)	**10^1** (deka is the American spelling, but deca is also used)
Hecto	(h)	10^2
Kilo	(k)	10^3
Mega	(M)	10^6
Giga	(G)	10^9
Tera	(T)	10^{12}

The prefixes for subdivisions are as follows:

Deci	(d)	**10^{-1}**
Centi	(c)	10^{-2}
Milli	(m)	10^{-3}
Micro	(μ)	10^{-6}
Nano	(n)	10^{-9}
Pico	(p)	10^{-12}

The rule of thumb is that prefixes greater than 10^3 are capitalized when abbreviating. Abbreviations do not need a period after them. A decimeter (dm) is a tenth of a meter, a deciliter (dL) is a tenth of a liter, and a decigram (dg) is a tenth of a gram. Pluralization is understood. For example, when referring to 5 mL of water, no "s" needs to be added to the abbreviation.

Basic SI Units of Measurement

SI uses **second(s)** to measure time. Fractions of seconds are usually measured in metric terms using prefixes such as millisecond ($\frac{1}{1,000}$ of a second) or nanosecond ($\frac{1}{1,000,000,000}$ of a second). Increments of time larger than a second are measured in **minutes** and **hours**, which are multiples of 60 and 24. An example of this is a swimmer's time in the 800-meter freestyle being described as 7:32.67, meaning 7 minutes, 32 seconds, and 67 one-hundredths of a second. One second is equal to $\frac{1}{60}$ of a minute, $\frac{1}{3,600}$ of an hour, and $\frac{1}{86,400}$ of a day. Other SI base units are the **ampere** (A) (used to measure electric current), the **kelvin** (K) (used to measure thermodynamic temperature), the **candela** (cd) (used to measure luminous intensity), and the **mole** (mol) (used to measure the amount of a substance at a molecular level). **Meter** (m) is used to measure length and **kilogram** (kg) is used to measure mass.

Significant Figures

The mathematical concept of **significant figures** or **significant digits** is often used to determine the accuracy of measurements or the level of confidence one has in a specific measurement. The significant figures of a measurement include all the digits known with certainty plus one estimated or uncertain digit. There are a number of rules for determining which digits are considered "important" or "interesting." They are:

- All non-zero digits are *significant.*
- Zeros between digits are *significant.*
- Leading and trailing zeros are *not significant* unless they appear to the right of the non-zero digits in a decimal.

For example, in 0.01230, the significant digits are 1230, and this number would be said to be accurate to the hundred-thousandths place. The zero indicates that the amount has actually been measured as 0. Other zeros are considered placeholders and are not important. A decimal point may be placed after zeros to indicate their importance (in "100." for example).

Graphs and Charts

Graphs and charts are effective ways to present scientific data such as observations, statistical analyses, and comparisons between dependent variables and independent variables. On a line chart, the **independent variable** (the one that is being manipulated for the experiment) is represented on the horizontal axis (the x-axis). Any **dependent variables** (the ones that may change as the independent variable changes) are represented on the y-axis. An **XY** or **scatter plot** is often used to plot many points. A "best fit" line is drawn, which allows outliers to be identified more easily. Charts and their axes should have titles. The x and y interval units should be evenly spaced and labeled. Other types of charts are **bar charts** and **histograms**, which can be used to compare differences between the data collected for two variables. A **pie chart** can graphically show the relation of parts to a whole.

Review Video: Identifying Variables
Visit mometrix.com/academy and enter code: 627181

Review Video: Data Interpretation of Graphs
Visit mometrix.com/academy and enter code: 200439

Data Presentation

Data collected during a science lab can be organized and **presented** in any number of ways. While **straight narrative** is a suitable method for presenting some lab results, it is not a suitable way to present numbers and quantitative measurements. These types of observations can often be better presented with **tables** and **graphs**. Data that is presented in tables and organized in rows and columns may also be used to make graphs quite easily. Other methods of presenting data include illustrations, photographs, video, and even audio formats. In a **formal report**, tables and figures are labeled and referred to by their labels. For example, a picture of a bubbly solution might be labeled Figure 1, Bubbly Solution. It would be referred to in the text in the following way: "The reaction created bubbles 10 mm in size, as shown in Figure 1, Bubbly Solution." Graphs are also labeled as figures. Tables are labeled in a different way. Examples include: Table 1, Results of Statistical Analysis, or Table 2, Data from Lab 2.

Statistical Precision and Errors

Errors that occur during an experiment can be classified into two categories: random errors and systematic errors. **Random errors** can result in collected data that is wildly different from the rest of the data, or they may result in data that is indistinguishable from the rest. Random errors are not consistent across the data set. In large data sets, random errors may contribute to the variability of data, but they will not affect the average. Random errors are sometimes referred to as noise. They may be caused by a student's inability to take the same measurement in exactly the same way or by outside factors that are not considered variables, but influence the data. A **systematic error** will show up consistently across a sample or data set, and may be the result of a flaw in the experimental design. This type of error affects the average, and is also known as bias.

Scientific Notation

Scientific notation is used because values in science can be very large or very small, which makes them unwieldy. A number in **decimal notation** is 93,000,000. In **scientific notation**, it is 9.3×10^7. The first number, 9.3, is the **coefficient**. It is always greater than or equal to 1 and less than 10. This number is followed by a multiplication sign. The base is always 10 in scientific notation. If the number is greater than ten, the exponent is positive. If the number is between zero and one, the exponent is negative. The first digit of the number is followed by a decimal point and then the rest of the number. In this case, the number is 9.3, and the decimal point was moved seven places to the right from the end of the number to get 93,000,000. The number of places moved, seven, is the exponent.

Statistical Terminology

- **Mean**—The average, found by taking the sum of a set of numbers and dividing by the number of numbers in the set.
- **Median**—The middle number in a set of numbers sorted from least to greatest. If the set has an even number of entries, the median is the average of the two in the middle.
- **Mode**—The value that appears most frequently in a data set. There may be more than one mode. If no value appears more than once, there is no mode.
- **Range**—The difference between the highest and lowest numbers in a data set.
- **Standard deviation**—Measures the dispersion of a data set, or how far from the mean a single data point is likely to be.
- **Regression analysis**—A method of analyzing sets of data and sets of variables. It involves studying how the typical value of the dependent variable changes when any one of the independent variables is varied and the other independent variables remain fixed.

Review Video: Mean, Median, and Mode
Visit mometrix.com/academy and enter code: 286207

Review Video: Standard Deviation
Visit mometrix.com/academy and enter code: 419469

The Role of Pedagogy and Scientific Inquiry in Science Education

Developing Scientific Understanding

Scientific understanding involves not merely the knowledge of scientific theories and equations, but a comprehension of how science is done, how we come to know these theories (and how confident we are in them), and how the different domains of science fit together. Students are unlikely to develop a good scientific understanding merely by being presented with isolated facts. Rather, research suggests that a scientific understanding is best fostered by **inquiry** and by **problem-based learning** approaches, which help students develop their own critical thinking and reasoning skills. In these methods, students are not just provided with facts and theories to memorize but are led to "discover" principles on their own, through experimentation and analogy. The instructor must still provide guidance in the process; if students are completely left to their own devices they may be confused or arrive at incorrect conclusions that may do more harm than good. Furthermore, assessments used in the classroom should promote **higher-order learning**, focusing not just on repetition of facts but on reasoning and evaluation of claims. It is critical that students understand that science is a process and a way of knowing, not a collection of facts.

Prior Knowledge

Students vary in their prior knowledge and capabilities, and science instruction is not a one-size-fits-all process. Sometimes prior knowledge helps student, in that they already have some knowledge about the subject in question, but sometimes prior knowledge may seem to conflict with the new information being taught—a dilemma sometimes called the "**paradox of continuity**." Learning therefore can require a **conceptual change**, in a way that allows the students to reformulate their understanding to fit new information.

Students' experience and developmental characteristics can also affect their science learning. Some students learn more effectively through different **learning styles**, or modalities: some learn best from what they see (**visual learners**), others from what they hear (**auditory learners**), still others from handling objects (**tactile learners**), and others from active participation (**kinesthetic learners**). **Abstract thinking** develops during adolescence and may develop more rapidly in some students than others; students who have not fully developed this capability may benefit from more structured teaching methods. Adolescents tend to be at a stage in their social development in which they learn well in cooperative group activities.

Planning Activities

Instructors should be aware of and sensitive to students' different preferred styles of learning and prepare lessons that engage all these styles. The instructor should also try to tie lessons to students' individual interests in order to promote active engagement. A **positive learning environment** is one that adapts to students' individual needs and that often involves students working cooperatively.

In science in particular it's important for instructors not to exclude women and minorities, since they have been excluded so much in the past that it's easy to do so unconsciously. The instructor should make an effort to mention scientists of different ethnicities and genders and make it clear that women and minorities can be and are capable scientists.

Students currently learning English have their own needs that must be addressed. The instructor can help English learners, for instance, by speaking slowly and clearly, by writing down and providing definitions of key terms, by using visual aids and graphic organizers (which also may help visual learners who are not English language learners), and by giving access to translating devices if necessary. English learners can also benefit from working in groups with capable English speakers who can help explain instructions and procedures they don't understand.

Motivation and Engagement

Regardless of how clearly and accurately an instructor explains the topic, the students may not learn if they're unengaged and not paying attention. Therefore, it's important for the teacher to engage the students' interest and keep their attention. One of the advantages of inquiry-based learning is that it actively involves the students and keeps them more engaged by relating the topic to their interests and goals and finding ways to tie the topics in to the students' own experiences, prior knowledge, and daily lives. This requires the teacher to get to know the students and their interests, but this has other benefits as well: the students are also more engaged when there is a good relationship between the teachers and students.

Students also tend to be more engaged by collaborative group activities than by working on their own. Adolescents are at a stage in their social development in which they are increasingly driven to form social attachments with their peers. They are comfortable working in groups and benefit from collaborative learning environments.

Texts Used in the Classroom

Science instruction often involves the students acquiring information from textbooks and handouts, but not all students may be able to effectively use these texts without guidance. Most textbooks have various features designed to make it easier to locate information: an **index**, a **table of contents**, and often a **glossary** and/or a list of important variables and formulas. An instructor can explain how to use these features at the beginning of the year and perhaps even assign an activity that involves making use of them.

It may also be helpful to teach **active reading** techniques. One such technique is **pre-reading**—skimming and reading the headings before reading the text in depth, making predictions and building background knowledge. The instructor can also encourage active reading techniques through providing graphic organizers or techniques like **SQ3R**—a method that involves the student first Surveying the chapter, then formulating Questions about each section, then Reading the section, Reciting the main ideas (putting them in their own words), and Reviewing the material.

In the modern classroom, textbooks aren't the only kind of text that students can take advantage of. An effective teacher can also show students how to find information online, through web searches and reference sites.

Total School Program

While the science teachers plan the curriculum for their classes, they must also be aware of the **total school program**—the overall objectives for the students' learning in all subjects. The science teacher must be aware of school-wide objectives, and make sure that they are being adequately met in his or her class. The science instructor may also have a role in *setting* those objectives, in conjunction with other teachers and administrators; the science instructor in this case should work cooperatively with the rest of the team and ensure that any issues unique or important to the science classroom are properly addressed and incorporated into the objectives.

The science teacher must also be mindful of the statewide objectives. State standards lay out the curriculum requirements for the course and specify topics that must be covered. Students must master these topics to be ready not only for standardized exams, but to ensure that no gaps in understanding exist prior to advancing to the next grade-level.

Supportive Learning Environment

Creating a learning environment that supports student inquiries involves both setting certain procedures and expectations in the class and providing resources that lend themselves to inquiry-based learning. To encourage inquiry-based learning, the instructor should encourage students to ask questions, but try to guide them toward finding answers for themselves rather than giving direct answers to their questions. The instructor should pose questions that require higher-order thinking rather than rote recall or yes or no answers and include a time for reflection in each lesson. Lessons in inquiry-based classrooms are centered around projects and experiments rather than lectures—in fact, one increasingly popular technique is to "**flip the classroom**," having the students read the lesson or watch video lectures you provide as their homework and freeing up class time for discussion and analysis.

An inquiry-centered classroom environment should put a priority on student collaboration. The instructor should give the students assignments that involve their working together as much as practical. It is helpful to have some online resources that facilitate collaboration and sharing of information, such as a class website, and perhaps a class blog and wiki. Many online resources allow students to share documents and work on them together.

Participation in Scientific Investigation

Scientific investigations are an important part of science teaching, and it is vital that all students are given the opportunity to participate. Ideally, there will be enough space and equipment for the students to work in small groups on an experiment, but in practice this may not be possible. In this case, one solution is to have rotating stations in the classroom, where for one day or for part of the period one group works on one experiment, while another group works on a different activity that uses different equipment; as they rotate through the different stations, all the students will have the opportunity to do every activity, just not in the same order.

Another important part of making it possible for all students to participate in scientific investigations is to ensure that they all have the means to understand and carry out the instructions. Going over the procedure in a lecture may not be enough; it may be better to have a written handout and/or a screencast that the students can watch and refer back to as needed. Students with special needs must also be accommodated; for instance, English language learners can be given definitions of key terms.

Active Learning, Inquiry, and Reflection

Active learning and inquiry-based learning are two related pedagogical techniques that have been shown by research to be effective in teaching science. **Active learning** refers to teaching by making the student an active participant in the learning process. A class in which the instructor lectures, the students take notes, and the students later demonstrate their learning of the topic by taking a written exam is *not* engaged in active learning, and is not likely to be as effective. Active learning can include experiments that the students perform, interactive online simulations of processes that they can't physically experience in the classroom, and having the students create presentations and projects rather than have exams and worksheets as the main assessments.

Inquiry-based learning is a form of teaching by asking questions, having discussions, and helping students do their own research rather than just presenting them with lists of facts and formulas to be learned. Inquiry-based learning is effective not only because it involves the students directly, but because allowing them to formulate their own questions engages their curiosity and critical thinking. **Reflection** is also an important part of inquiry-based learning, having students think back on what they learned and how they learned it.

Modeling Scientific Thought

Modeling, in a pedagogical context, refers to *showing* the students what they should do, rather than telling them. This doesn't mean just demonstrating an activity at the front of the classroom while the students watch passively; effective modeling also involves the students as active participants. The important thing is that the teacher sets an example of the principles he or she wants to convey.

To model scientific attitudes, therefore, means to demonstrate and embody those attitudes. To instill curiosity and skepticism in students, the teacher should display those attributes. If the teacher doesn't know the answer to a question, the teacher should not be afraid to say "I don't know"—but should follow that by trying to find the answer, by looking it up online or by performing an experiment. When discussing a topic and coming up with questions about it, the instructor should come up with questions as well—ideally questions the instructor honestly doesn't know the answer to. On the other hand, the instructor should not be too quick to accept answers—not, for instance, immediately latching onto the first answer found online, but looking for multiple sources of information and analyzing their credibility.

Inquiry-Based Scientific Investigation

An **inquiry-based scientific investigation** is one that follows the **scientific method**. While the scientific method is often formalized in different ways, there are some essential aspects. The investigator formulates a specific **question** that the investigation will answer. Usually this question is based on an **observation** that the investigation is intended to explain. The investigator then does some background **research**, reviewing previously published information on the subject in question. For a professional scientist, this will usually involve reading articles in scientific journals; in a classroom setting, a web search may suffice. The investigator may formulate a **hypothesis**—a proposed possible answer to the question.

The investigator decides how to **gather evidence** to find an answer to the question and prove or disprove the hypothesis, designing an **experiment** that will test the hypothesis, and selecting the proper tools to carry it out. The investigator makes **predictions** as to what will happen in the experiment if the hypothesis is true or if it is not. The investigator then carries out the experiment, gathers data, and analyzes the results, drawing **conclusions** based on the data.

There remain other important steps: **communication** of the results to others, defending the results, and possibly formulating further questions.

Formulating Scientific Questions

Formulating scientific questions is an important part of an inquiry-based investigation; an investigation starts with a specific question, and then an experiment is designed to answer that question. The question usually is based on an observation: the student observes a phenomenon and then formulates a question about what was observed. The question should be as concrete, objective, quantitative, and measurable as possible. "Why did this object move?" is a vague and abstract question that cannot be easily answered. "Did this object move because of this force?" is more concrete. "What is the relationship between this force and the motion of this object?" is a good quantitative question that can potentially be answered by experiment.

To help the student to formulate a question, the instructor can first guide students through an observation, encouraging the students to think of anything about the observation they're curious about or that they don't understand. The instructor can then help the students come up with questions addressing the subject of their curiosity, and then gradually guide the students into making the questions more specific and measurable.

HYPOTHESES

The **hypothesis** is an educated guess as to the answer to the central question of a scientific investigation. It is an important part of the investigation because it helps guide the inquiry and suggest specific lines of investigation that can prove or disprove the hypothesis: the experiment at the heart of the investigation should be designed such that it will have different results depending on whether or not the hypothesis is correct.

It is important that the hypothesis is an *educated* guess; the student may not know the answer to the question, but there should be some basis for choosing the hypothesis—by extrapolation from known cases, or by analogy with similar scenarios. If the student has trouble coming up with a hypothesis, the instructor might prompt the student to think of similar situations the student understands better, or to research such situations that have been investigated before, and then to consider what those situations imply about the present question. Even a very loose analogy can be enough to make a hypothesis—for the purposes of the investigation, it doesn't matter that the student chooses a hypothesis that turns out to be *right*, only that it relates to the question.

SCIENTIFIC RESULTS

There are many methods that can be used to analyze and evaluate scientific results. Often **graphs** help investigators and readers visualize data better. If one variable is plotted against another and the points seem to form a straight line, that is evidence that a linear relationship may exist between these variables; if they form a parabola, they may have a quadratic relationship; and so on. In more advanced classes, **statistical methods** may be useful, from methods as simple as taking the **mean** of multiple measurements and comparing the means of sets of data rather than the individual points, to methods as complex as calculating **standard deviations** and **correlation coefficients**. All of these methods help show the relationships between quantities and can help to evaluate possible explanations of a result.

Error analysis is another important part of evaluating results. Students should have an idea of what possible sources of error exist in the experiment, and whether they are **random** or **systematic**. Random error can be identified by taking repeated measurements and seeing how close they are; identifying systematic error involves a more thoughtful consideration of what could lead results to be off in one direction or the other.

HIGHER-LEVEL THINKING SKILLS

Students should be encouraged to engage in not just rote memorization and learning of procedures, but in higher-order thinking as well that involves putting together what they've learned in constructive ways. The most commonly used model of different levels of thinking in education is **Bloom's taxonomy**, which divides cognitive processes into six categories or levels. The lowest level, **Remember**, involves simple recall of data. The next, **Understand**, requires students to be able to explain or discuss concepts in their own words. Then come **Apply**, using the concepts in practice; **Analyze**, drawing connections and comparisons between ideas; **Evaluate**, judging and justifying ideas; and **Create**, synthesizing something new from the concepts.

It's easy to design activities that utilize the lower levels of Bloom's Taxonomy. Engaging the higher orders of thinking is more difficult, but it is important for developing a more thorough understanding of a topic. Some verbs commonly associated with each level of Bloom's Taxonomy give clues as to how to promote them. "Create", for example, is associated with the verbs "construct," "plan," and "design" (among others)—certainly designing an experiment to answer a specific question fits here. "Evaluate" is associated with "appraise," "argue," and "justify"—students could be asked to assess a scientific claim and argue for or against it.

Systematic Observations and Measurements

In a scientific investigation, observations are not haphazard; there are certain systematic principles that must be followed for useful observations. As far as possible, the observations should be **quantitative**; there should be some measured value recorded, and not simply a qualitative observation such as "it is longer". Measurements should be taken by a consistent method and recorded with proper units—and with an estimate of their **uncertainty**. A measurement taken with a meter stick with markings every millimeter, for instance, has an uncertainty of ±0.5 mm.

It is also important when making observations to vary only one quantity at a time. If you want to measure how a plant's growth is affected by temperature and by amount of light, it isn't useful to change both factors for each measurement—that would make it impossible to see how much of the effect was produced by each change. Rather, it is better to do at least one set of measurements in which the temperature is held constant and the amount of light is changed, and another where the reverse is true, so that the effects of each factor can be isolated. In many cases, an **experimental control** is also desirable.

Students' Prior Knowledge

Prior knowledge refers to the knowledge the student has about the subject matter before it's covered in class. This may come from previous classes, from books and television, from peers or parents, from experience, or from other sources. It's useful to know what prior knowledge students possess before the lesson begins, and there are a number of ways of finding out. One way is through **formative assessments**, assessments that are designed not to test what the student has learned but to test what the students already know in order to guide lesson planning. Another popular way of testing prior knowledge is a **K-W-L chart**, in which students write down what they *know* about the topic, what they *want* to know, and, after the lesson, what they *learned*.

The instructor can use the students' prior knowledge as a starting point for the lesson; having the students share what they already know can help introduce the topic. Prior knowledge may also guide the instructor's approach to the topic, since it may carry some assumptions or preconceptions that will affect the way the student might react to different presentations. In some cases, prior knowledge may even lead to misconceptions that must be overcome.

Performance in Inquiry-Based Investigations

The stereotypical classroom assessment may be a multiple-choice quiz, but this is not generally the most effective way of assessing student learning in an inquiry-based classroom. There may be a place for written exams as summative assessments, but more effective assessment methods will engage students' higher-order thinking processes and may involve collaboration and active participation.

For example, in a science class, a lab report can be a useful assessment; after performing an experiment, students may be asked to turn in a written account of the procedure and results. Along similar lines, a laboratory journal that students keep during an experiment can also be used for assessment, or a field journal for longer-term projects. The instructor may require students to compile all their work in a portfolio, to be turned in at the end of the semester or at shorter intervals; this can serve as a summative assessment in lieu of or in addition to a traditional exam. To assess the student's participation in a classroom activity as objectively as possible, rather than make a subjective judgment call the instructor can use checklists or a detailed rubric prepared ahead of time.

Assessment and Instruction

An **assessment** is an activity designed to measure students' knowledge, learning, or abilities, such as an exam. Assessments are not limited to testing how much the student has learned after a lesson; there are also formative assessments used before or during a lesson to test the student's prior knowledge and how well they are learning the topic.

There are important relationships between assessment and instruction, and the two must be designed together. Formative assessments guide instruction, since the instructor should take into account students' prior knowledge in planning a lesson, and if a formative assessment shows that students are not learning what the instructor expects, the instructor should use that information to try a different pedagogical approach. As for summative assessments, they should be designed to match the learning objectives; the instructor should make sure that the summative assessment is designed to test that the students have met the specific instructional goals of the lessons.

Ongoing Assessment

Ongoing assessment is vital in science instruction for several reasons. For one thing, formative assessments are important so that the instructor can be informed of the students' prior knowledge and plan the lesson accordingly. If the instructor learns from a formative assessment that the students lack some prior knowledge necessary to the lesson, then the instructor will have to be sure to cover that first; if the instructor learns that the students have a significant misconception about the topic, then the instructor may have to plan for a conceptual change. During the lesson, further formative assessments can monitor students' learning and inform the instructor whether the students are absorbing the information and methodologies that the instructor intends them to absorb, or whether the pace of the lesson should be changed or different pedagogical methods adopted.

Ongoing assessments can also benefit the students by reinforcing the subject matter. The assessments give the students another opportunity to put what they have learned to use, and may help them better retain it. They also give the students an idea of how well they are learning, and what topics they might need to review or about which they should ask more questions.

Types of Assessments

Assessments are divided into two main categories: **summative assessments** that measure how well students have learned the subject matter at the end of a unit, and **formative assessments** that are used before or during a lesson to test the student's prior knowledge and how well they are learning the topic. Both these types of assessment are important, and both can be carried out in a number of ways. Assessments can also be **formal**—data-driven, standardized assessments the results of which can be compared against preset benchmarks—or **informal**—less structured assessments based around performance and content. An effective science classroom utilizes a variety of different assessment methods.

For example, a **performance assessment** is an assessment that requires the student to demonstrate skills by completing a task, rather than by selecting a pre-set answer or filling in a blank. A **self-assessment** is an activity in which the student assesses his or her own work, perhaps using a rubric provided by the instructor; these are often not graded and serve to inform the student of his or her own learning. A **peer assessment** is an activity in which the student's work is assessed not by the instructor, but by a fellow student.

Review Video: Formative and Summative Assessments
Visit mometrix.com/academy and enter code: 804991

Combatting Misconceptions

One of the reasons it's important to gauge students' prior knowledge of a topic is because some of that prior knowledge may be incorrect or misleading, and the student may have misconceptions about the topic that must be overcome. Simply telling the students that their prior beliefs were incorrect is unlikely to be effective, and it may in fact be counterproductive, leading to their misconceptions being reinforced instead of removed. Rather, a better goal is to bring about a **conceptual change**, a gradual revision and rearrangement of prior knowledge to accommodate new ideas, in which the student is an active participant.

There are several research-based methods of bringing about conceptual change. One method is to promote **cognitive conflict**: presenting data or demonstrations that contradict the students' prior conceptions, and guiding the students into finding a resolution to the conflict. Another is the use of **refutational texts** that discuss and refute various views on the topic. Other methods include **collaborative argumentation**, in which students are encouraged to discuss, defend, and evaluate their positions; and **persuasive pedagogy**, applying methods of persuasion such as response shaping and reinforcing.

Reliability and Validity

Two measurements of the soundness of an assessment are reliability and validity. An assessment is **reliable** if it yields consistent results; students' scores on the assessment should not depend on external circumstances and should be similar for different questions that test the same skill. An assessment is **valid** if it measures what it is meant to measure. These two qualities can vary independently; it is possible for an exam to have a high reliability but a low validity, or vice versa.

The reliability of an assessment can be affected by many factors. Longer tests tend to be more reliable; tests with a short time limit so that many students cannot complete all the questions, or must rush to do so, tend to be less reliable. Reliability is also affected by difficulty; a test is most reliable when the questions are not so easy that almost every student answers the questions correctly, but not so hard that almost none do. It requires finding a suitable middle ground of difficulty. An assessment will tend to be more valid if it is designed to cover all the material that it is supposed to cover, but only that material. It will be less valid if it has hidden biases against certain categories of student.

Assessment as a Learning Experience

Though an obvious purpose of assessments is to allow the instructor to assign students a grade in the class, the assessments themselves can provide learning experiences. For one thing, as the students see what questions on the assessment they are unable to answer, or do not answer correctly, this helps them see what topics they have not fully learned and may need to further review. On the other hand, the questions that the students got right will help build their confidence and perhaps help them better remember in the future what they learned about those topics. Assessments also give students further practice with the methods and concepts they are testing, which may further work to reinforce them. They may also help students to learn new problem-solving strategies; as students go over the assessment after the fact and discuss how they were supposed to solve a particular problem, the answer might give them information about a strategy they were previously unaware of or underutilizing.

Equitable Use of Assessments

One important consideration that must be kept in mind in designing assessments is that they must be **equitable**—they must not be biased toward or against any part of the student population. Every student must have an adequate opportunity to demonstrate his or her skills and knowledge. There are many biases that may carelessly enter into assessments: cultural biases, language biases, biases against students with special needs.

There are a number of steps that instructors can take to ensure that assessments are equitable. Questions should not rely on "common knowledge" that may not be common to students of different cultures. Students with special needs must be provided with adequate accommodations. English language learners should be given definitions or paraphrases of difficult words and sentences. Other steps that can be taken toward making assessments more equitable include clearly laying out learning outcomes and grading rubrics, using many different methods of assessment that allow students to show their accomplishments in different ways, and ensuring that the subject matter covered in assessments is closely matched to what the instructor teaches in class.

Sharing Criteria and Results

It's important to share the evaluation criteria of assessments with students so that the students will know what to expect from the assessments and prepare accordingly, and so that during the assessment they will know where to best focus their time and attention. If the students have no idea how an assessment will be graded, then the assessment is not fair or equitable; students will not know what aspects of the assessment they should focus on the most and doing well on the assessment may be largely a matter of luck. Sharing the rubric for the assessment ahead of time makes the instructor's expectations clear and ensures that the students know what specifically they will be tested on and can prepare accordingly.

It is also important to share the results of assessments with the students. If the students know the results of their assessments, they can gauge their own progress and learning, and decide where they need to focus in the future and what topics they may need to revisit. Knowing their assessment results may also help students evaluate their study strategies and judge whether or not they are working and how or if they might need to be revised.

Scientific Inquiry Skills for Elementary Students

The six abilities that **grades K-4 students** should acquire are as follows:

- They should be able to ask questions about objects, organisms, and events in the environment.
- They should be able to devise a simple investigation to answer a question.
- They should be able to use tools such as magnifying glasses, rulers, and balances to gather data and make observations.
- They should be able to use the gathered data and observations to provide an explanation.
- They should be able to talk about, draw pictures, or use another method to communicate the results of an investigation and what they learned.
- With respect to the nature of scientific inquiry and scientists, students should understand that investigations involve formulating questions and answers, using different methods of discovering and disclosing answers, using basic tools, observing, sharing answers, and looking at and understanding others' work.

Scientific Inquiry Skills for Middle Grade Students

The five abilities that **grades 5–8 students** should acquire are as follows:

- They should be able to reformulate and clarify questions until they can be answered through scientific investigation.
- They should be able to create and carry out a scientific investigation, interpret the data to provide explanations, and use further data to revise explanations.
- They should be able to identify the tools necessary to gather and analyze data. They should be able to use computer hardware and software to store, organize, and gather data.
- They should be able to provide descriptions and explanations, create models, and make predictions based on the body of knowledge they possess.
- They should be able to explain cause and effect relationships using explanations and data from experiments.

Scientific Inquiry Skills for Older Students

The six abilities that **grades 9–12 students** should acquire are as follows:

- They should be able to identify questions and concepts that guide scientific investigation. In other words, they should be able to create a hypothesis and an appropriate experiment to test that hypothesis.
- They should be able to design and conduct a scientific investigation from start to finish. This includes being able to guide the inquiry by choosing the proper technologies and methods, determining variables, selecting an appropriate method for presenting data, and conducting peer review.
- They should be able to use technology and mathematics in investigations.
- They should be able to formulate and revise scientific explanations and models.
- They should be able to recognize and analyze alternative explanations. In other words, they should be able to devise other possibilities based on the current body of knowledge.
- They should be able to communicate and defend a scientific argument in both written and oral form.

Chapter Quiz

Ready to see how well you retained what you just read? Scan the QR code to go directly to the chapter quiz interface for this study guide. If you're using a computer, simply visit the online resources page at **mometrix.com/resources719/gacechemistry** and click the Chapter Quizzes link.

Nature of Matter and Energy

Temperature, Scales, Heat, and Heat Capacity

Temperature Scales

Empirical or relative temperature scales, like Celsius (°C) and Fahrenheit (°F), can have a corresponding **absolute temperature scale**, which in this case would be Kelvin (K) and Rankine (R), respectively. A temperature of 0 K or 0 R is known as **absolute zero**, at which point atomic motion and thermal energy are, theoretically, at a minimum. Kelvins and degrees Celsius are related by the equation, $T_K = T_C + 273.15$. Similarly, Rankines and degrees Fahrenheit are related as $T_R = T_F + 459.67$. From these relations, we can see that within both individual pairs of temperature scales, the magnitude of the unit is the same; that is, an increase of 1 °C is the same an increase of 1 K, while an increase of 1 °F equals an increase of 1 R. Converting from Fahrenheit to Celsius is slightly more complicated: $T_C = \frac{5}{9}(T_F - 32)$, or in reverse, $T_F = \frac{9}{5}T_C + 32$. From these equations, we can see that a change of 1 °C is greater than a change of 1 °F .

Relationship between Heat and Temperature

It is often useful to know how much heat is required to cause a certain amount of material to reach a desired temperature. Each material has a property called specific heat, which allows this calculation. To bring about a temperature increase ΔT to a mass m made of a material with specific heat c, the required heat input is found by the equation $Q = mc\Delta T$. This equation can also be used to calculate the amount of heat absorbed during a given temperature increase. The amount of heat required to raise the temperature of 1 gram of water by 1 degree Celsius, or 1 Kelvin, is 1 calorie or 4.184 joules. Thus, the specific heat of water is 1 $\frac{\text{cal}}{\text{g K}}$ or 4.184 $\frac{\text{J}}{\text{g K}}$.

Note that since Kelvin and Celsius scales use the same unit size and the heat equation uses *change* in temperature, it is equally valid to use units of $\frac{\text{J}}{\text{g K}}$ or $\frac{\text{J}}{\text{g °C}}$.

Latent Heat and Specific Heat

Suppose we wish to convert ice initially at –5 °C to water at 5 °C. We must provide heat to accomplish this. The amount of heat energy required to raise the temperature of a given quantity of a material is a property known as **specific heat**. This is most often given on a mass basis, with units of $\frac{\text{J}}{\text{g K}}$, but may also be given as a molar property as $\frac{\text{J}}{\text{mol K}}$. If the given quantity of material and the given specific heat are not unit compatible, it will be necessary to multiply or divide by the molar weight of the material to achieve compatibility. Returning to the problem at hand, in order for ice initially at –5 °C to reach 5 °C, it must undergo a phase change from a solid to a liquid. When the ice is heated, it does not simply become water when it reaches 0 °C. In order for the ice to become water, additional heat must be added to break the bonds of the solid. This heat is called the **latent heat of fusion** and, like the specific heat, may be given on a mass or a molar basis, with common units of kJ/g or kJ/mol, respectively. This heat input for the phase change occurs while the material remains at a constant temperature. Once the phase change has been completed, the water temperature will begin to rise again with heat input, though the specific heat of liquid water will be different from that of ice. If the water need be heated above 100 °C, it will have to undergo a second phase change, overcoming the **latent heat of vaporization**, and its temperature will subsequently be governed by a third specific heat, that of the gas phase.

Thermal Expansion and Contraction

When the temperature of most materials changes, they will undergo some amount of size change called **thermal expansion**. Though generally quite small, it is important to know how much of an impact thermal expansion might have on the size of an object. Each material has a linear coefficient of thermal expansion α, generally having units of $°C^{-1}$ or $°F^{-1}$, that relates the change in length to the original length. The percentage change in length is found by the equation $\frac{\Delta L}{L_0} = \alpha\Delta T$, and the absolute change is found by a rearrangement of that equation, $\Delta L = L_0\alpha\Delta T$. Negative thermal expansion means that either ΔT is negative (i.e., getting colder) or the material has a negative α (some materials in specific conditions have this property).

Assuming that the material is able to expand in all directions, there will similarly be a change in **areas** and **volumes**. The change in an area A_0 will be $\Delta A = 2\alpha A_0\Delta T + \alpha^2\Delta T^2$. Because α is generally much less than 1, $\alpha^2\Delta T^2$ will most often be negligible. Thus, the change in area becomes $\Delta A = 2\alpha A_0\Delta T$. From this we can see that the area coefficient of thermal expansion is $\gamma = 2\alpha$, and $\Delta A = \gamma A_0\Delta T$. By making similar assumptions with the equation for change in volume, we find that the volume coefficient of thermal expansion is $\beta = 3\alpha$ and that $\Delta V = \beta V_0\Delta T$.

Various Sample Temperature Conversions

Convert 200.0 Degrees Fahrenheit to the Celsius Scale.

To convert from 200.0 °F to °C, use the equation $T_C = \frac{5}{9}(T_F - 32)$. Substituting 200.0 in for T_F yields $T_C = \frac{5}{9}(200.0 - 32) = \frac{5}{9}(168.0) = 93.33\ °C$.

Convert 24.0 Degrees Celsius to the Fahrenheit Scale.

To convert from 24.0 °C to °F, use the equation $T_F = \frac{9}{5}T_C + 32$. Substituting 24.0 in for T_C yields $T_F = \frac{9}{5}(24.0) + 32 = 43.2 + 32 = 75.2\ °F$

Convert 21.5 Degrees Celsius to the Kelvin Scale.

To convert from 21.5 °C to K, use the equation $T_K = T_C + 273.15$. Substituting 21.5 in for T_C yields $T_K = 21.5 + 273.15 = 294.65\ K$.

Thermal Energy

Thermal energy is part of a system's **total internal energy**, which consists of potential and kinetic energy. Thermal energy is the total internal kinetic energy of a system due to the random motions of the particles. The thermal energy of a system is measured by its temperature, which is the average kinetic energy of the particles in that system. The flow of thermal energy is referred to as heat. Appropriate units for thermal energy include the joule (J), British thermal unit (Btu), calorie (cal), and kilocalorie (kcal).

$$1\ \text{Btu} = 1{,}055\ \text{J}$$
$$1\ \text{cal} = 4.184\ \text{J}$$
$$1{,}000\ \text{cal} = 1\ \text{kcal}$$

Heat Capacity and Specific Heat

Heat capacity is the amount of heat required to raise a sample of matter by 1 °C. Heat capacity is an extensive property and varies with the amount of matter in the sample. The greater the mass of the sample, the higher the heat capacity of the sample. This means that a specific type of matter will have different heat capacities depending on the size of the sample. Heat capacity may be represented by the formula $C = \frac{Q}{\Delta T}$, where Q is the heat in joules and ΔT is the change in temperature in degrees Celsius. Specific heat is the amount of heat required to raise the temperature of a unit mass by 1 °C. The formula for specific heat is $c = \frac{Q}{m\Delta T}$, where Q is the heat in joules, ΔT is the change in temperature in degrees Celsius, and m is the mass of the sample. Because the specific heat formula incorporates the mass of the sample, a specific type of substance will have a constant specific heat, making specific heat an intensive property.

> **Review Video: Specific Heat Capacity**
> Visit mometrix.com/academy and enter code: 736791

Explain How to Calculate the Amount of Heat Lost By a Piece of Copper with a Mass of 100.0 g When it Cools from 100.0°C to 20.0°C. The Specific Heat of Copper is 0.380 J/(g·°C).

To calculate the amount of heat lost by a piece of copper with a mass of 100.0 g when it cools from 100.0 °C to 20.0 °C, use the equation $Q = mc\Delta T$, where Q is the amount of heat lost in joules, m is the mass of the copper in grams, c is the specific heat of copper, and ΔT is the change in temperature $(T_2 - T_1)$ in degrees Celsius. Substituting these known values yields:

$$Q = (100.0\text{ g})\left(0.380\ \frac{\text{J}}{\text{g °C}}\right)\left((20.0\text{°C}) - (100.0\text{°C})\right) = -3{,}040\text{ J}$$

The negative value confirms that heat was lost as the copper cooled.

Finding the Specific Heat of a Substance with a Calorimeter

The specific heat of a substance can be determined using a calorimeter. A known amount of the substance is heated to a known temperature. In the classroom setting, this can be accomplished by placing the metal in a loosely stoppered test tube and then placing the test tube in boiling water. The calorimeter is prepared by placing water of a known amount and temperature in the calorimeter. The heated metal is carefully placed into the water in the calorimeter. The temperature of the water is carefully monitored until it stops rising. The final temperature of the metal will be equal to the final temperature of the water. The heat lost by the metal equals the heat gained by the water:

$$-Q_{\text{metal}} = Q_{\text{water}}$$

$$-m_{\text{metal}}c_{\text{metal}}\Delta T_{\text{metal}} = m_{\text{water}}c_{\text{water}}\Delta T_{\text{water}}$$

In these equations, Q is the amount of heat lost or gained in joules, m is the mass in grams, c is the specific heat, and ΔT is the change in temperature $T_2 - T_1$ in degrees Celsius.

> **Review Video: Using a Calorimeter**
> Visit mometrix.com/academy and enter code: 703935

Calculating the Specific Heat of an Unknown Metal:

- In a calorimetry experiment, the specific heat of an unknown metal dropped 20.0 °C.
- The mass of the unknown metal is 100.0 g.
- The temperature of the water with a mass of 100.0 g in the calorimeter increased 1.00 °C.
- The specific heat of water is 4.184 $\frac{\text{J}}{\text{g °C}}$.

The heat lost by the metal must equal the heat gained by the water, as shown in the equation $Q_{lost\ by\ metal} = Q_{gained\ by\ the\ water}$, where Q is the amount of heat lost or gained in joules. To calculate the specific heat of the metal, use $-m_{metal}c_{metal}\Delta T_{metal} = m_{water}c_{water}\Delta T_{water}$, where m is the mass of the metal or water in grams, c is the specific heat of the metal or water, and ΔT is the change in temperature $(T_2 - T_1)$ in degrees Celsius in the metal or water. Solving the equation for c_{metal} results in:

$$c_{metal} = -\frac{m_{water}c_{water}\Delta T_{water}}{m_{metal}\Delta T_{metal}}$$

Substituting in the given information yields:

$$c_{\text{metal}} = -\frac{(100.0\ \text{g})\left(4.184\ \frac{\text{J}}{\text{g °C}}\right)(1.00\ \text{°C})}{(100.0\ \text{g})(-20.0\ \text{°C})} = 0.209\ \frac{\text{J}}{\text{g °C}}$$

Types of Energy

Chemical, Electrical, Electromagnetic, Nuclear, and Thermal Energy

Different types of energy may be associated with systems:

- **Chemical energy** is the energy that is stored in chemical bonds and intermolecular forces.
- **Electrical energy** is the energy associated with the movement of electrons or ions through a material.
- **Electromagnetic energy** is the energy of electromagnetic waves of several frequencies including radio waves, microwaves, infrared light, visible light, ultraviolet light, x-rays, and gamma rays.
- **Nuclear energy** is the binding energy that is stored within an atom's nucleus.
- **Thermal energy** is the total internal kinetic energy of a system due to the random motions of the particles.

Phase Transitions

States of Matter

The four states of matter are solid, liquid, gas, and plasma. **Solids** have a definite shape and a definite volume. Because solid particles are held in fairly rigid positions, solids are the least compressible of the four states of matter. **Liquids** have definite volumes but no definite shapes. Because their particles are free to slip and slide over each other, liquids take the shape of their containers, but they still remain fairly incompressible by natural means. **Gases** have no definite shape or volume. Because gas particles are free to move, they move away from each other to fill their containers. Gases are compressible. **Plasmas** are high-temperature, ionized gases that exist only under very high temperatures at which electrons are stripped away from their atoms.

Review Video: States of Matter
Visit mometrix.com/academy and enter code: 742449

Review Video: Properties of Liquids
Visit mometrix.com/academy and enter code: 802024

Review Video: States of Matter [Advanced]
Visit mometrix.com/academy and enter code: 298130

The following table shows similarities and differences between solids, liquids, and gases:

	Solid	Liquid	Gas
Shape	Fixed shape	No fixed shape (assumes shape of container)	No fixed shape (assumes shape of container)
Volume	Fixed	Fixed	Changes to assume volume of container
Fluidity	Does not flow easily	Flows easily	Flows easily
Compressibility	Hard to compress	Hard to compress	Compresses

Six Different Types of Phase Change

A substance that is undergoing a change from a solid to a liquid is said to be melting. If this change occurs in the opposite direction, from liquid to solid, this change is called freezing. A liquid which is being converted to a gas is undergoing vaporization. The reverse of this process is known as condensation. Direct transitions from gas to solid and solid to gas are much less common in everyday life, but they can occur given the proper conditions. Solid to gas conversion is known as sublimation, while the reverse is called deposition.

Review Video: Chemical and Physical Properties of Matter
Visit mometrix.com/academy and enter code: 717349

Phase Diagram and Critical Point

A **phase diagram** is a graph or chart of pressure versus temperature that represents the solid, liquid, and gaseous phases of a substance and the transitions between these phases. Typically, **pressure** is located on the vertical axis, and temperature is located along the horizontal axis. The curves drawn on the graph represent points at which different phases are in an equilibrium state. These curves indicate at which pressure and temperature the phase changes of sublimation, melting, and boiling occur. Specifically, the curve between the liquid and gas phases indicates the pressures and temperatures at which the liquid and gas phases are in equilibrium. The curve between the solid and liquid phases indicates the temperatures and pressures at which the solid and liquid phases are in equilibrium. The open spaces on the graph represent the distinct phases solid, liquid, and gas. The point at which the solid–liquid, solid–gas, and liquid–gas phase boundaries intersect is called the triple point. At the triple point, the solid, liquid, and gas phases all exist in equilibrium. The critical point, by contrast, is the endpoint of the liquid–gas coexistence curve, where the liquid and gas phases become indistinguishable and form a supercritical fluid.

Lettered Regions of a Phase Diagram

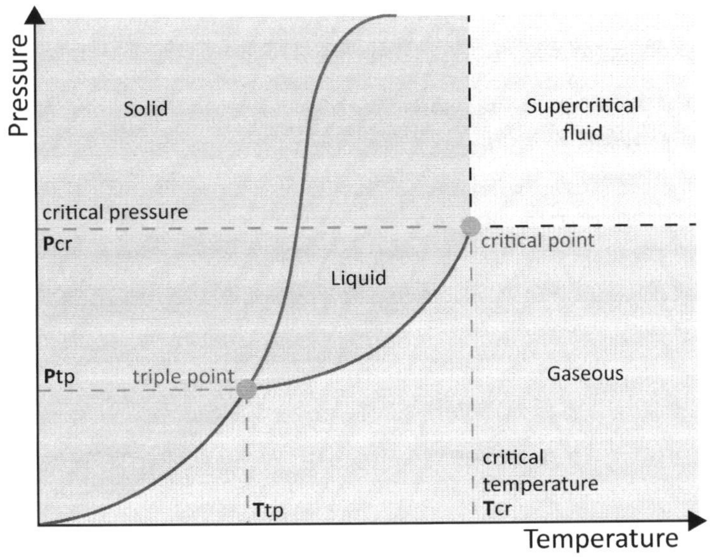

A—**Solid phase**: This is a region of high pressure and low temperature where the substance always exists as a solid.

B—**Liquid phase**: This is a region of pressure and temperature where the substance is in the liquid phase.

C—**Gas phase**: This is a region of pressure and temperature where the substance is in the gaseous phase.

D—**Sublimation point**: The portion of the curve that contains point D shows all the combinations of pressure and temperature at which the solid phase is in equilibrium with the gaseous phase.

E—**Triple point**: The point at which the solid, liquid, and gaseous phases are all in equilibrium.

F—**Boiling point**: The line that contains point F indicates all the combinations of pressure and temperature at which the liquid phase and gas phase are in equilibrium.

Calculating Phase Transitions

Heating Curve of Water from −40 °C to 140 °C

In the first portion of the curve, the graph slants up and to the right as the ice is a solid that is increasing in temperature from −40 °C to 0 °C. In the second portion of the curve, the graph remains horizontal during the phase change from solid to liquid as the temperature remains constant at 0 °C. In the third portion of the curve, the graph slants up and to the right as the water now is in the liquid state and is increasing in temperature from 0 °C to 100 °C. In the fourth portion of the curve, the graph remains horizontal during the phase change from liquid to gas as the temperature remains at 100 °C. In the last portion of the curve, the graph slants up and to the right as water now is in the gaseous state and the steam is increasing in temperature from 100 °C to 140 °C

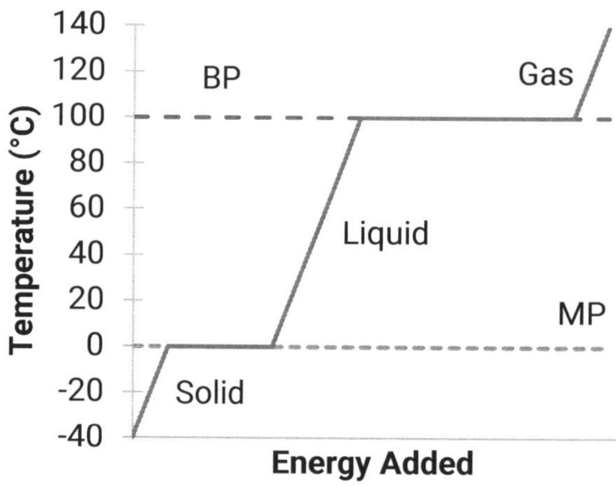

Calculating the Amount of Heat Corresponding to Each Portion of a Heating Curve

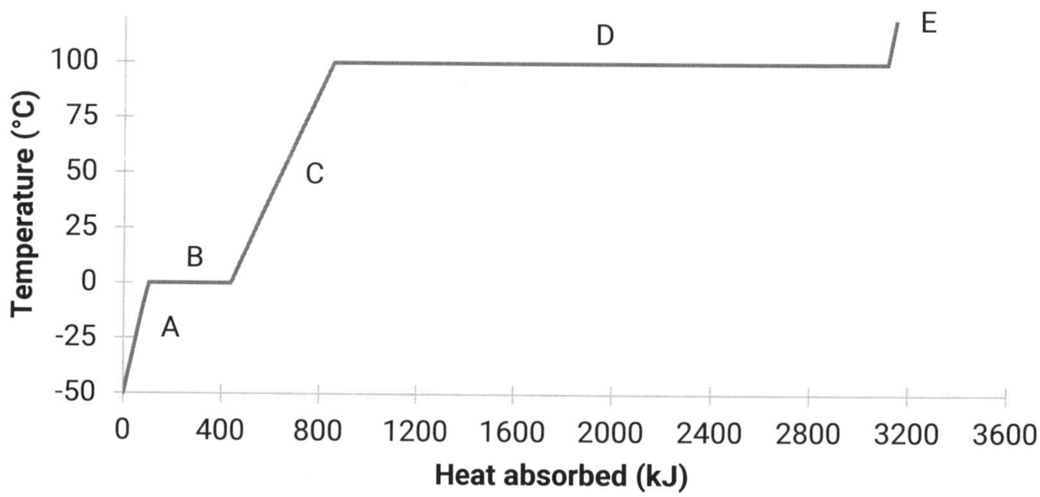

For portion A, $Q = mc_{\text{ice}}\Delta T$, where Q is the amount of heat gained in joules, m is the mass of the ice in grams, c_{ice} is the specific heat of ice, and ΔT is the temperature change in degrees Celsius.

For portion B, $Q = m\Delta H_{\text{fus}}$, where Q is the amount of heat gained in joules, m is the mass of the ice/water in grams, and ΔH_{fus} is the heat of fusion for water in joules per gram, $\frac{\text{J}}{\text{g}}$.

For portion C, $Q = mc_{\text{water}}\Delta T$, where Q is the amount of heat gained in joules, m is the mass of the water in grams, c_{water} is the specific heat of water, and ΔT is the temperature change in degrees Celsius.

For portion D, $Q = m\Delta H_{\text{vap}}$, where Q is the amount of heat gained in joules, m is the mass of the water/steam in grams, and ΔH_{vap} is the heat of vaporization for water in joules per gram, $\frac{\text{J}}{\text{g}}$.

For portion E, $Q = mc_{\text{steam}}\Delta T$, where Q is the amount of heat gained in joules, m is the mass of the steam in grams, c_{steam} is the specific heat of steam, and ΔT is the temperature change in degrees Celsius.

HEAT OF VAPORIZATION, HEAT OF FUSION, AND HEAT OF SUBLIMATION

- The **heat of vaporization** (ΔH_{vap}) is the amount of heat that must be added to one mole of a substance to change the substance from the liquid phase to the gaseous phase.
- The **heat of fusion** (ΔH_{fus}) is the amount of heat that must be added to one mole of a substance to change the substance from the solid phase to the liquid phase.
- The **heat of sublimation** (ΔH_{sub}) is the amount of heat that must be added to one mole of a substance to change the substance directly from the solid phase to the gaseous phase without passing through the liquid phase.

Explain How to Calculate the Amount of Heat Required to Change 100.0 g of Ice at -10.0 °C to Water at 10.0 °C. $\left[\Delta H_{fus} = 334\ \frac{J}{g}; c_{water} = 4.18\ \frac{J}{g\,°C}, c_{ice} = 2.06\ \frac{J}{g\,°C}\right]$**.**

To calculate the amount of heat required to change 100.0 g of ice at −10.0 °C to water at 10.0 °C, it is necessary to calculate the heat required for each step along the way. Step 1 is to calculate the heat required to raise the temperature of the ice from −10.0 °C to 0.0 °C. Step 2 is to calculate the amount of heat required to melt the ice. Finally, step 3 is to calculate the amount of heat required to raise the temperature of the water from 0.0 °C to 10.0 °C.

For steps 1 and 3, the required equation is $Q = mc\Delta T$.

Because step 2 is a phase change, the required equation is $Q = m\Delta H_{fus}$.

For step 1: $Q_1 = (100.0\text{ g})\left(2.06\ \frac{J}{g\,°C}\right)(0.0°C - (-10.0°C)) = 2{,}060\text{ J}$.

For step 2: $Q_2 = m\Delta H_{fus} = (100.0\text{ g})\left(334\ \frac{J}{g}\right) = 33{,}400\text{ J}$.

For step 3: $Q_3 = (100.0\text{ g})\left(4.18\ \frac{J}{g\,°C}\right)(10.0\text{ °C} - 0.0\text{ °C}) = 4{,}180\text{ J}$.

Adding $Q_1 + Q_2 + Q_3 = 2{,}060\text{ J} + 33{,}400\text{ J} + 4{,}180\text{ J} = 39{,}640\text{ J}$.

Explain How to Calculate the Amount of Heat Required to Change 100.0 g of Water at 90.0 °C to Steam at 110.0 °C. $\left[\Delta H_{vap} = 2,260\ \frac{J}{g}; c_{steam} = 1.86\ \frac{J}{g\,°C}, c_{water} = 4.18\ \frac{J}{g\,°C}\right]$**.**

To calculate the amount of heat required to change 100.0 g of water at 90.0 °C to steam at 110.0 °C, it is necessary to calculate the heat required at each step along the way. Step 1 is to calculate the heat required to raise the temperature of the water from 90.0 °C to 100.0 °C. Step 2 is to calculate the amount of heat required to change the water to steam. Finally, step 3 is to calculate the amount of heat required to raise the temperature of the steam from 100.0 °C to 110.0 °C.

For steps 1 and 3, the required equation is $Q = mc\Delta T$.

Because Step 2 is a phase change, the required equation is $Q = m\Delta H_{vap}$.

For step 1: $Q_1 = (100.0\text{ g})\left(4.18\ \frac{J}{g\,°C}\right)(100.0\text{ °C} - 90.0\text{ °C}) = 4{,}180\text{ J}$.

For step 2: $Q_2 = m\Delta H_{vap} = (100.0\text{ g})\left(2{,}260\ \frac{J}{g}\right) = 226{,}000\text{ J}$.

For step 3: $Q_1 = (100.0\text{ g})\left(1.86\ \frac{J}{g\,°C}\right)(110.0°C - 100.0°C) = 1{,}860\text{ J}$.

Adding $Q_1 + Q_2 + Q_3 = 4{,}180\text{ J} + 226{,}000\text{ J} + 1{,}860\text{ J} = 232{,}040\text{ J}$.

Gas Laws

Kinetic Molecular Theory

The **kinetic molecular theory of gases** states that the pressure exerted by a gas is due to numerous collisions of molecules with one another and with container walls. This assertion led to the development of what is now known as the ideal gas law: $PV = nRT$, where P is **pressure**, V is **volume**, T is **temperature**, n is the number of moles of gas present, and R is the universal gas constant. Different aspects of this law have different names, but there are many simple relations that may be derived from it. For instance, if an ideal gas is contained such that no molecules can escape, then it may be said that $\frac{P_1V_1}{T_1} = \frac{P_2V_2}{T_2}$, where the subscripts indicate distinct sets of conditions. Generally, one of the three variables will be held constant while the other two change. If an ideal gas in a container with a constant volume is heated, the effect this has on the pressure can be determined both analytically and numerically. Additional energy imparted to the gas particles will cause them to move faster, and, according to the kinetic molecular theory, faster particles mean more collisions and a higher resulting pressure. This can be expressed numerically as $\frac{P_1}{T_1} = \frac{P_2}{T_2}$. This means that if T_2 is higher than T_1, then P_2 must be equivalently higher than P_1 to maintain the same ratio.

Other derivations from the ideal gas law include calculating molarity or moles per unit volume $\left(\frac{n}{V} = \frac{P}{RT}\right)$, gas density if the molecular weight (M) is known $\left(\rho = \frac{PM}{RT}\right)$, or molecular weight if the density is known $\left(M = \frac{\rho RT}{P}\right)$.

Ideal Gases

An **ideal gas** is a hypothetical or theoretical gas. Ideal gases are assumed to be a set of randomly moving point particles that do not interact with each other. The collisions of ideal gases are assumed to be completely elastic, and the intermolecular forces are assumed to be zero. Real gases show far more complex behaviors. The ideal gas laws tend to fail at low temperatures and high pressures when the effects of the particle size and intermolecular forces are more apparent. Also, the ideal gas assumptions do not account for phase transitions.

Avogadro's Law

Avogadro's law describes the relationship between the **volume** and **number of moles** of an ideal gas at a constant pressure and temperature. For an ideal gas, the volume and the number of moles are directly related. If the volume increases, the number of moles would have to increase in order to maintain the pressure and temperature. If the number of moles in the container increases, the volume will also need to increase to maintain the same pressure and temperature. The relationship between volume and the number of moles of a gas is represented by $V \propto n$, $V = kn$, or $\frac{V}{n} = k$. Because the quotient of the volume and the number of moles is a constant, Avogadro's law can be stated as:

$$\frac{V_i}{n_i} = \frac{V_f}{n_f}$$

Review Video: Avogadro's Hypothesis
Visit mometrix.com/academy and enter code: 968309

Boyle's Law

Boyle's law describes the relationship between the **volume** and **pressure** of an ideal gas at a constant temperature for a given amount of gas. For an ideal gas, volume and pressure are inversely related. Because gases are compressible, if the pressure of a gas sample is increased, the volume will decrease. If the pressure of a gas sample is decreased, the volume will increase. Conversely, if the volume of a gas sample is increased, the pressure will decrease. If the volume of a gas sample is decreased, the pressure will increase. For example, if the pressure of a gas sample is doubled, the volume decreases to one-half of the original volume. If the pressure of a gas sample is tripled, the volume decreases to one-third of the original volume. The relationship between volume and pressure is represented by $V \propto \frac{1}{P}$, $V = k\frac{1}{P}$, or $PV = k$. Because the product of the pressure and the volume is a constant, Boyle's law can be stated as $P_iV_i = P_fV_f$.

Review Video: Boyle's Law
Visit mometrix.com/academy and enter code: 115757

Charles's Law

Charles's law describes the relationship between the **volume** and **temperature** of an ideal gas at a constant pressure for a given amount of gas. For an ideal gas, volume and temperature are directly related. Because the kinetic energy of a gas is directly proportional to the absolute temperature, if the temperature increases, the average kinetic energy of the gas molecules increases. As the molecules move faster, they will spread farther apart as long as the pressure remains constant, which increases the volume. If the volume of the container were to increase, the temperature would also have to increase if it were to maintain a constant pressure, since the molecules must move faster to strike the container as often. The relationship between volume and temperature is represented by $V \propto T$, $V = kT$, or $\frac{V}{T} = k$. Because the quotient of the volume and the temperature is a constant, Charles's law can be stated as $\frac{V_i}{T_i} = \frac{V_f}{T_f}$, where the temperature is stated in Kelvin.

Combined Gas Law

The **combined gas law** combines Boyle's law and Charles's law. According to Boyle's law, **volume** and **pressure** are inversely related, or $V \propto \frac{1}{P}$. According to Charles's law, **volume** and **temperature** are directly related, or $V \propto T$. Combining these relationships into one yields $V \propto \frac{T}{P}$ or $V = k\frac{T}{P}$. Solving for k yields $\frac{PV}{T}$. Because $k = \frac{P_1V_1}{T_1}$ and $k = \frac{P_2V_2}{T_2}$, the combined gas law can be written as:

$$\frac{P_1V_1}{T_1} = \frac{P_2V_2}{T_2}$$

For situations in which $V_1 = V_2$, the combined gas law yields a relationship of $P \propto T$, indicating that for a constant volume, the pressure and temperature are directly related.

Ideal Gas Law

The **ideal gas law** combines Boyle's law, Charles's law, and Avogadro's law. According to Boyle's law, $V \propto \frac{1}{P}$. According to Charles's law, $V \propto T$. According to Avogadro's law, $V \propto n$. Combining these three relationships into one relationship yields $V \propto \frac{nT}{P}$. Multiplying through by P yields $PV \propto nT$, or $PV = nRT$, where R is the ideal gas constant of $0.0821\ \frac{\text{L atm}}{\text{K mol}}$, P is the pressure in atmospheres, V is the volume in liters, n is the number of moles, and T is the temperature in Kelvin.

Behavior of Real Gases

Although assuming that gases are ideal is appropriate for many situations, **real gases** behave differently than **ideal gases**. The collisions of real gases are not elastic. Real gases do have attractive and repulsive forces. Real gases have **mass**, whereas ideal gases do not. The atoms or molecules of real gases are not point particles, and they do interact with each other, especially under high pressures and low temperatures. Under the right conditions of pressure and temperature, real gases will undergo phase transitions and become liquids. The pressure of real gases is less than those of ideal gases due to the small attractive forces between the particles in the gases.

> **Review Video: Ideal Gas vs Real Gas**
> Visit mometrix.com/academy and enter code: 619477

A 5.0 L Gas Sample Has a Pressure of 1.0 Standard Atmosphere (atm). If the Pressure Is Increased to 2.0 atm, Find the New Volume. Assume That the Temperature Is Constant.

To find the new volume, use the equation associated with Boyle's law, $P_iV_i = P_fV_f$. Solving the equation for the unknown V_f yields $V_f = \frac{P_iV_i}{P_f}$. Substituting the given values, $P_i = 1.0$ atm, $V_i = 5.0$ L, and $P_f = 2.0$ atm, into the equation yields $V_f = \frac{(1.0 \text{ atm})(5.0 \text{ L})}{(2.0 \text{ atm})} = 2.5$ L. This checks out because the pressure increased and the volume decreased. More specifically, because the pressure was doubled, the volume was reduced to one-half of the original volume.

A Gas Sample Has a Volume of 10.0 L at 200.0 K. Find Its Volume If the Temperature Is Increased to 300.0 K.

To find the new volume, use the equation associated with Charles's law, $\frac{V_i}{T_i} = \frac{V_f}{T_f}$. Solving the equation for the unknown V_f yields $V_f = \frac{T_fV_i}{T_i}$. Substituting the given values, $V_i = 10.0$ L, $T_i = 200.0$ K, and $T_f = 300.0$ K, into the equation yields $V_f = \frac{(300.0 \text{ K})(10.0 \text{ L})}{(200.0 \text{ K})} = 15.0$ L. This checks out because the temperature increased and the volume increased. Also, note that if the temperature had not been stated in Kelvin, it would have to be converted to Kelvin before substituting the values into the equation.

Explain How to Find the Pressure That 0.500 mol of H_2 (g) Will Exert on a 500.0 mL Flask at 300.0 K.

To calculate the pressure that 0.500 mol of $H_2(g)$ will exert on a 500.0 mL flask at 300.0 K, use the ideal gas equation $PV = nRT$, where R is the ideal gas constant of $0.0821 \frac{\text{L atm}}{\text{K mol}}$, P is the pressure in atmospheres, V is the volume in liters, n is the number of moles, and T is the temperature in Kelvin. Solving the ideal gas equation for P yields $P = \frac{nRT}{V}$. First, convert the 500.0 mL to 0.500 L. Substituting in $n = 0.500$ mol, $V = 0.500$ L, $T = 300.0$ K, and $R = 0.0821 \frac{\text{L atm}}{\text{K mol}}$ yields:

$$P = \frac{(0.500 \text{ mol})\left(0.0821 \frac{\text{L atm}}{\text{K mol}}\right)(300.0 \text{ K})}{(0.500 \text{ L})} = 24.6 \text{ atm}$$

Thermodynamic Processes of Gases

In discussing thermodynamic processes applied to gases, it is important to understand what is meant by some of the different types of processes that can take place. Most real processes do not strictly hold to one of these types, but most can be reasonably approximated by one of them. A process in which the pressure remains constant is known as an isobaric process. In this type of process, the volume-to-absolute-temperature ratio remains constant. In an isothermal process, the temperature remains constant, as does the product of the pressure and volume. For isothermal processes, the internal energy of the gas is constant, and, according to the first law of thermodynamics, the heat added is equal to the work done by the gas. An adiabatic process is one in which no heat is transferred between the gas or its surroundings. This does not mean that the temperature of the gas remains the same; rather, any temperature changes are due to changes in pressure or volume. According to the first law of thermodynamics, the change in internal energy of the gas is equal to the amount of work done on the gas by its surroundings.

Review Video: What is the Difference between Heat and Temperature?
Visit mometrix.com/academy and enter code: 879095

Heat Engines and the Carnot Cycle

A **heat engine** is a mechanical device that **takes in heat energy** (Q_H) from a high-temperature region and uses that energy to **produce work** (W). It then **expels heat** (Q_C) to a lower-temperature region. When the machine is operating at a steady state, such that it does not change temperature, the first law of thermodynamics tells us that the net heat input is equal to the work achieved:

$$Q_H - Q_C = W$$

We can define the efficiency of a heat engine as the work received divided by the work put in, or $\eta = \frac{W}{Q_H}$. The rejected heat Q_C is not considered work received because it is not usable for work. The efficiency may also be calculated as $\eta = 1 - \frac{Q_C}{Q_H}$. From this, we can see that 100% efficiency can only be achieved if $Q_C = 0$; however, constructing a heat engine that expels no heat is impossible.

A **Carnot engine** is a heat engine that operates on the Carnot cycle, an ideal reversible gas cycle that consists of the following processes: high-temperature isothermal expansion, adiabatic expansion, low-temperature isothermal compression, and adiabatic compression. The efficiency of this ideal engine is given as $\eta = 1 - \frac{T_C}{T_H}$, where T_C and T_H are the low and high temperatures of the gas during the cycle. Carnot's theorem states that no heat engine operating between T_C and T_H can have a higher efficiency than that of the Carnot engine.

Chemical Reactions and Energy

Exothermic and Endothermic Reactions

Exothermic reactions **release** heat energy, whereas endothermic reactions **absorb** energy. Exothermic reactions can be represented by $reactants \rightarrow products + heat$. Endothermic reactions can be represented by $reactants + heat \rightarrow products$. The change in enthalpy for exothermic reactions is negative, whereas the change in enthalpy for endothermic reactions is positive. An example of an exothermic reaction is the burning of propane. An example of an endothermic reaction is the reaction that takes place in a first-aid cold pack.

Hess's Law

Bond energy is the energy needed to **break** or **form** a bond. Hess's law can be used to calculate bond energy. Usually, Hess's law is used to state the relationship between the enthalpies of formations of the reactants and the enthalpies of formation of the products of a reaction. Basically, Hess's law states that when reactants are converted to products, the total sum of the energy required to break the bonds of the reactants minus the total sum of energy required to form the bonds of the products is equal to the heat of the reaction. Enthalpies of formation are generally used in place of the actual bond energies because enthalpies of formation have been standardized whereas the bond energies of individual molecules vary. Hess's law is given by the equation $\Delta H^{\circ}_{reaction} = \sum \Delta H^{\circ}_{f(products)} - \sum \Delta H^{\circ}_{f(reactants)}$. It is important to note that in these equations the state of the components is important. The superscript ° means they are in the state of standard temperature and pressure.

> **Review Video: Standard Temperature and Pressure (STP)**
> Visit mometrix.com/academy and enter code: 995054

Explain How to Calculate the ΔH° for the Following Reaction: $3H_2(g) + N_2(g) \rightarrow 2NH_3(g)$ (Ammonia: $\Delta H^{\circ}_f = -46.19 \frac{kJ}{mol}$).

To calculate the ΔH° for the following reaction: $3H_2(g) + N_2(g) \rightarrow 2NH_3(g)$ given that for ammonia $\Delta H^{\circ}_f = -46.19 \frac{kJ}{mol}$, use the equation given by Hess's law:

$$\Delta H^{\circ}_{reaction} = \sum \Delta H^{\circ}_{f(products)} - \sum \Delta H^{\circ}_{f(reactants)}$$

Recall that the enthalpy of formation (ΔH°_f) of an element in its uncombined state is zero. The number of moles of each reactant and product is the coefficients from the balanced chemical equation. Substituting this information and the given information into the equation yields:

$$\begin{aligned}\Delta H^{\circ}_{reaction} &= \sum \Delta H^{\circ}_{f(products)} - \sum \Delta H^{\circ}_{f(reactants)} \\ &= \left[(2\text{ mol})\left(-46.19\ \frac{\text{kJ}}{\text{mol}}\right)\right] - \left[(3\text{ mol})\left(0\frac{\text{kJ}}{\text{mol}}\right) + (1\text{ mol})\left(0\ \frac{\text{kJ}}{\text{mol}}\right)\right] \\ &= -92.38\text{ kJ}\end{aligned}$$

Laws of Thermodynamics

First Law

The **first law of thermodynamics** states that energy cannot be **created** or **destroyed**, but only **converted** from one form to another. It is generally applied as $Q = \Delta U + W$, where Q is the net heat energy added to a system, ΔU is the change in internal energy of the system, and W is the work done by the system. For any input of heat energy to a system, that energy must be either converted to internal energy through a temperature increase or expended in doing work. For a system that gives off heat, either the temperature of the system must decrease or work must be done on the system by its surroundings. By convention, work done by the system is positive while work done on the system is negative.

For instance, suppose a gas is compressed by a piston while the gas temperature remains constant. If we consider the gas to be the system, the work is negative, since the work is being performed on the gas. Since the temperature remains constant, $\Delta U = 0$. Thus, Q must be a negative quantity, indicating that heat is lost by the gas. Conversely, if the gas does positive work on the piston while remaining at a constant temperature, the gas must be receiving heat input from the surroundings.

SECOND LAW

The **second law of thermodynamics** is primarily a statement of the natural tendency of all things toward disorder rather than order. It deals with a quantity called **entropy**, which is an inverse measure of the remaining useful energy in a system. If we take a system of a pot of hot water and an ice cube, the system entropy initially has a value of s_1. After the ice cube melts in the water and the system reaches an equilibrium temperature, the system has larger entropy value s_2, which is the maximum entropy for the system. The system cannot return to its initial state without work put into the system to refreeze the ice cube and reheat the water. If this is done and the system returns to a state with entropy s_1, then the entropy of the surroundings must at the same time increase by more than $s_2 - s_1$, since the net entropy from any process is always greater than zero. Reversible processes are those that may be accomplished in reverse without requiring additional work input. These processes do not exist in the real world, but can be useful for approximating some situations. All real processes are irreversible, meaning they require additional work input to accomplish in reverse. Another important concept is that of spontaneity, the ability of a process to occur without instigation. An ice cube located in an environment at a temperature above the freezing point will spontaneously melt. Although some processes can decrease system entropy at a cost to the entropy of the surroundings, all spontaneous processes involve an increase in the total entropy of the universe.

THIRD AND ZEROTH LAWS

The **third law of thermodynamics** regards the behavior of systems as they **approach absolute zero temperature**. Actually reaching a state of absolute zero is impossible. According to this law, all activity disappears as molecules slow to a standstill near absolute zero, and the system achieves a perfect crystal structure while the system entropy approaches its minimum value. For most systems, this would in fact be a value of zero entropy. Note that this does not violate the second law since causing a system to approach absolute zero would require an immense increase in the entropy of the surroundings, resulting in a positive net entropy. This law is used to determine the value of a material's standard entropy, which is its entropy at the standard temperature of 25 °C.

The **zeroth law of thermodynamics** deals with thermal equilibrium between two systems. It states that if two systems are both in thermal equilibrium with a third system, then they are in thermal equilibrium with each other. This may seem intuitive, but it is an important basis for the other thermodynamic laws.

Review Video: Laws of Thermodynamics
Visit mometrix.com/academy and enter code: 253607

ENTROPY

Entropy (S) is the amount of **disorder** or **randomness of a system**. According to the second law of thermodynamics, systems tend toward a state of greater entropy. The second law of thermodynamics can also be stated as $\Delta S > 0$. Processes with positive changes in entropy tend to be spontaneous. For example, melting is a process with a positive ΔS. When a solid changes into a liquid state, the substance becomes more disordered; therefore, entropy increases. Entropy also will increase in a reaction in which the number of moles of gases increases due to the amount of disorder increasing. Entropy increases when a solute dissolves into a solvent due to the increase in the number of particles. Entropy increases when a system is heated due to the particles moving faster and the amount of disorder increasing.

Spontaneous / Reversible Processes

Some chemical processes are **spontaneous**. According to the second law of thermodynamics, systems or processes always **tend to a state of greater entropy** or lower potential energy. Some exothermic chemical systems are spontaneous because they can increase their stability by reaching a lower potential energy. If processes or reactions have products at a lower potential energy, these processes tend to be spontaneous. Spontaneous reactions have only one direction as given by the second law of thermodynamics. Spontaneous processes go in the direction of greater entropy and lower potential energy. To be reversible, a reaction or process has to be able to go back and forth between two states. A spontaneous process is irreversible.

Concept of Change in Enthalpy

All chemical processes involve either the release or the absorption of heat. Enthalpy is this heat energy. **Enthalpy** is a state function that is equivalent to the amount of heat a system exchanges with its surroundings. For **exothermic processes**, which release heat, the change in enthalpy (ΔH) is negative because the final enthalpy is less than the initial enthalpy. For **endothermic processes**, which absorb heat, the change in enthalpy (ΔH) is positive because the final enthalpy is greater than the initial enthalpy.

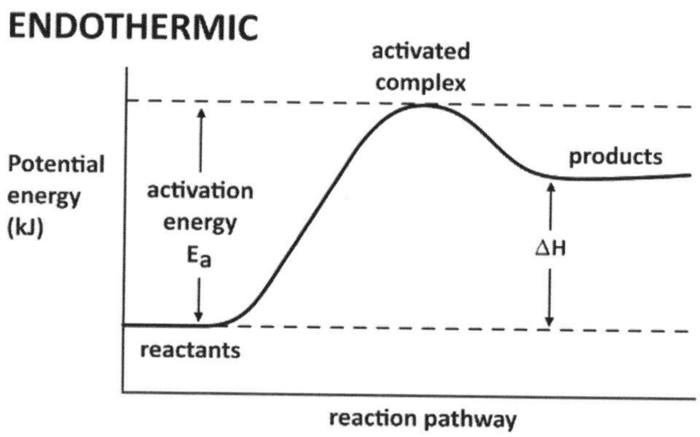

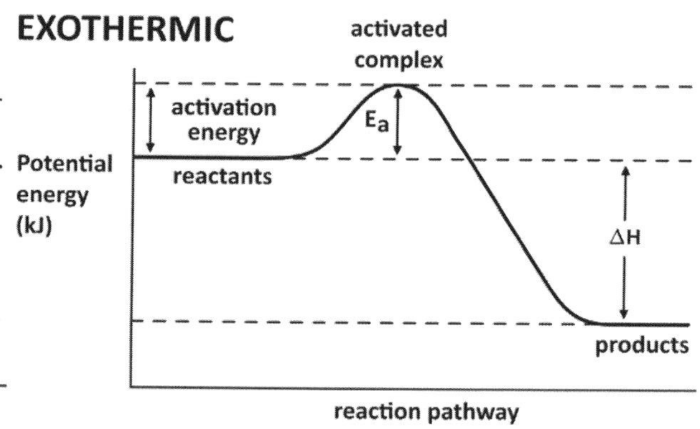

Review Video: Enthalpy
Visit mometrix.com/academy and enter code: 233315

Gibbs Energy

Gibbs energy (G), also known as Gibbs free energy, is the energy of the system that is available to do work. Gibbs energy determines the **spontaneity** of chemical and physical processes. Some processes are spontaneous because $\Delta H < 0$ or because $\Delta S > 0$. If one of the conditions is favorable but the other condition is not favorable, Gibbs energy can be used to determine if a process is spontaneous. Gibbs energy is given by $G = H - TS$. For processes that occur at constant temperature, $\Delta G = \Delta H - T\Delta S$. If ΔG is equal to zero, then the reaction is at equilibrium and neither the forward nor the reverse reaction is spontaneous. If ΔG is less than zero, then the forward reaction is spontaneous. If ΔG is greater than zero, then the reverse reaction is spontaneous.

Historical Models of the Atom

Atomic Models and Theories

There have been many theories regarding the **structure** of atoms and their particles. Part of the challenge in developing an understanding of matter is that atoms and their particles are too small to be seen. It is believed that the first conceptualization of the atom was developed by **Democritus** in 400 B.C. Some of the more notable models are the solid sphere or billiard ball model postulated by **John Dalton**, the plum pudding or raisin bun model by **J.J. Thomson**, the planetary or nuclear model by **Ernest Rutherford**, the Bohr or orbit model by **Niels Bohr**, and the electron cloud or quantum mechanical model by **Louis de Broglie** and **Erwin Schrödinger**. Rutherford directed the alpha scattering experiment that discounted the plum pudding model. The shortcoming of the Bohr model was the belief that electrons orbited in fixed rather than changing elliptical orbits.

Review Video: Atomic Models
Visit mometrix.com/academy and enter code: 434851

Review Video: John Dalton
Visit mometrix.com/academy and enter code: 565627

Thomson "Plum Pudding" Model

J.J. Thomson, the discoverer of the electron, suggested that the arrangement of protons and electrons within an atom could be approximated by dried fruit in a **plum pudding**. Thomson, whose discovery of the electron preceded that of the proton or neutron, hypothesized that an atom's electrons, the dried plums, were **positioned uniformly** inside the atom within a cloud of positive charge, the pudding. This model was later disproved.

Rutherford Scattering

Ernest Rutherford concluded from the work of Geiger and Marsden that the majority of the atom's mass was concentrated in a minute, positively charged region, the **nucleus**, which was surrounded by **electrons**. When a positive alpha particle approached close enough to the nucleus, it was strongly repelled, enough so that it had the ability to rebound at high angles. The small nucleus size explained the small number of alpha particles that were repelled in this fashion. The scattering led to development of the **planetary model of the atom**, which was further developed by Niels Bohr into what is now known as the Bohr model.

Bohr Model

Niels Bohr postulated that the electrons orbiting the nucleus must occupy **discrete orbits**. These discrete orbits also corresponded to discrete levels of energy and angular momentum. Consequently, the only way that electrons could move between orbits was by making nearly instantaneous jumps between them. These jumps, known as **quantum leaps**, are associated with the absorption or emission of a quantum of energy, known as a **photon**. If the electron is jumping to a higher energy state, a photon must be absorbed. Similarly, if the electron is dropping to a lower energy state, a photon must be emitted.

Review Video: Structure of Atoms
Visit mometrix.com/academy and enter code: 905932

Atomic and Subatomic Structure

Basic Organization of Matter

An **element** is the most basic type of matter. It has unique properties and cannot be broken down into other elements. The smallest unit of an element is the **atom**. Most elements are found somewhere in nature in single-atom form, but a few elements only exist naturally in pairs. These are called diatomic elements, and some of the most common of these are hydrogen, nitrogen, and oxygen. A chemical combination of two or more types of elements is called a compound. **Compounds** often have properties that are very different from those of their constituent elements. The smallest independent unit of an element or compound of two or more atoms is known as a **molecule**. Elements and compounds are represented by chemical symbols, one or two letters, most often the first in the element name. More than one atom of the same element in a compound is represented with a subscript number designating how many atoms of that element are present. Water, for instance, contains two hydrogens and one oxygen. Thus, the chemical formula is H_2O. Methane contains one carbon and four hydrogens, so its formula is CH_4.

Review Video: Molecules
Visit mometrix.com/academy and enter code: 349910

Protons, Neutrons, and Electrons

The three major subatomic particles are the proton, neutron, and electron. The **proton**, which is located in the nucleus, has a relative charge of +1. The **neutron**, which is located in the nucleus, has a relative charge of 0. The **electron**, which is located outside the nucleus, has a relative charge of −1. The proton and neutron, which are essentially the same mass, are much more massive than the electron and make up the mass of the atom. The electron's mass is insignificant compared to the mass of the proton and neutron.

Orbits and Orbitals

An orbit is a definite path, but an orbital is a region in space. The Bohr model described electrons as orbiting or following a definite path in space around the nucleus of an atom. But, according to **Heisenberg's uncertainty principle**, it is impossible to determine the location and the momentum of an electron simultaneously. Therefore, it is impossible to draw a definite path or orbit of an electron. An **orbital**, as described by the quantum-mechanical model or the electron-cloud model, is a region in space that is drawn in such a way as to indicate the probability of finding an electron at a specific location. The distance an orbital is located from the nucleus corresponds to the principal quantum number. The orbital shape corresponds to the subshell or azimuthal quantum number. The orbital orientation corresponds to the magnetic quantum number.

Quantum Numbers

The **principal quantum number** (n) describes an electron's shell or energy level and actually describes the size of the orbital. Electrons farther from the nucleus are at higher energy levels. The **subshell** or azimuthal quantum number (l) describes the electron's sublevel or subshell $(s, p, d,$ or $f)$ and specifies the shape of the orbital. Typical shapes include spherical, dumbbell, and clover leaf.

The **magnetic quantum number** (m_l) describes the orientation of the orbital in space. The spin or magnetic moment quantum number (m_s) describes the direction of the spin of the electron in the orbital.

Atomic Number and Mass Number

The **atomic number** of an element is the number of protons in the nucleus of an atom of that element. This is the number that identifies the type of an atom. For example, all oxygen atoms have eight protons, and all carbon atoms have six protons. Each element is identified by its specific atomic number.

The **mass number** is the number of protons and neutrons in the nucleus of an atom. Although the atomic number is the same for all atoms of a specific element, the mass number can vary due to the varying numbers of neutrons in various isotopes of the atom.

Isotopes

Isotopes are atoms of the same element that vary in their number of neutrons. Isotopes of the same element have the same number of protons and thus the same atomic number. Because isotopes vary in the number of neutrons, they are identified by their mass numbers. For example, two naturally occurring carbon isotopes are carbon-12 and carbon-13, which have mass numbers 12 and 13, respectively. The symbols $^{12}_{6}C$ and $^{13}_{6}C$ also represent the carbon isotopes. The general form of the symbol is $^{M}_{A}X$, where X is the element symbol, M is the mass number, and A is the atomic number.

Average Atomic Mass

The **average atomic mass** is the weighted average of the masses of all the naturally occurring isotopes of an atom in comparison to the carbon-12 isotope. The unit for average atomic mass is the atomic mass unit (u). Atomic masses of isotopes are measured using a mass spectrometer by bombarding a gaseous sample of the isotope and measuring its relative deflections. Atomic masses can be calculated if the percent abundances and the atomic masses of the naturally occurring isotopes are known.

Cathode Ray Tube (CRT)

Electrons were discovered by Joseph John Thomson through scientific work with cathode ray tubes (CRTs). **Cathode rays** had been studied for many years, but it was Thomson who showed that cathode rays were **negatively charged particles**. Although Thomson could not determine an electron's charge or mass, he was able to determine the ratio of the charge to the mass. Thomson discovered that this ratio was constant regardless of the gas in the CRT. He was able to show that the cathode rays were actually streams of negatively charged particles by deflecting them with a positively charged plate.

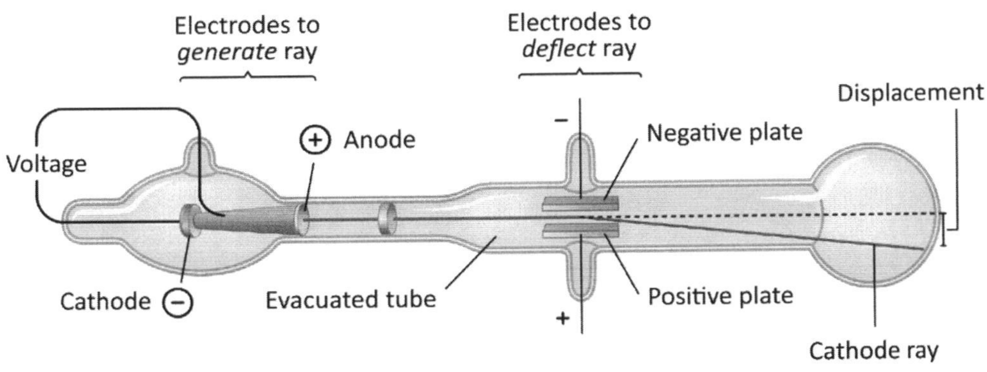

GOLD FOIL EXPERIMENT

After Thomson determined the ratio of the charge to the mass of an electron from studying cathode rays, he proposed the plum pudding model, in which he compared electrons to the raisins embedded in plum pudding. This model of the atom was disproved by the gold foil experiment. The gold foil experiment led to the discovery of the nucleus of an atom. Scientists at Rutherford's laboratory bombarded a thin gold foil with high-speed helium ions. Much to their surprise, some of the ions were reflected by the foil. The scientists concluded that the atom has a **hard central core**, which we now know to be the **nucleus**.

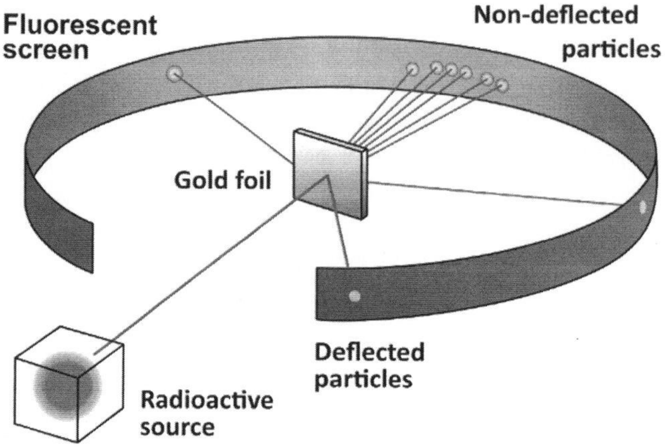

PROBLEMS THAT RUTHERFORD'S MODEL HAD WITH SPECTRAL LINES

Rutherford's model allowed for the electrons of an atom to be in an **infinite number of orbits** based on Newton's laws of motion. Rutherford believed that electrons could orbit the nucleus at any distance from the nucleus and that electrons could change velocity and direction at any moment. But, according to Rutherford's model, the electrons would lose energy and spiral into the nucleus. Unfortunately, if this was in fact true, then every atom would be **unstable**. Rutherford's model also does not correspond to the spectral lines emitted from gases at low pressure. The **spectral lines** are discrete bands of light at specific energy levels. These spectral lines indicate that electrons must be at specific distances from the nucleus. If electrons could be located at any distance from the nucleus, then these gases should emit continuous spectra instead of spectral lines.

Electron Configuration and the Periodic Table

Electron Configuration

The chemical and physical properties of atoms are related to the number of **valence electrons** the atom possesses. Atoms (except hydrogen and helium) seek to have **eight electrons in their outer shell** as stated in the octet rule. A full octet corresponds to full *s* and *p* orbitals. Noble gases have full *s* and *p* orbitals and are inert. To fulfill the octet rule, elements in groups 1A (alkali metals) and 2A (alkaline earth metals) tend to lose one or two electrons, respectively, forming cations. Elements in group 6A (chalcogens) and group 7A (halogens) tend to gain one or two electrons, respectively, forming anions. Other elements such as carbon (group 4A) tend to form covalent bonds to satisfy the octet rule.

Review Video: Electron Configuration
Visit mometrix.com/academy and enter code: 565113

Review Video: Anion, Cation, and Octet Rule
Visit mometrix.com/academy and enter code: 303525

Aufbau Principle

The **Aufbau principle** is named from the German word for "building up," and it describes how electrons fill the energy levels or **shells of an atom**. In general, electrons will fill the $n = 1$ energy level before filling the $n = 2$ energy level, and electrons will fill the $n = 2$ energy level before filling the $n = 3$ energy level. The *s* subshell of an energy level will fill before the *p* subshell, which fills before the *d* and *f* subshells.

Hund's Rule

Hund's rule describes how electrons fill the orbitals in a sublevel. Less energy is required for an electron to occupy an orbital alone than the energy needed for an electron to pair up with another electron in an orbital. Therefore, electrons will occupy each orbital in a subshell before electrons will begin to pair up in those orbitals. For example, in the $2p$ subshell, one electron will occupy each of the three orbitals before pairing begins. In the $3d$ subshell, one electron will occupy each of the five orbitals before pairing begins.

Pauli Exclusion Principle

The **Pauli exclusion principle** describes the unique address or location of each electron in an atom. Each electron has a unique or exclusive set of four quantum numbers indicating the electron's energy level, subshell, orbital orientation, and magnetic moment. Every orbital can hold a maximum of two electrons, but even if two electrons occupy the same orbital resulting in identical energy levels, subshells, and orbital orientations, they must have opposite spins, which means that their magnetic moment quantum numbers will differ.

Correlation Between the Electron Configuration and the Periodic Table

Electron configurations show a direct correlation to the periodic table. The periodic table can be divided into blocks representing *s*, *p*, *d*, and *f* subshells. The **energy level** corresponds to the row or period of the periodic table. The **subshells,** *s*, *p*, *d*, or *f* are related to the block's group numbers. The *s* block corresponds to groups 1A and 2A. The *p* block corresponds to groups 3A–8A. The *d* block corresponds to the 10 groups of transition metals, and the *f* block corresponds to the two rows of inner transition metals (14 groups) located at the bottom of the table.

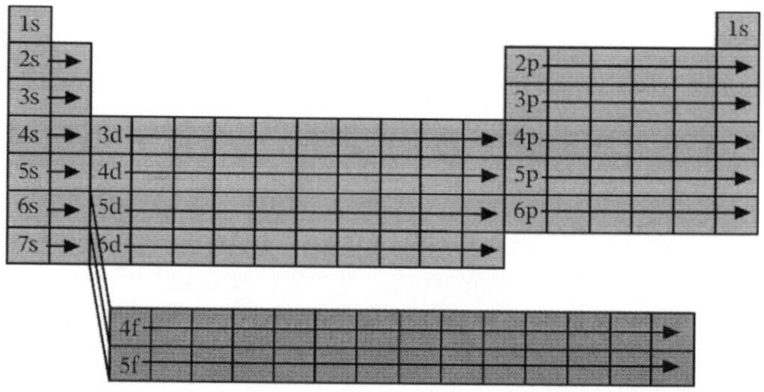

Pure Substances and Mixtures

Pure Substances

Pure substances are substances that cannot be further broken down into simpler components or pieces and still retain their characteristics. Pure substances are categorized as either **elements** or **compounds**. Elements consist of only one type of atom may be monatomic, diatomic, or polyatomic. For example, helium (He) and copper (Cu) are monatomic elements, and hydrogen (H_2) and oxygen (O_2) are diatomic elements. Phosphorus (P_4) and sulfur (S_8) are polyatomic elements. Compounds consist of molecules of more than one type of atom. For example, pure water (H_2O) is made up of molecules consisting of two atoms of hydrogen bonded to one atom of oxygen, and glucose ($C_6H_{12}O_6$) is made up of molecules of six carbon atoms and twelve hydrogen atoms bonded together with six oxygen atoms.

Mixtures

Mixtures can be classified as either homogeneous or heterogeneous. The molecules of a **homogeneous mixture** are distributed uniformly throughout the mixture, whereas the molecules of a **heterogeneous mixture** are not. Air is an example of a homogeneous mixture, and a pile of sand and rock is an example of a heterogeneous mixture. Solutions are homogeneous mixtures consisting of a **solute** (the substance that is dissolved) and a **solvent** (the substance doing the dissolving).

Suspensions

Suspensions are heterogeneous mixtures in which the particle size of the substance **suspended** is too large to be kept in suspension by Brownian motion. Once left undisturbed, suspensions will settle out to form layers. An example of a suspension is sand stirred into water. Left undisturbed, the sand will fall out of suspension and the water will form a layer on top of the sand.

Mixtures with Compounds

Mixtures are similar to compounds in that they are produced when two or more substances are combined. However, there are some key differences as well. Compounds require a chemical combination of the constituent particles, while mixtures are simply the interspersion of particles. Unlike compounds, mixtures may be **separated** without a chemical change. A mixture retains the chemical properties of its constitutent particles, while a compound acquires a new set of properties. Given compounds can exist only in specific ratios, while mixtures may be any ratio of the involved substances.

Chemical and Physical Properties and Changes

Chemical and Physical Properties

Matter has both physical and chemical properties. **Physical properties** can be seen or observed without changing the identity or composition of matter. For example, the mass, volume, and density of a substance can be determined without permanently changing the sample. Other physical properties include color, boiling point, freezing point, solubility, odor, hardness, electrical conductivity, thermal conductivity, ductility, and malleability.

Chemical properties cannot be measured without changing the identity or composition of matter. Chemical properties describe how a substance reacts or changes to form a new substance. Examples of chemical properties include flammability, corrosivity, oxidation states, enthalpy of formation, and reactivity with other chemicals.

Intensive and Extensive Properties

Physical properties are categorized as either intensive or extensive. **Intensive properties** *do not* depend on the amount of matter or quantity of the sample. This means that intensive properties will not change if the sample size is increased or decreased. Intensive properties include color, hardness, melting point, boiling point, density, ductility, malleability, specific heat, temperature, concentration, and magnetization.

Extensive properties *do* depend on the amount of matter or quantity of the sample. Therefore, extensive properties do change if the sample size is increased or decreased. If the sample size is increased, the property increases. If the sample size is decreased, the property decreases. Extensive properties include volume, mass, weight, energy, entropy, number of moles, and electrical charge.

Atomic Properties of Neutral Atoms, Anions, and Cations

Neutral atoms have the same number of protons as electrons. **Cations** are positively-charged ions that are formed when atoms lose electrons. For example, the alkali metals sodium and potassium form the cations Na^+ and K^+, and the alkaline earth metals magnesium and calcium form the cations Mg^{2+} and Ca^{2+}. These elements easily lose electrons because the resulting ion is left with a full valence shell.

Anions are negatively-charged ions that are formed when atoms gain electrons. For example, the halogens fluorine and chlorine form the anions F^- and Cl^-. These elements easily gain electrons because the resulting ion has a full valence shell.

Chemical and Physical Changes

Physical changes do not produce new substances. The atoms or molecules may be rearranged, but no new substances are formed. **Phase changes**—changes of state such as melting, freezing, and sublimation—are physical changes. For example, physical changes include the melting of ice, the boiling of water, sugar dissolving into water, and the crushing of a piece of chalk into a fine powder.

Chemical changes involve a **chemical reaction** and do produce new substances. When iron rusts, iron oxide is formed, indicating a chemical change. Other examples of chemical changes include baking a cake, burning wood, digesting food, and mixing an acid and a base.

Conservation of Energy and Matter

Law of Conservation of Energy

The **law of conservation of energy** states that in a closed system, energy cannot be created or destroyed but only changed from one form to another. This is also known as the first law of thermodynamics. Another way to state this is that the **total energy in an isolated system is constant**. Energy comes in many forms that may be transformed from one kind to another, but in a closed system, the total amount of energy is conserved or remains constant. For example, potential energy can be converted to kinetic energy, thermal energy, radiant energy, or mechanical energy. In an isolated chemical reaction, there can be no energy created or destroyed. The energy simply changes forms.

Law of Conservation of Mass

The **law of conservation of mass** is also known as the **law of conservation of matter**. This law states that for a chemical reaction in a closed system, the total mass of the products must equal the total mass of the reactants. This could also be stated that in a closed system, mass never changes. A consequence of this law is that matter is never created or destroyed during a typical chemical reaction. The atoms of the reactants are only rearranged to form the products. The number and type of each specific atom involved in the reactants is identical to the number and type of atoms in the products. This is the key principle used when balancing chemical equations. In a balanced chemical equation, the number of moles of each element on the reactant side equals the number of moles of each element on the product side.

Review Video: Balancing Chemical Equations
Visit mometrix.com/academy and enter code: 341228

Conversion of Energy Within Chemical Systems

Chemical energy is the energy stored in molecules in the bonds between the atoms of those molecules and the energy associated with the intermolecular forces. This stored **potential energy** may be converted into **kinetic energy** and then into heat. During a chemical reaction, atoms may be rearranged and chemical bonds may be formed or broken accompanied by a corresponding absorption or release of energy, usually in the form of heat. According to the first law of thermodynamics, during these energy conversions, the **total amount of energy must be conserved**.

Kinetic and Potential Energy in Chemistry

Kinetic and Potential Energy

The internal energy of a system may be categorized as kinetic energy or potential energy. **Kinetic energy** is the energy of a system associated with movement. In chemical systems, this movement is described by the **kinetic theory of matter** and is due to the random movement of the particles that make up the system. The kinetic energy of a particle may be calculated by the following formula: $KE = \frac{1}{2}mv^2$, where KE is the kinetic energy in joules, m is the mass of the particle in kilograms, and v is the velocity of the particle in meters per second.

Potential energy is the stored energy in a system associated with position or configuration. In chemical systems, this energy is the energy associated with the chemical bonds and intermolecular forces of the matter contained in the system.

Basics of Radioactivity

Radioactivity

Radioisotopes: Also known as radionuclides or radioactive isotopes, radioisotopes are atoms that have an unstable nucleus. This is a nucleus that has excess energy and the potential to undergo radioactive decay, which most often results in the emission of alpha, beta, or gamma radiation. Many radionuclides occur naturally but others have only been produced artificially.

Radioactive decay: This occurs when an unstable atomic nucleus spontaneously loses energy by emitting ionizing particles and radiation. Decay is a form of energy transfer, as the energy lost by the nucleus is given to the particles or radiation emitted. It also results in products that are different from the initial atoms. Before decay there is one type of atom, called the **parent nuclide**. After decay there are one or more different products, called the **daughter nuclide(s)**.

Radioactivity: This refers to particles or energy that are emitted from nuclei as a result of nuclear instability.

Review Video: Radioactivity
Visit mometrix.com/academy and enter code: 537142

Radiation is the term for energy emitted or transmitted as waves or particles. Radiation is classified as either ionizing (able to detach an electron from an atom) or non-ionizing. Nuclear weapons, nuclear reactors, and radioactive substances are all examples of things that involve ionizing radiation. Acoustic radiation and electromagnetic radiation (with wavelength greater than 125 nm) are types of non-ionizing radiation.

Radioactive half-life is the time it takes for half of the radioactive nuclei in a sample to undergo radioactive decay. Radioactive decay rates are usually expressed in terms of half-lives. The different types of radioactivity lead to different decay paths, which transmute the nuclei into other chemical elements. **Decay products** (or daughter nuclides) make radioactive dating possible. **Decay chains** are a series of decays that result in different products. For example, uranium-238 is often found in granite. Its decay chain includes 14 daughter products. It eventually becomes a stable isotope of lead, which is why lead is often found with deposits of uranium ore. Its first half-life is equivalent to the approximate age of the earth, about 4.5 billion years. One of its products is radon, a radioactive gas.

Isotopes that have not been observed to decay are **stable**, or non-radioactive, isotopes. It is not known whether some stable isotopes may have such long decay times that observing decay is not possible. Currently, 80 elements have one or more stable isotopes. There are 256 known stable isotopes in total. Carbon, for example, has three isotopes. Two (carbon-12 and carbon-13) are stable and one (carbon-14) is radioactive.

Ionizing radiation comes in three types: alpha (α), beta (β), and gamma (γ). Alpha particles are positive, beta particles are negative, and gamma rays are neutral. **Alpha particles** are larger than beta particles and can cause severe damage if a source of alpha particles is ingested. Because of their large mass, however, they can be easily stopped. Even paper can protect against this type of radiation. **Beta particles** can be beta-minus or beta-plus. Beta-minus particles contain an energetic electron, while beta-plus particles are emitted by positrons. Beta particles can be stopped with a thin sheet of metal. **Gamma rays** are a type of high energy electromagnetic radiation. Gamma radiation is one of the ways a decaying nucleus emits excess energy after it has emitted either alpha or beta radiation. Gamma rays can cause serious damage when absorbed by living tissue, and it takes a lot of shielding (typically lead) to stop them. Alpha, beta, and gamma radiation can also have positive applications.

Nuclear fission and nuclear fusion are similar in that they occur in the nucleus of an atom, can release great amounts of energy, and result in the formation of different elements (nuclear transmutation). They are different in that **nuclear fission** is the splitting of a nucleus into smaller particles, and **nuclear fusion** is the joining of nuclei to form a heavier nucleus. It requires immense pressures and temperatures, but when fusion occurs, energy can either be absorbed or released, depending on the resultant nucleus. Fusion occurs naturally in stars, and is thought to be the process responsible for the generation of all naturally occurring elements (stellar nucleosynthesis).

Radioactive waste is a waste product that is considered dangerous because of either low levels or high levels of radioactivity. Radioactive waste could include discarded clothing that was used as protection against radiation, or decay products of substances used to create electricity through nuclear fission. Small amounts of radioactive material can be ingested as a method of tracing how the body distributes certain elements. Other radioactive materials are used as light sources because they glow when heated. Uncontrolled radiation or even small amounts of radioactive material can cause sickness and cancer in humans. **Gamma wave radiation** is fast-moving radiation that can cause cancer and damage genetic information by crashing into DNA molecules or other cells. Low-level radiation also occurs naturally. When related to everyday occurrences, radiation is measured in millirems per hour (mrem/hr). Humans can be exposed to radiation from stone used to build houses, cosmic rays from space, x-rays and other medical devices, and nuclear energy products.

Nuclear Chemistry and Radioactivity

Alpha Particles

Alpha particles are the products of **alpha decay**. They are identical to helium nuclei. An alpha particle consists of two protons and two neutrons. Because they have two protons but zero electrons, alpha particles have a net +2 charge. They are represented by the Greek letter alpha as α, α^{2+}, or ${}^{4}_{2}\alpha^{2+}$. Because they are identical to helium nuclei, they may also be written as He^{2+}, ${}^{4}_{2}He$, or ${}^{4}_{2}He^{2+}$. Because alpha particles have a strong charge and travel slowly, they interact significantly with matter that they pass through and may therefore be stopped by a sheet of paper or a few inches of air. Alpha particles cannot penetrate the skin.

Beta Particles

Beta particles are the products of **beta decay**. Beta particles may be high-speed electrons or high-speed positrons. These two forms of beta decay are designated by the Greek letter beta as β^- and β^+ or ${}_{-1}^{0}e$ and ${}_{+1}^{0}e$, respectively. Negative beta particles are created during radioactive decay when a neutron changes into a proton and an electron. Positive beta particles are created when a proton changes into a neutron and a positron. Beta particles have a greater penetrating ability than alpha particles. Beta particles can be stopped by thin plywood or metal or several feet of air.

Gamma Radiation

Gamma radiation (represented by the Greek letter gamma γ) is released during **gamma decay**. Often, atoms that have just undergone alpha or beta decay then undergo gamma decay. An atom produced during alpha or beta decay may still be in an excited state. The atom then releases this energy in a burst of gamma rays as high-energy photons. Gamma radiation is part of the electromagnetic spectrum and consists of electromagnetic waves that travel at the speed of light with frequencies higher than x-rays. Because gamma radiation has no charge, it easily penetrates solid substances. Gamma decay is useful in medical procedures, including cancer treatment.

Energy, Frequency, and Wavelength

The properties of energy, frequency, and wavelength can be used to describe electromagnetic waves. These properties also have a mathematical relationship with each other. Energy (E) is directly related to frequency (f) as given by $E = hf$, where h represents Planck's constant (6.626×10^{-34} J-s). As the frequency increases, the energy increases. For example, gamma rays, which have the highest frequency of the electromagnetic spectrum, also have the highest energy. The speed (v) of the wave is equal to the product of wavelength (λ) and frequency (f). Because the speed of light (c) is constant in a vacuum at 3.00×10^8 m/s, wavelength and frequency are inversely related. As wavelength decreases, frequency increases. For example, gamma rays have the shortest wavelength of the electromagnetic spectrum and the highest frequency.

Radioactive Decay and Half-Life

Radioactivity or **radioactive decay** occurs when an unstable atom splits to form a new atom and emits some type of radiation. An atom's nucleus contains protons and neutrons. The protons have positive charges and repel each other, but with the help of neutrons the repulsive force between protons is overcome by the strong nuclear force, which holds the nucleus together. With elements of greater atomic number, the repulsive force is increasingly a match for the strong force. All atoms with atomic number greater than 83 are unstable. The three basic types of **radioactive decay** are alpha decay, beta decay, and gamma decay. The **half-life** of an isotope is the length of time it takes for one-half of the atoms of a radioactive substance to decay into a new type of atom.

Typical Fission Reaction

A typical fission reaction is the fission of uranium-235 from neutron bombardment:

$$^{235}_{92}\text{U} + ^{1}_{0}\text{n} \rightarrow ^{139}_{56}\text{Ba} + ^{94}_{36}\text{Kr} + 3[^{1}_{0}\text{n}]$$

The uranium-235 atom ($^{235}_{92}\text{U}$) is bombarded by a neutron ($^{1}_{0}\text{n}$). This neutron is absorbed, forcing the uranium-235 atom into an excited, unstable state. This excited, unstable uranium-235 atom splits into smaller more stable pieces, which consist of a barium-139 atom ($^{139}_{56}\text{Ba}$), a krypton-94 atom ($^{94}_{36}\text{Kr}$), and three neutrons ($^{1}_{0}\text{n}$). These neutrons in turn may bombard other uranium-235 atoms causing the nuclear fission to continue.

Review Video: Reading Nuclear Equations
Visit mometrix.com/academy and enter code: 688890

Nuclear Fusion

Nuclear fusion is the process in which the nuclei of atoms that are light and unstable will unite or fuse to form a heavier, more stable atom. Fusion requires extremely high temperatures and often pressures that force the atoms into a plasma state. In this high-energy state, the atoms collide frequently and are able to fuse together. In this process, some mass is lost and released as large quantities of energy. The Sun's heat and light are produced by a fusion reaction in the Sun's core, in which four hydrogen atoms fuse into a helium nucleus.

Review Video: Nuclear Fusion
Visit mometrix.com/academy and enter code: 381782

Alpha Emission

In alpha emission, the parent nuclide splits into **two parts** consisting of the daughter nuclide and an alpha particle. The alpha particle is identical to a helium nucleus and consists of two protons and two neutrons, represented by ${}^{4}_{2}\text{He}$ or ${}^{4}_{2}\text{He}^{2+}$. The daughter nuclide has a mass number that is four less than the parent nuclide and an atomic number that is two less than the parent nuclide. An example of alpha emission is the decay of a uranium-238 atom into a thorium-234 atom and an alpha particle, as shown below:

$${}^{238}_{92}\text{U} \rightarrow {}^{234}_{90}\text{Th} + {}^{4}_{2}\text{He}$$

Positive and Negative Beta Decay

In **positive beta decay**, also known as **positron emission**, the parent nuclide splits into two parts consisting of the daughter nuclide and a positron. The positron is represented by ${}^{0}_{+1}\text{e}$ because its mass is negligible compared to a neutron or proton, and its charge is $+1$. The daughter nuclide has the same mass number as the parent nuclide and an atomic number of one less than the parent nuclide. An example of positive beta decay is when a carbon-11 atom splits into a boron-11 atom and a positron, as given by the equation shown here:

In **negative beta decay**, also simply called **beta decay**, the parent nuclide splits into two parts consisting of the daughter nuclide and an electron. The electron is represented by ${}^{0}_{-1}\text{e}$ because its mass is negligible compared to a neutron or proton, and its charge is -1. An example of negative beta decay is when a carbon-14 atom splits into a nitrogen-14 atom and an electron, as given by the following equation:

$${}^{14}_{6}\text{C} \rightarrow {}^{14}_{7}\text{N} + {}^{0}_{-1}\text{e}$$

Electron Capture

In electron capture, an electron from an atom's own electron cloud impacts the atom's nucleus and causes a **decay reaction.** The parent nuclide absorbs the electron, and a proton is converted to a neutron. A neutrino is emitted from the nucleus. Gamma radiation is also emitted. The daughter nuclide has the same mass number as the parent nuclide, and the atomic number of the daughter nuclide is one lower than the atomic number of the parent nuclide. An example of electron capture is when a nitrogen-13 atom absorbs an electron and converts to a carbon-13 atom while emitting a neutrino (${}^{0}_{0}\nu$) and gamma radiation (γ), as shown by the following equation:

$${}^{13}_{7}\text{N} + {}^{0}_{-1}\text{e} \rightarrow {}^{13}_{6}\text{C} + {}^{0}_{0}\nu + \gamma$$

Transmutation

Transmutation is a type of nuclear decay in which an atom is bombarded by **high-speed particles** to cause it to convert from one type of atom to another type of atom. Ernest Rutherford was the first to accomplish this, with the transmutation of the nitrogen-14 atom into an oxygen-17 atom by bombardment with a beam of high-speed helium ions. In this transmutation, the helium-4 ion is also converted to a hydrogen-1 ion:

$${}^{14}_{7}\text{N} + {}^{4}_{2}\text{He} \rightarrow {}^{17}_{8}\text{O} + {}^{1}_{1}\text{H}$$

Neutron Radiation

Neutron radiation is a type of **transmutation** that is used to create many isotopes that do not occur naturally. In neutron radiation, an atom is bombarded by high-speed neutrons (${}^{1}_{0}\text{n}$) to cause nuclear decay. In neutron radiation, the daughter nuclide has a mass number one higher than the parent nuclide, but the atomic number remains the same. The daughter is an atom of the same element as the parent nuclide, but it has one more neutron, which makes it a different isotope of that element. An example of neutron radiation is when a cobalt-59 atom is bombarded by a high-speed neutron and converts to a cobalt-60 atom, as shown in the following equation:

$$^{59}_{27}\text{Co} + ^{1}_{0}\text{n} \rightarrow ^{60}_{27}\text{Co}$$

Balancing a Nuclear Reaction

When balancing a nuclear reaction, two key principles must be applied. First, the **mass number must be conserved**. Second, the **atomic number must be conserved**. To determine the products formed, the mass numbers and atomic numbers of the particles emitted or absorbed must be known. Alpha decay emits alpha particles ($^{4}_{2}\text{He}$). Beta decay emits electrons ($^{0}_{-1}\text{e}$). Positron decay emits positrons ($^{0}_{+1}\text{e}$). Neutron radiation absorbs neutrons ($^{1}_{0}\text{n}$). In alpha decay, the mass number decreases by four, and the atomic number decreases by two. In negative beta decay, the mass number stays the same, and the atomic number increases by one. In positive beta decay, the mass number stays the same, and the atomic number decreases by one. In neutron radiation, the mass number increases by one, and the atomic number stays the same.

Complete or Balance the Following Nuclear Reactions:

The key principles to completing or balancing nuclear reactions are that the mass number is conserved and the atomic number is conserved.

$$^{230}_{90}\text{Th} \leftrightarrow ^{4}_{2}\text{He} + \underline{\quad}$$

In this reaction, thorium-230 under goes alpha decay and emits an alpha particle with a mass number of 4 and an atomic number of 2. Balancing the atomic numbers $(90 - 2)$ yields an atomic number of 88, which corresponds to radium. Balancing the mass numbers $(230 - 4)$ yields 226. Therefore, the missing product is $^{226}_{88}\text{Ra}$.

$$^{40}_{19}\text{K} \leftrightarrow ^{0}_{-1}\text{e} + \underline{\quad}$$

In this reaction, potassium-40 undergoes beta decay and emits an electron with an assigned mass number of 0 and an assigned atomic number of -1. Balancing the atomic numbers $\big(19 - (-1)\big)$ yields an atomic number of 20, which indicates calcium. Balancing the mass numbers $(40 - 0)$ yields a mass number of 40. Therefore, the missing product is $^{40}_{20}\text{Ca}$.

Conversions between Forms of Energy

Conversion of Energy

There are many different types of energy that exist. These include mechanical, sound, magnetic, electrical, light, heat, and chemical. From the **first law of thermodynamics**, we know that no energy can be created or destroyed, but it may be **converted** from one form to another. This does not mean that all forms of energy are useful. Indeed, the **second law** states that net useful energy **decreases** in every process that takes place. Most often this occurs when other forms of energy are converted to heat through means such as friction. In these cases, the heat is quickly absorbed into the surroundings and becomes unusable. There are many examples of energy conversion, such as in an automobile. The chemical energy in the gasoline is converted to mechanical energy in the engine. Subsequently, this mechanical energy is converted to kinetic energy as the car moves. Additionally, the mechanical energy is converted to electrical energy to power the radio, headlights, air conditioner, and other devices. In the radio, electrical energy is converted to sound energy. In the headlights, it is converted to heat and light energy. In the air conditioner, it does work to remove heat energy from the car's interior. It is important to remember that a portion of the energy is lost from its intended purpose in all of these processes.

Electronic Absorption and Emission Spectra

Electronic Energy Transition (Emission/Absorption of Energy) in Atoms

An electron must gain or absorb energy to **transition** to a higher or excited state, and the electron will emit that energy when it transitions back to the ground state. The **ground state** of an electron is the electron's lowest state of energy or when the electron is in the energy level that it normally occupies. An electron can gain energy if it absorbs a photon or collides with another particle. When an electron occupies an energy level higher that its normal level or ground state, it is in an excited state. The excited state is an unstable state, and the electron will return to the ground state as quickly as possible.

Absorption Spectroscopy and Emission Spectroscopy

When an electron makes a **quantum leap** from one electron shell to another, a **photon** is either **absorbed** or **emitted**. Because the energy levels of these shells are discrete, the energy of an absorbed or emitted photon is unique to a particular pair of shells. Thus, any element can be positively identified by the energy levels of the photons it emits.

Absorption Spectroscopy

Spectroscopy is most commonly used to determine the **composition of unknown compounds**. In absorption spectroscopy, a compound is bombarded with a full spectrum of photons, causing the compound to absorb those photons corresponding to its constituent elements' electron shell energy levels. By capturing and measuring the wavelengths of the photons **not absorbed**, it can be determined which wavelengths, and thus which energy levels, were absorbed, giving the identity of the elements contained in the compound. The resulting visible spectrum consists of color from red to violet with black bands at the wavelength of the absorbed photons.

Emission Spectroscopy

Emission spectroscopy works in a similar fashion. The compound's electrons are excited by an application of energy and allowed to decay back down to lower energy levels. This decay is necessarily accompanied by an emission of photons, whose wavelengths are measured to determine the identity of the elements. The resulting visible spectrum consists of colored bands at the wavelengths of the emitted photons.

Chapter Quiz

Ready to see how well you retained what you just read? Scan the QR code to go directly to the chapter quiz interface for this study guide. If you're using a computer, simply visit the online resources page at **mometrix.com/resources719/gacechemistry** and click the Chapter Quizzes link.

Nomenclature, Chemical Composition, and Bonding and Structure

Nomenclature for Inorganic Compounds

Binary Molecular Compounds

The names of binary molecular compounds follow this pattern:

prefix + first element name (space) prefix + root of second element name + -ide.

If a prefix ends with *a* or *o* and the element name begins with *a* or *o*, the ending *a* or *o* of the prefix is dropped. For example, N_2O_5 is named dinitrogen pentoxide. The prefix *mono-* is usually dropped unless more than one binary compound may be formed from the two elements involved.

Numeric Prefixes			
#	**Prefix**	**#**	**Prefix**
1	*mono-*	6	*hexa-*
2	*di-*	7	*hepta-*
3	*tri-*	8	*octa-*
4	*tetra-*	9	*nona-*
5	*penta-*	10	*deca-*

Naming Binary Ionic Compounds

The names of binary ionic compounds follow this pattern: cation name (space) anion name.

The name of **simple cations** is usually the element name. For example, the K^+ cation is named potassium. Some cations exist in more than one form. In those cases, the charge of the ion follows the element as a Roman numeral in parentheses. For example, the Cu^+ ion is named copper(I), and the Cu^{2+} ion is named copper(II). **Simple anions** are named with the root of the element name followed by the suffix *-ide.* For example, the O^{2-} anion is named oxide, and the F^- ion is named fluoride. The following are some examples of names of binary ionic compounds: KI is named potassium iodide, and FeO is named iron(II) oxide.

Naming Binary Compounds Examples

$$N_2O_4$$

The example above is a binary molecular compound. Using the prefixes *di-* for 2 and *tetra-* for 4, this compound is named dinitrogen tetroxide. Note that the entire element name is retained for the cation, but the root plus *-ide* is used for the anion name.

$$S_2F_{10}$$

This is a binary molecular compound. Using the prefixes *di-* for 2 and *deca-* for 10, this compound is named disulfur decafluoride. Note that the entire element name is retained for the cation, but the root plus *-ide* is used for the anion name.

$$Fe_2O_3$$

This is a binary ionic compound. Iron forms two types of cations Fe^{2+} and Fe^{3+}, but because the anion is O^{2-}, this must be the Fe^{3+} ion in order to balance the charges. This compound is named iron(III) oxide.

$$CuCl_2$$

This is a binary ionic compound. Copper forms two types of cations Cu^{+} and Cu^{2+}, but because the anion is Cl^{-}, this must be the Cu^{2+} ion in order to balance the charges. This compound is named copper(II) chloride.

Naming Acids

Acids are generally categorized as binary acids or oxyacids. **Binary acids** are named by the pattern: *hydro-* + root of element + *-ic* (space) acid. For example, HI is named hydroiodic acid, and HCl is named hydrochloric acid. One exception is that in hydrosulfuric acid (H_2S), the entire element name *sulfur* is used. The names of **oxyacids** depend on the endings of their polyatomic anions. If the polyatomic anions end in *-ate*, then the acid names end in *-ic*. If the anions end in *-ite*, the acid names end in *-ous*. The naming pattern for an oxyacid is as follows: anion root + ending (space) acid. For example, H_2CO_3 is named carbonic acid because the carbonate ion ends in *-ate*, and H_2SO_3 is named sulfurous acid because the sulfite ion ends in *-ite.*

Naming Hydrates

Hydrates form from salts (ionic compounds) that attract water. Hydrates are named from their salt (ionic compound) name and the number of water molecules involved, in the following pattern:

For example, the name of $CuSO_4 \cdot 5H_2O$ is copper(II) sulfate pentahydrate, and the name of $CoCl_2 \cdot 6H_2O$ is cobalt(II) chloride hexahydrate.

Hydrates			
#	**Prefix**	**#**	**Prefix**
1	mono-	6	hexa-
2	di-	7	hepta-
3	tri-	8	octa-
4	tetra-	9	nona-
5	penta-	10	deca-

Naming Salts

Salts are ionic compounds with any cation except H^{+} from an aqueous base and any anion except OH^{-} from an aqueous acid. Salts are named like regular ionic compounds, with the name of the cation followed by the name of the anion. Examples of salts include sodium chloride (NaCl), potassium fluoride (KF), magnesium iodide (MgI_2), sodium acetate ($NaC_2H_3O_2$), and ammonium carbonate ($(NH_4)_2CO_3$).

Naming Bases

Bases are typically ionic compounds with a hydroxide anion and are named following the conventions of naming ionic compounds. For example, NaOH is named sodium hydroxide, and $Mg(OH)_2$ is named magnesium hydroxide.

Nomenclature for Organic Compounds

Alkanes, Alkenes, and Alkynes

Alkanes, alkenes, and alkynes are organic compounds called **hydrocarbons**, which consist only of carbon and hydrogen. **Alkanes** have only single bonds between their carbon atoms. Alkanes are saturated hydrocarbons because they contain as many hydrogen atoms as possible due to their single bonds. Alkanes include methane (CH_4), ethane (C_2H_6), propane (C_3H_8), and butane (C_4H_{10}).

Alkenes have at least one double bond between two of their carbon atoms. Alkenes are unsaturated hydrocarbons. Alkenes include ethene or ethylene (C_2H_4), propene (C_3H_6), 1-butene (C_4H_8), and 1-pentene (C_5H_{10}).

Alkynes have at least one triple bond between two of their carbon atoms. Like alkenes, alkynes are unsaturated hydrocarbons. Alkynes include ethyne or acetylene (C_2H_2), 1-propyne (C_3H_4), 1-butyne (C_4H_6), and 1-pentyne (C_5H_8).

Review Video: Properties of Alkanes
Visit mometrix.com/academy and enter code: 903333

Review Video: Basics for Alkenes
Visit mometrix.com/academy and enter code: 916284

Review Video: Basics of Alkynes
Visit mometrix.com/academy and enter code: 963837

Naming Alkanes, Alkenes, and Alkynes

The prefixes of alkanes, alkenes, and alkynes are based on the number of carbon atoms. These prefixes are given by the table below. For example, an alkane with one carbon atom is named methane. An alkane with two carbon atoms would be named ethane. An alkene with two carbon atoms is named ethene. An alkene with five carbon atoms is named pentene. An alkyne with four carbon atoms is named butyne. An alkyne with eight carbon atoms is named octyne.

Hydrocarbons			
#	**Prefix**	**#**	**Prefix**
1	meth-	6	hexa-
2	eth-	7	hepta-
3	prop-	8	octa-
4	but-	9	nona-
5	penta-	10	deca-

Review Video: Rules for Naming Alkanes, Alkenes, and Alkynes
Visit mometrix.com/academy and enter code: 441567

Alcohol

An **alcohol** is a substituted hydrocarbon compound with a hydroxyl group (—OH) bound to a saturated carbon. To name an alcohol, drop the *-e* from the name of the hydrocarbon and add *-ol.*

For example, when the functional group for an alcohol replaces one hydrogen in methane, then the name is changed to methanol (left). Likewise, ethane becomes ethanol (right).

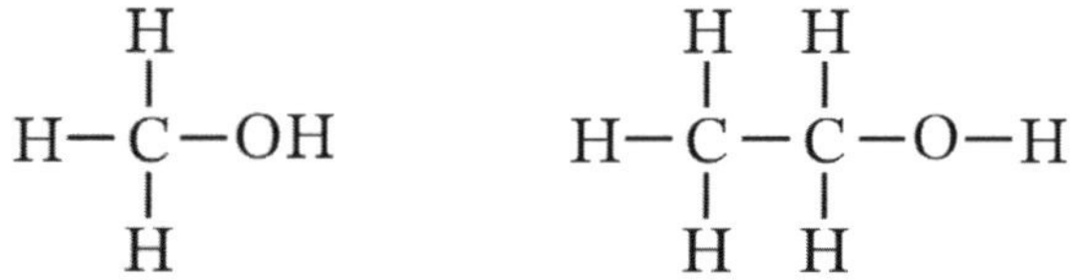

Review Video: Naming of Alcohols
Visit mometrix.com/academy and enter code: 737321

ETHER

An **ether** is a substituted hydrocarbon compound containing an oxygen molecule linking two hydrocarbon groups. Ethers are named for the two hydrocarbons that flank the functional group. The root of the shorter of the two chains is named first. This is followed by *-oxy-*, which is then followed by the name of the longer chain. For example, $CH_3OCH_2CH_3$ (below) is named methoxyethane.

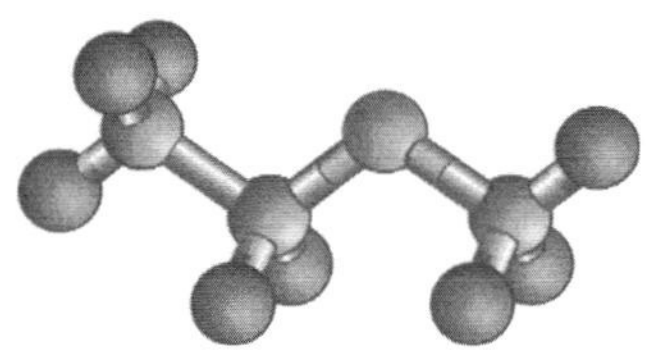

ALDEHYDE

An **aldehyde** is a substituted hydrocarbon compound with an oxygen molecule that is double bonded to the CH group at an end of a hydrocarbon chain. To name an aldehyde, drop the *-e* from the name of the hydrocarbon and add *-al*. For example, when the functional group for an aldehyde is substituted into methane, the aldehyde name would be methanal (below).

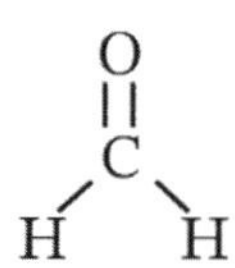

KETONE

A **ketone** is a substituted hydrocarbon compound containing an oxygen that is double bonded to a carbon atom somewhere within the hydrocarbon chain. The difference between a ketone and an aldehyde is that in an aldehyde the = O will be at one or both ends of the hydrocarbon molecule, whereas in a ketone the = O will be somewhere other than the end of the hydrocarbon molecule. To name a ketone, drop *-e* from the name of the hydrocarbon and add *-one*. For example, when the functional group for a ketone is inserted into propane, the name is changed to propanone, which is commonly known as acetone (below).

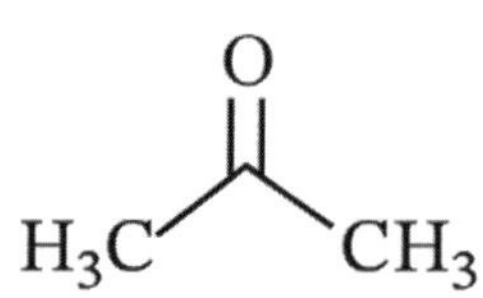

CARBOXYLIC ACIDS

Carboxylic acids are organic compounds that contain a carboxyl functional group that consists of a carbon atom double-bonded to an oxygen and single-bonded to a hydroxyl (−OH). For example, the simplest carboxylic acid is formic acid, HCO_2H (left). Acetic acid or ethanoic acid, CH_3CO_2H (right), is commonly known as vinegar. Fatty acids and amino acids are also examples of carboxylic acids.

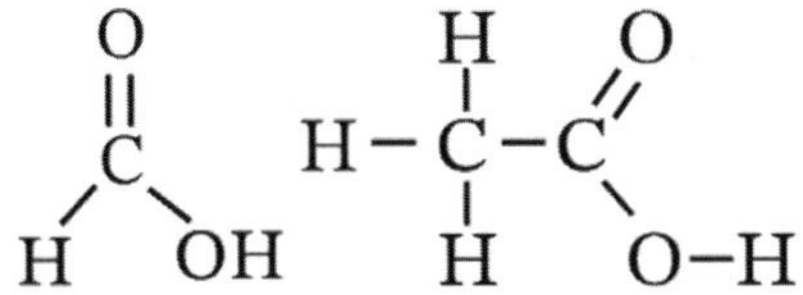

BENZENE

Benzene is an organic compound that is an aromatic hydrocarbon. Benzene has a molecular formula of C_6H_6, where the six carbon atoms are arranged in a "ring" shaped like a hexagon. Each carbon is single-bonded to two other carbons and single-bonded to one hydrogen. The remaining valence electrons from the six carbon atoms are delocalized electrons that are shared among all the carbons in the molecule.

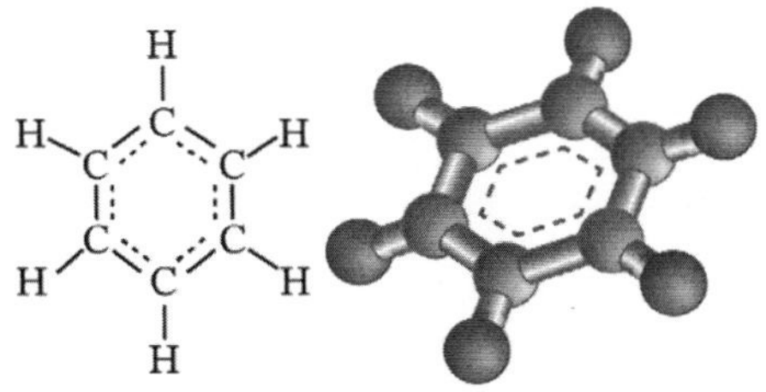

Derivatives of benzene include phenol, which is used in producing carbonates; toluene, which is used as a solvent and an octane booster in gasoline; and aniline, which is used in the production of polyurethane.

AMINE

An **amine** is a compound with a nitrogen atom that contains a lone pair of electrons and is bound to one or more hydrocarbon groups. Amines may be named in more than one way. The two most common ways are either with the prefix *amino-* or the suffix *-amine.* Two simple amines are methylamine (CH_3NH_2) and ethylamine ($CH_3CH_2NH_2$).

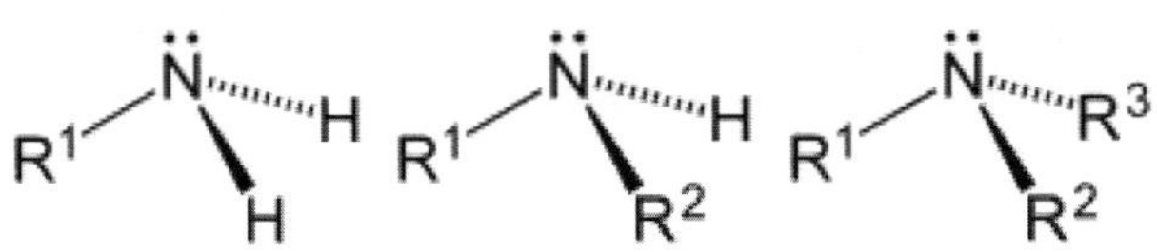

Molarity

Avogadro's Number, Molar Mass, and the Mole

Avogadro's number is equivalent to the number of atoms in 12 g of the carbon-12 isotope and is the definition of the quantity 1 mole. Avogadro's number is numerically equal to approximately 6.022×10^{23}. Just like a dozen eggs represents 12 eggs and a pair of shoes represents 2 shoes, a **mole** of atoms represents 6.022×10^{23} atoms. **Molar mass** is the mass of one mole of a substance in grams. As such, molar mass has units of grams per mole (g/mol).

Review Video: The Mole Concept
Visit mometrix.com/academy and enter code: 593205

Explain How to Determine the Mass of 2.50 Moles of O_2. (The Atomic Mass of Oxygen is 16.0 u.)

To convert from moles of O_2 to mass in grams of O_2, use the dimensional analysis method with the molar mass of O_2. The molar mass of O_2 is 2(16.0 g/mol) or 32.0 g/mol. This molar mass can be written as the conversion factor $\left(\frac{32.0 \text{ g } O_2}{\text{mol } O_2}\right)$. Then, using dimensional analysis, multiply $(2.50 \text{ mol } O_2)\left(\frac{32.0 \text{ g } O_2}{\text{mol } O_2}\right)$. The "mol O_2" cancels from the numerator of the first factor and the denominator of the second factor, resulting in 80.0 g O_2.

Explain How to Determine the Number of Moles of $C_{12}H_{22}O_{11}$ in 100.0 g of This Substance. (The Atomic Masses of C, H, and O are 12.0 u, 1.0 u, and 16.0 u, Respectively.)

To find the number of moles in a sample of $C_{12}H_{22}O_{11}$, first calculate the molar mass to be used in dimensional analysis. The molar mass of $C_{12}H_{22}O_{11}$:

$$12(12.0 \text{ g}) + 22(1.0 \text{ g}) + 11(16.0 \text{ g}) = 144.0 \text{ g} + 22.0 \text{ g} + 176.0 \text{ g} = 342 \text{ g}$$

This means that every mole of $C_{12}H_{22}O_{11}$ has a molar mass of 342 g. To convert from grams to moles, use dimensional analysis as follows:

$$(100.0 \text{ g } C_{12}H_{22}O_{11})\left(\frac{1 \text{ mol } C_{12}H_{22}O_{11}}{342 \text{ g}}\right) = 0.292 \text{ mol}$$

Given the Reaction $3H_2(g) + N_2(g) \rightarrow 2NH_3(g)$, Determine How Many Grams of Nitrogen Gas Are Needed to Produce 100.0 g of Ammonia. (The Molar Mass of $N_2 = 28.0$ g; the Molar Mass of $NH_3 = 17.0$ g.)

One approach to working out this problem is to use the dimensional analysis method all the way through the work of the problem. Conversion factors using the molar masses of NH_3 and N_2 are used, as well as a mole ratio from the balanced chemical equation. The approach is to convert from grams of NH_3 to moles of NH_3, then to convert moles of NH_3 to moles of N_2, and finally to convert the moles of N_2 to grams of N_2.

$$\left(\frac{100.0 \text{ g } NH_3}{1}\right)\left(\frac{1 \text{ mol } NH_3}{17.0 \text{ g}}\right)\left(\frac{1 \text{ mol } N_2}{2 \text{ mol } NH_3}\right)\left(\frac{28.0 \text{ g } N_2}{1 \text{ mol } N_2}\right) = 82.4 \text{ g } N_2$$

Review Video: Concept of a Mole Ratio
Visit mometrix.com/academy and enter code: 747963

Calculating the Empirical Formula and the Molecular Formula of a Compound

To find the **empirical formula of a compound**, first, calculate the masses of each element in the compound based on the percent composition that is given. Then, convert these masses to moles by dividing by the molar masses of those elements. Next, divide these amounts in moles by the smallest calculated value in moles and round to the nearest tenth. These calculations provide the subscripts for each element in the empirical formula. To find the **molecular formula**, divide the actual molar mass of the compound by the molar mass of the empirical formula.

Show How to Find the Empirical Formula and the Molecular Formula for Hydrogen Peroxide Given That it Has a Composition of 5.94% Hydrogen and 94.1% Oxygen. (The Atomic Mass for Hydrogen Is 1.008 u; The Atomic Mass of Oxygen Is 16.00 u.)

To find the empirical formula, calculate the masses of each element in hydrogen peroxide for a sample size of 100.0 g. Calculating 5.94% of 100.0 g yields 5.94 g of hydrogen. Calculating 94.1% of 100.0 g yields 94.1 g of oxygen. Next, convert the masses of these elements to moles.

For hydrogen:

$$(5.94\text{ g})\left(\frac{\text{mol}}{1.008\text{ g}}\right) = 5.89\text{ mol}$$

For oxygen:

$$(94.1\text{ g})\left(\frac{\text{mol}}{16.00\text{ g}}\right) = 5.88\text{ mol}$$

Now, divide these amounts by the smallest value of moles that was calculated and round to the nearest tenth. For hydrogen, $\left(\frac{5.89}{5.88}\right) = 1.00$, and for oxygen, $\left(\frac{5.88}{5.88}\right) = 1.00$. These calculations are the subscripts for the empirical formula. Therefore, the empirical formula of hydrogen peroxide is HO. To find the molecular formula, find the molar mass of the empirical formula (HO) by adding $1.008\text{ g} + 16.00\text{ g} = 17.008\text{ g}$. To perform the calculation, the molar mass of hydrogen peroxide would need to be given. If the problem states that the actual molar mass of hydrogen peroxide is 34.016 g, divide this molar mass by the molar mass of the empirical formula: $\frac{34.016}{17.008} = 2$. Multiply each subscript of the empirical formula by 2. The molecular formula for hydrogen peroxide is H_2O_2.

Calculating Percent Composition When Given the Molecular Formula

Percent composition of a substance is a measure of the contibution of each element by mass to the total mass of the compound. To find the **percent composition** of a compound when given the molecular formula, start by finding find the molar mass of the compound. Then, find the percent contribution of each element of the compound by dividing the molar mass of the element (remembering to multiply through by the subscripts of the molecular formula) by the molar mass of the compound. Finally, check the calculations by totaling these individual percentages to ensure their combined total is 100%. This may be slightly off if any of the numbers used were rounded, but it should be very close.

Explain How to Find the Percent Composition of Methane (CH_4). (The Atomic Mass of Carbon = 12.01 u; the Atomic Mass of Hydrogen = 1.008 u.)

To find the percent composition of methane, first find the molar mass of methane. The molar mass of methane is given by $12.01\text{ g} + 4(1.008\text{ g}) = 16.042\text{ g}$. Next, find the percent contributed by the carbon and the percent contributed by the hydrogen. For the carbon, $\frac{12.01 \text{ g/mol}}{16.042 \text{ g/mol}} \times 100\% = 74.87\%$. For the hydrogen, $\frac{4(1.008) \text{ g/mol}}{16.042 \text{ g/mol}} \times 100\% = 25.13\%$. Finally, check to see that the total of the calculated percentages sum to approximately 100%. For methane, $74.87\% + 25.13\% = 100\%$.

Properties of Bonds

Relative Bond Length and Strength of Covalent Bonds

The **bond length of a covalent bond** is the distance between the nuclei of two covalently bonded atoms. The higher the bond order, the shorter the bond length. **Single bonds** are between one pair of electrons, and they are the weakest. Because single bonds (bond order 1) are the weakest, they are the longest of the three types of covalent bonds. **Double bonds** are between two pairs of electrons. Because double bonds (bond order 2) are stronger than single bonds, double bonds are shorter than single bonds. **Triple bonds** are between three pairs of electrons. Because triple bonds (bond order 3) are stronger than double bonds and single bonds, triple bonds have the shortest bond length.

Bond Types

Bonds

Chemical bonds are the attractive forces that bind atoms together into molecules. Atoms form chemical bonds in an attempt to satisfy the octet rule. These bond types include covalent bonds, ionic bonds, and metallic bonds. **Covalent bonds** are formed from the sharing of electron pairs between two atoms in a molecule. **Ionic bonds** are formed from the transferring of electrons between one atom and another, which results in the formations of cations and anions. **Metallic bonding** results from the sharing of delocalized electrons among all of the atoms in a molecule.

Ionic Bonding

Ionic bonding results from the transfer of electrons between atoms. A **cation** or positive ion is formed when an atom loses one or more electrons. An **anion** or negative ion is formed when an atom gains one or more electrons. An ionic bond results from the electrostatic attraction between a cation and an anion. One example of a compound formed by ionic bonds is sodium chloride or NaCl. Sodium (Na) is an alkali metal and tends to form Na^+ ions. Chlorine (Cl) is a halogen and tends to form Cl^- ions. The Na^+ ion and the Cl^- ion are attracted to each other. This electrostatic attraction between these oppositely charged ions is what results in the ionic bond between them.

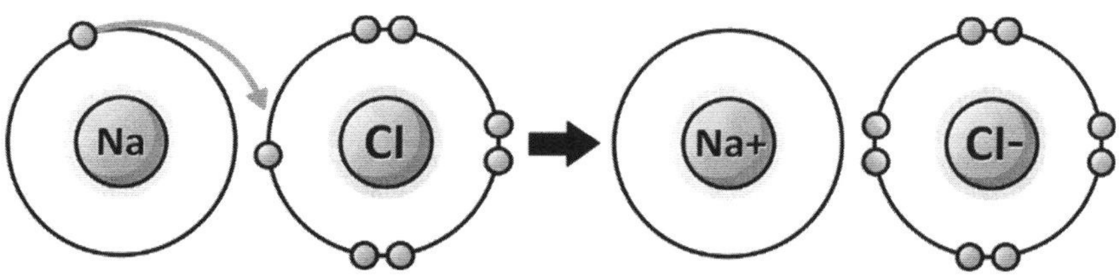

Review Video: Ionic Bonds
Visit mometrix.com/academy and enter code: 116546

Covalent Bonding

Covalent bonding results from the sharing of electrons between atoms. Atoms seek to fill their valence shell and will share electrons with another atom in order to have a full octet (except hydrogen and helium, which only hold two electrons in their valence shells). **Molecular compounds** have covalent bonds. **Organic compounds** such as proteins, carbohydrates, lipids, and nucleic acids are molecular compounds formed by covalent bonds. Methane (CH_4) is a molecular compound in which one carbon atom is covalently bonded to four hydrogen atoms as shown below.

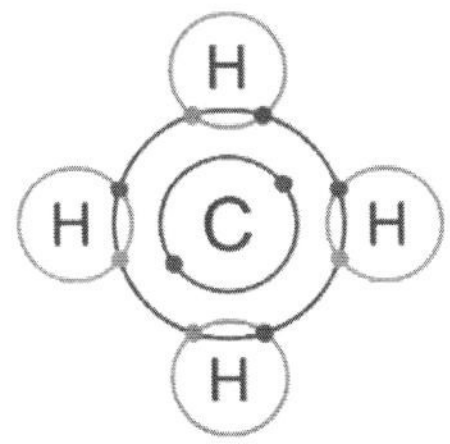

Polar Covalent Bonds, Nonpolar Covalent Bonds, and Hybridization

Polar covalent bonds result when electrons are shared unequally between atoms. **Nonpolar covalent bonds** result when electrons are shared equally between atoms. The unequal sharing of electrons is due to the differences in the electronegativities of the two atoms sharing the electrons. Partial charges develop due to this unequal sharing of electrons. The greater the difference in electronegativities between the two atoms, the stronger the dipole is. For example, the covalent bonds formed between the carbon atom and the two oxygen atoms in carbon dioxide are polar covalent bonds because the electronegativities of carbon and oxygen differ slightly. If the electronegativities are equal, then the covalent bonds are nonpolar. For example, the covalent double bond between two oxygen atoms is nonpolar because the oxygen atoms have the same electronegativities.

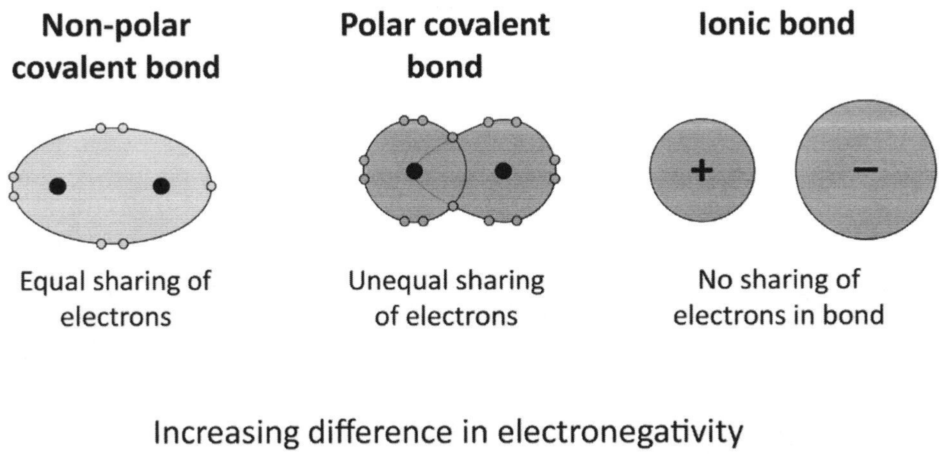

Review Video: Nonpolar Covalent Bonds
Visit mometrix.com/academy and enter code: 986465

Review Video: Covalent Bonds
Visit mometrix.com/academy and enter code: 482899

Metallic Bonding

Metallic bonding is a type of bonding between metals. Metallic bonds are similar to covalent bonds in that they are a type of sharing of electrons between atoms. However, in covalent bonding, the electrons are shared with only one other atom. In metallic bonding, the electrons are shared with all the surrounding atoms. These electrons are referred to as delocalized electrons. Metallic bonding is responsible for many of the characteristics in metals including conductivity, malleability, and ductility. An example of metallic bonding is the metallic bond between the copper atoms in a piece of copper wire.

Review Video: Metallic Bonds
Visit mometrix.com/academy and enter code: 230855

Shape of Bonds

Drawing a Lewis Structure

In order to draw a **Lewis structure** for a molecule, determine the number of **valence electrons** for each atom in the molecule and the number of valence electrons each atom needs in order to have a full outer shell. All atoms except hydrogen and helium seek to have eight electrons in their outer shells. Hydrogen and helium only have room for two valence electrons. Next, determine the **central atom**. Usually, the central atom is the atom with the largest number of valence openings. Draw the skeletal structure with the central atom. Each single bond represents two electrons. Each double bond represents four electrons. Each triple bond represents six electrons. Start with single bonds and change to double or triple bonds as needed to satisfy the octet rule. But remember, atoms may only share what they have available. For example, elements in group IIIA have three valence electrons and need an additional five electrons to make eight, but they may only share the three that they have available. Add the remaining valence electrons to all the atoms. Check to make sure that each atom (except hydrogen, helium, and boron) satisfies the octet rule.

Examples of Lewis Structures:

NH_3	H_2O
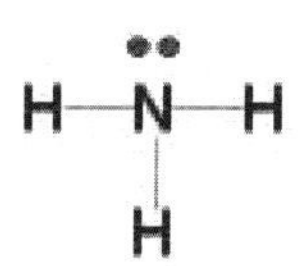	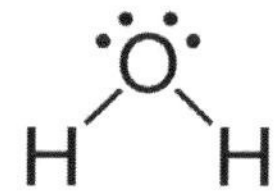
CCl_4	BF_3
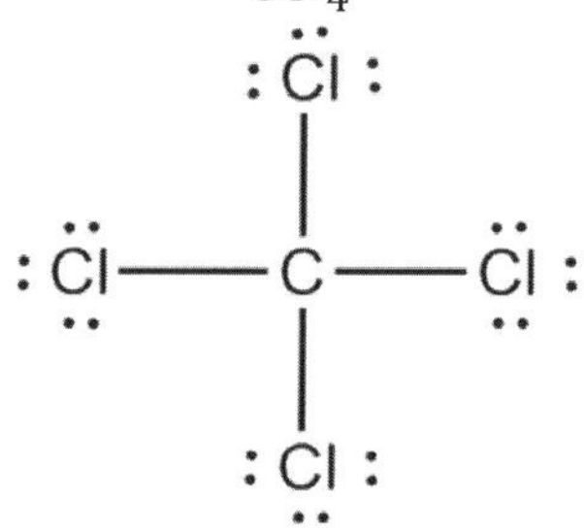	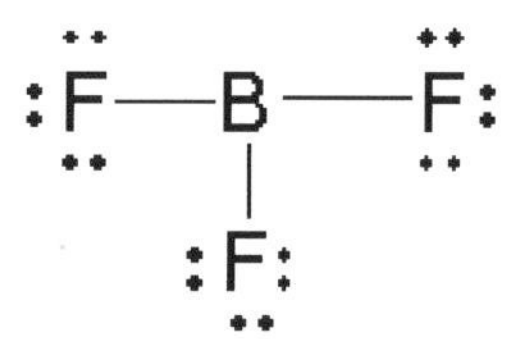

Resonance Structures

For some molecules, more than one Lewis structure may be drawn due to the delocalization of electrons. In order to determine which resonance structure is the most stable, calculate the formal charge of each structure. The structure with the lowest formal charge is the most stable. The actual molecule is a hybrid of all the possible Lewis structures. An example of resonance occurs in benzene, C_6H_6. The two possible Lewis structures for benzene are shown below. The only difference between the two Lewis structures is the placement of the single and double bonds between the carbon atoms.

Studies show that in reality, **neither Lewis structure is correct**. In fact, all the bonds between the carbon atoms are exactly the same. The structure of the resonance hybrid of benzene is often represented by the drawing shown below. The circle inside the ring of carbons represents the delocalized electrons that are shared among all the carbon atoms of the ring.

Possible Lewis Structures Resonance Hybrid

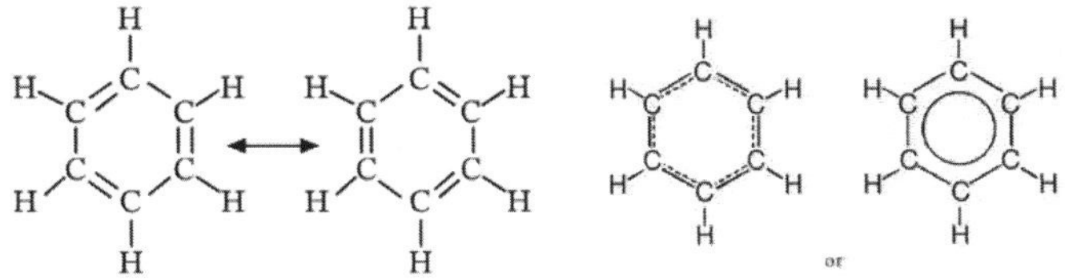

Linear Molecular Geometry

Linear: All diatomic molecules are linear molecules. Also, molecules with two bonding groups and two nonbonding pairs of electrons are linear. The bond angle measurement for linear molecules is 180°. Nitric oxide (also called nitrogen monoxide) is an example of a linear molecule.

Trigonal Planar Molecular Geometry

Trigonal planar: For a trigonal planar molecule, the central atom has three bonding pairs of electrons and zero nonbonding pairs. These molecules are an exception to the octet rule. The bond angle measurement for trigonal planar molecules is 120°. Boron trifluoride (BF_3), which has has three bonding pairs and zero nonbonding pairs around the central atom, is an example of a trigonal planar molecule.

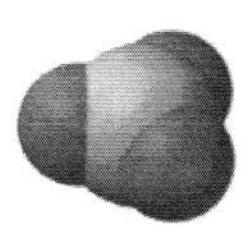

Angular Molecular Geometry

Angular: For an angular molecule, the central atom has two bonding pairs of electrons and one or two nonbonding pairs. The bond angle measurement for angular molecules is less than 120° if there is one nonbonding pair, and less than 109° if there are two. Oxygen difluoride (OF_2), which has two bonding pairs and two nonbonding pairs around the central angle, is an example of an angular molecule.

Tetrahedral Molecular Geometry

Tetrahedral: For a tetrahedral molecule, the central atom has four bonding pairs of electrons and zero nonbonding pairs. The bond angle measurement for tetrahedral molecules is 109.5°. Methane

(CH_4), which has four bonding pairs and zero nonbonding pairs around the central angle, is an example of a tetrahedral molecule.

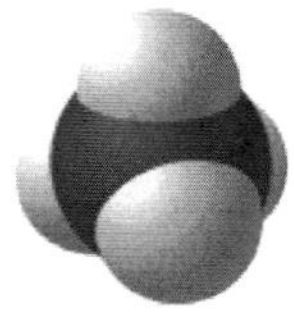

Trigonal Pyramidal Molecular Geometry

Trigonal pyramidal: For a trigonal pyramidal molecule, the central atom has three bonding pairs and one nonbonding pair. The bond angle measurement for trigonal pyramidal molecules is less than 109.5°. Ammonia (NH_3), which has three bonding pairs and one nonbonding pair around the central atom, is an example of a trigonal pyramidal molecule.

Polar and Nonpolar Molecules

Covalently bonded molecules are either **polar** or **nonpolar** depending on the type and arrangement of their covalent bonds. **Covalent bonds** are polar if the electronegativities of the two atoms sharing the pair of electrons differ. With differing electronegativities, the electrons are shared unequally, with the pair of electrons displaced more toward the more electronegative atom. This results in a polar covalent bond. **Covalent molecules** always have polar covalent bonds. If the bonds are arranged symmetrically around a central atom, the polar bonds will "cancel" each other out, resulting in a nonpolar molecule. If a molecule contains polar covalent bonds that are not arranged symmetrically in a way to "cancel" each other out, the molecule is polar. Molecules with only nonpolar covalent bonds are always nonpolar. Only molecules with polar covalent bonds can be polar.

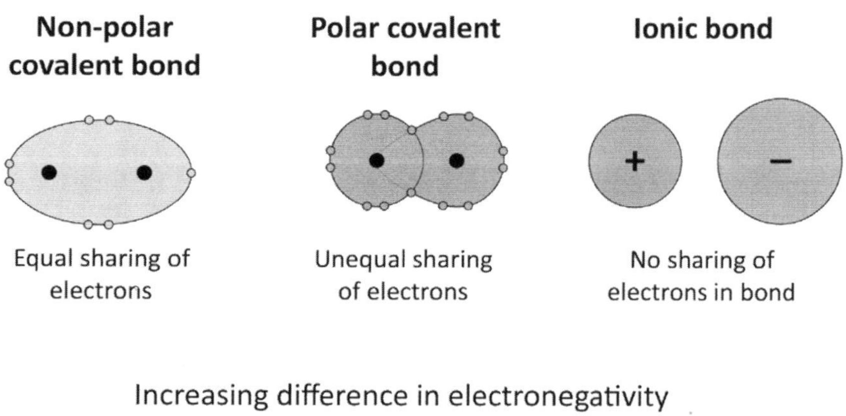

Identifying Polar or Nonpolar Examples:

CH_4

Nonpolar: Methane, or CH_4 has a tetrahedral geometry with four hydrogen atoms covalently bonded around the central carbon atom. These four bonds are polar covalent bonds, but because they are arranged symmetrically around the central carbon atom, the molecule is nonpolar.

CO_2

Nonpolar: Carbon dioxide, or CO_2, is a linear molecule with two oxygen atoms covalently double bonded to a central carbon atom. These two double bonds are polar covalent bonds, but because they are arranged symmetrically around the carbon atom, the molecule is nonpolar.

H_2S

Polar: Dihydrogen sulfide, or H_2S, is an angular molecule with the two hydrogen atoms covalently bonded to a sulfur atom. This molecule has two bonding pairs and one nonbonding pair. Because of the nonbonding pair, the molecule is bent or angular. Because the polar bonds do not cancel each other out in this arrangement, the molecule is polar.

NH_3

Polar: Ammonia, or NH_3, is a trigonal pyramidal molecule with the three hydrogen atoms bonded asymmetrically around the central nitrogen atom. The molecule has three bonding pairs and one nonbonding pair of electrons. Because the polar covalent bonds are arranged asymmetrically, the molecule is polar.

BF_3

Nonpolar: Boron trifluoride, or BF_3, is a trigonal planar molecule with three fluorine atoms bonded symmetrically around the central boron atom. Because the molecule is an exception to the octet rule and only has three bonding pairs and no nonbonding pairs around the central boron atom, these fluorine atoms are arranged symmetrically around the boron atom canceling out the effect of the polar covalent bonds and resulting in a nonpolar molecule.

Intermolecular Interactions

Hydrogen Bonding

Hydrogen bonding is a type of intermolecular force present between molecules containing hydrogen atoms covalently bonded to oxygen, fluorine, or nitrogen. Hydrogen bonding is the strongest of the intermolecular forces. When hydrogen from one molecule is near a highly electronegative atom such as oxygen, fluorine, or nitrogen in another molecule and acts as a bridge between another highly electronegative atom, a hydrogen bond is formed. Hydrogen bonding is responsible for the high boiling point in water and for the crystalline structure of ice.

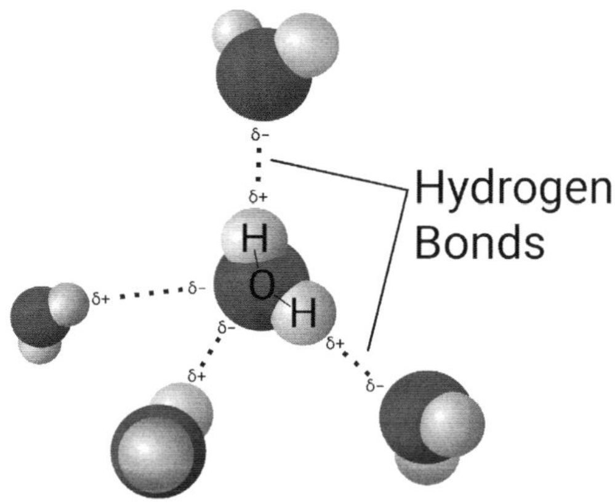

Dipole-Induced Dipole Intermolecular Forces

Whereas **dipole–dipole intermolecular forces** are between two polar molecules, **a dipole-induced intermolecular force** is between a polar molecule and a nonpolar molecule. Dipole-induced dipole intermolecular forces are forces that occur when a dipole induces a temporary dipole in a molecule that is nonpolar. The electron cloud of the nonpolar molecule is distorted when it comes near the electron cloud of a dipole. This is typically a weak intermolecular force. However, this dipole-induced dipole intermolecular force is responsible for the stability of hydrates formed from hydrocarbons and some of the noble gases.

Dipole–Dipole Intermolecular Forces

Dipole–dipole forces are intermolecular forces that occur only between polar molecules. Polar molecules have positive and negative ends because of an unequal sharing of electrons due to differences in electronegativities between the atoms of the molecules. The positive end of one molecule is attracted to the negative end of the other molecules. Dipole–dipole forces are stronger than London (dispersion) forces but weaker than hydrogen bonds. In the figure below, the dipole–dipole force between the positive end of one hydrogen chloride molecule and the negative end of another hydrogen chloride molecule is indicated by the dashed line.

$$\overset{\delta+}{H}—\overset{\delta-}{Cl}\text{- - - -}\overset{\delta+}{H}—\overset{\delta-}{Cl}$$

London Forces

London forces are intermolecular forces that exist between all molecules due to the temporary instantaneous dipoles induced by an unequal distribution of electrons around a molecule. London forces are present between all molecules of liquids, solids, and gases. London forces are the weakest of the intermolecular forces and the only intermolecular forces present between nonpolar molecules. London forces are also known as London dispersion forces or dispersion forces. London forces are weaker than both dipole–dipole forces and hydrogen bonds.

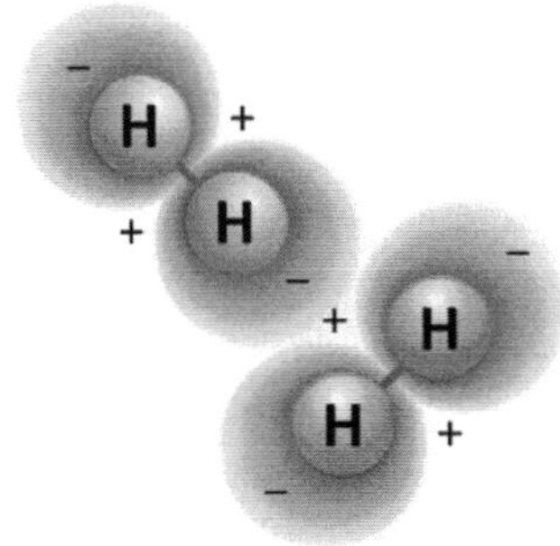

Intermolecular Interactions Examples

NH_3

The intermolecular forces present in a sample of NH_3 are London forces and hydrogen bonds. London forces are present between all molecules. Hydrogen bonds are present between molecules with hydrogen covalently bonded to nitrogen, fluorine, and oxygen.

CH_4

The intermolecular forces present in a sample of CH_4 are only London forces. London forces are present between all molecules. Because CH_4 is a nonpolar molecular molecule, no dipole–dipole forces are present.

H_2S

The intermolecular forces present in a sample of H_2S are London forces and dipole–dipole forces. London forces are present between all molecules. Dipole–dipole forces are present between polar molecules, and because H_2S is a polar molecule, dipole–dipole forces are present.

Effect of Bonds on Physical Properties

Bonding and Structure

Properties Affected by Bonding and Structure

Bonding and structure determine whether a substance exists naturally as a solid, liquid, or gas. Properties that are affected by bonding and structure include boiling point, freezing point, and vapor pressure. Bonding and structure determine if a substance is soluble in water or in nonpolar solvents. Also affected are the viscosity of liquids, whether a solid material is hard or soft, and whether or not a substance forms crystals or is amorphous. Bonding affects the conductivity of heat and electricity and thus whether a substance is a good insulator or conductor.

Effect of Bonding and Structure on Boiling Points and Melting Points

The types of bonds within molecules affect boiling and melting points. **Compounds with ionic bonds** typically have high melting and boiling points, whereas **compounds with covalent bonds** typically have low melting and boiling points. Intermolecular forces also affect these points.

Substances with hydrogen bonds typically have high boiling and melting points. For example, hydrogen bonds are responsible for the high boiling and melting points of water.

Review Video: Differences in Boiling Points
Visit mometrix.com/academy and enter code: 810110

Effect of Bonding and Structure on Solubility

Bonding and structure affect **solubility**. The basic idea behind solubility is *like dissolves like.* This means that solutes with polar molecules typically dissolve in solvents with polar molecules. The polarity of the molecules is determined by the type of bonds and the arrangement of those bonds in the molecules. For example, both salt and table sugar (sucrose) dissolve in water because salt, table sugar, and water are all polar molecules. Solutes with nonpolar molecules typically dissolve in solvents with nonpolar molecules. For example, a grease stain will not rinse out with water because water consists of polar molecules and grease is a nonpolar lipid.

Effect of Bonding and Structure on Equilibrium Vapor Pressure

Vapor pressure is related to the **boiling point** of a substance. The boiling point of a substance is the temperature at which the vapor pressure equals the atmospheric pressure. In general, as the vapor pressure increases, the boiling point decreases. Compounds with ionic bonds typically have high boiling points and low vapor pressures. Compounds with covalent bonds typically have low boiling points and high vapor pressures. Substances with the strongest intermolecular forces, hydrogen bonds, typically have high boiling points and low vapor pressures.

Chapter Quiz

Ready to see how well you retained what you just read? Scan the QR code to go directly to the chapter quiz interface for this study guide. If you're using a computer, simply visit the online resources page at **mometrix.com/resources719/gacechemistry** and click the Chapter Quizzes link.

Periodicity and Chemical Reactions

Periodic Table Layout

Groups and Periods in the Periodic Table

A **group** is a vertical column of the periodic table. Elements in the same group have the same number of **valence electrons**. For the representative elements, the number of valence electrons is equal to the group number. Because of their equal valence electrons, elements in the same groups have similar physical and chemical properties. A **period** is a horizontal row of the periodic table. Atomic number increases from left to right across a row. The period of an element corresponds to the **highest energy level** of the electrons in the atoms of that element. The energy level increases from top to bottom down a group.

Period ↓ / Group →	1	2	3	4	5	6	7	8	9	10	11	12	13	14	15	16	17	18
1	1 H																	2 He
2	3 Li	4 Be											5 B	6 C	7 N	8 O	9 F	10 Ne
3	11 Na	12 Mg											13 Al	14 Si	15 P	16 S	17 Cl	18 Ar
4	19 K	20 Ca	21 Sc	22 Ti	23 V	24 Cr	25 Mn	26 Fe	27 Co	28 Ni	29 Cu	30 Zn	31 Ga	32 Ge	33 As	34 Se	35 Br	36 Kr
5	37 Rb	38 Sr	39 Y	40 Zr	41 Nb	42 Mo	43 Tc	44 Ru	45 Rh	46 Pd	47 Ag	48 Cd	49 In	50 Sn	51 Sb	52 Te	53 I	54 Xe
6	55 Cs	56 Ba	*	72 Hf	73 Ta	74 W	75 Re	76 Os	77 Ir	78 Pt	79 Au	80 Hg	81 Tl	82 Pb	83 Bi	84 Po	85 At	86 Rn
7	87 Fr	88 Ra	**	104 Rf	105 Db	106 Sg	107 Bh	108 Hs	109 Mt	110 Ds	111 Rg	112 Cn	113 Uut	114 Fl	115 Uup	116 Lv	117 Uus	118 Uuo

*	57 La	58 Ce	59 Pr	60 Nd	61 Pm	62 Sm	63 Eu	64 Gd	65 Tb	66 Dy	67 Ho	68 Er	69 Tm	70 Yb	71 Lu
**	89 Ac	90 Th	91 Pa	92 U	93 Np	94 Pu	95 Am	96 Cm	97 Bk	98 Cf	99 Es	100 Fm	101 Md	102 No	103 Lr

Review Video: Periodic Table
Visit mometrix.com/academy and enter code: 154828

Atomic Number and Atomic Mass in the Periodic Table

The elements in the periodic table are arranged in order of **increasing atomic number**, first left to right and then top to bottom across the periodic table. The **atomic number** represents the number of protons in the atoms of that element. Because of the increasing numbers of protons, the atomic mass typically also increases from left to right across a period and from top to bottom down a row. The **atomic mass** is a weighted average of all the naturally occurring isotopes of an element.

Atomic Symbols

The **atomic symbol** for many elements is simply the first letter of the element name. For example, the atomic symbol for hydrogen is H, and the atomic symbol for carbon is C. The atomic symbol of other elements is the first two letters of the element name. For example, the atomic symbol for helium is He, and the atomic symbol for cobalt is Co. The atomic symbols of several elements are derived from Latin. For example, the atomic symbol for copper (Cu) is derived from *cuprum,* and the atomic symbol for iron (Fe) is derived from *ferrum.* The atomic symbol for tungsten (W) is derived from the German word *wolfram.*

Arrangement of Metals, Nonmetals, and Metalloids in the Periodic Table

The **metals** are located on the left side and center of the periodic table, and the **nonmetals** are located on the right side. The **metalloids** or **semimetals** form a zigzag line between the metals and nonmetals as shown below. Metals include the alkali metals, such as lithium, sodium, and potassium, and the alkaline earth metals, such as beryllium, magnesium, and calcium. Metals also include the transition metals, such as iron, copper, and nickel, and the inner transition metals, such as thorium, uranium, and plutonium. Nonmetals include the chalcogens, such as oxygen and sulfur; the halogens, such as fluorine and chlorine; and the noble gases, such as helium and argon. Carbon, nitrogen, and phosphorus are also nonmetals. Metalloids or semimetals include boron, silicon, germanium, antimony, and polonium.

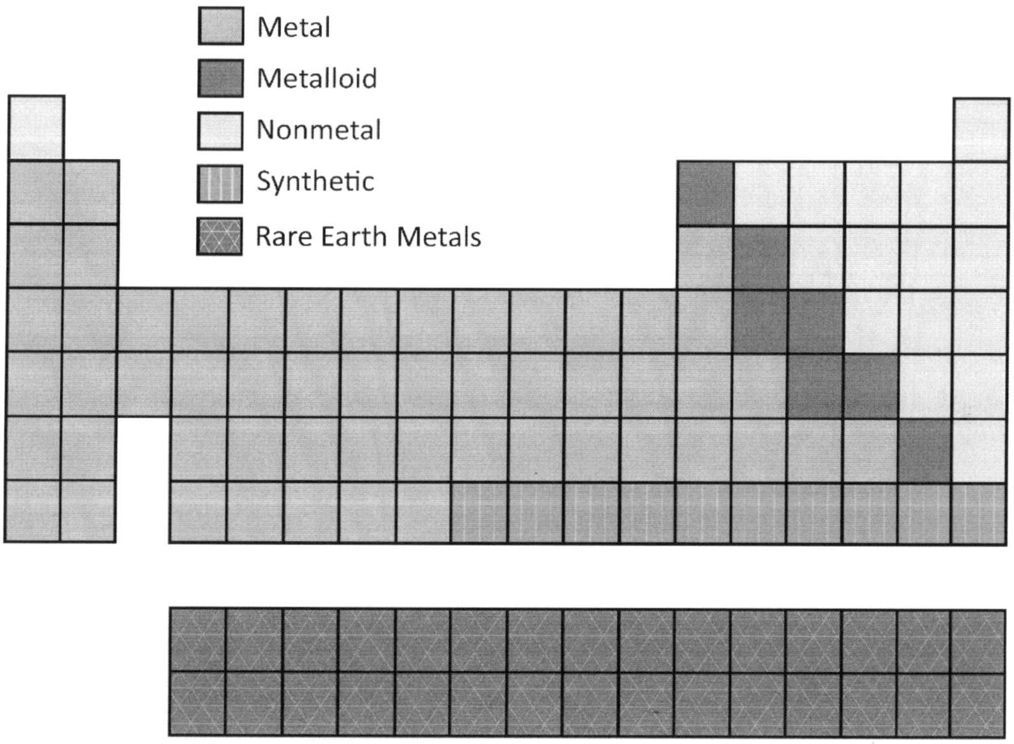

Arrangement of Transition Elements

The **transition elements** belong to one of two categories—transition metals or inner transition metals. The **transition metals** are located in the middle of the periodic table, and the inner transition metals are typically set off as two rows by themselves at the bottom of the periodic table. The transition metals correspond to the "*d* block" for orbital filling, and the inner transition metals correspond to the "*f* block" for orbital filling. Examples of transition metals include iron, copper, nickel, and zinc. The **inner transition metals** consist of the lanthanide or rare-earth series, which corresponds to the first row, and the actinide series, which corresponds to the second row of the inner transition metals. The **lanthanide series** includes lanthanum, cerium, and praseodymium. The **actinide series** includes actinium, uranium, and plutonium.

Periodic Trends

Atomic Radius Size

Atomic radius size decreases across a period from left to right and increases down a group from top to bottom. The atomic radius decreases across a period due to the increasing number of protons and the attraction between those protons and the orbiting electrons. The atomic radius increases down a group due to the increasing energy levels. Atoms in the top-right corner of the periodic table (including hydrogen) have the smallest atomic radii, and atoms in the bottom-left corner of the periodic table have the largest atomic radii. Helium has the smallest atomic radius, and cesium has the largest confirmed atomic radius.

Ionic Radius Size

The **ionic radius size** increases down a group of the periodic table. This is due to the increasing energy levels and the fact that electrons are orbiting farther and farther from the nucleus. The trend seen across the periods of the periodic table is due to the formation of cations or anions. Metals form cations or positive ions. Cations are smaller than their neutral atoms due to the loss of one or more electrons. Nonmetals except the noble gases form anions or negative ions. Anions are larger than their neutral atoms due to the gain of one or more electrons.

Ionization Energy

Ionization energy is the amount of energy needed to remove an electron from an isolated atom. Ionization energy decreases down a group of the periodic table because the electrons get farther and farther from the nucleus, making it easier for the electron to be removed. Ionization energy increases across a period of the periodic table due to the decreasing atomic size, which is due to the increasing number of protons attracting the electrons towards the nucleus. These trends of ionization energy are the opposite of the trends for atomic radius.

Electron Affinity

Electron affinity is the energy required to add an electron to a neutral atom in the gaseous phase of an element. If electrons are added to a halogen such as fluorine or chlorine, energy is released and the electron affinity is negative. If electrons are added to an alkaline earth metal, energy is absorbed and the electron affinity is positive. In general, electron affinity becomes more negative from left to right across a period in the periodic table. Electron affinity becomes less negative from the top to the bottom of a group of the periodic table.

Electronegativity

Electronegativity is a measure of the ability of an atom that is chemically combined to at least one other atom in a molecule to attract electrons to it. The Pauling scale is commonly used to assign values to the elements, with fluorine, which is the most electronegative element, being assigned a value of 4.0. Electronegativity increases from left to right across a period of the periodic table and decreases from top to bottom down a group of the periodic table.

Review Video: Electron Configuration
Visit mometrix.com/academy and enter code: 565113

Review Video: Electronegativity
Visit mometrix.com/academy and enter code: 823348

Physical Properties of the Elements in Relation to the Periodic Table

The **boiling point**, **melting point**, and **conductivity** of the elements depend partially on the number of valence electrons of the atoms of those elements. For the representative elements in groups 1A–8A, the number of valence electrons matches the group number. Because all of the elements in each individual group contain the same number of valence electrons, elements in the same groups tend to have similar boiling points, melting points, and conductivity. Boiling points and melting points tend to decrease moving down the column of groups 1A–4A and 8A but increase slightly moving down the column of groups 5A–7A.

Chemical Reactivity in Relation to the Periodic Table

Atoms of elements in the same **group** or **family** of the periodic table tend to have **similar chemical properties** and **similar chemical reactions**. For example, the alkali metals, which form cations with a charge of +1, tend to react with water to form hydrogen gas and metal hydroxides. The alkaline earth metals, which form cations with a charge of +2, react with oxygen gas to form metal oxides. The halogens, which form anions with a charge of −1, are highly reactive and toxic. The noble gases are unreactive and never form compounds naturally.

Balancing Chemical Equations

Balancing a Chemical Equation

According to the law of conservation of mass, the **mass of the products** must always equal the **mass of the reactants** in a **chemical reaction**. Because mass is conserved and it is a chemical reaction (as opposed to a nuclear reaction), the number of each type of atom in the products must equal the number of each type of atom in the reactants. The key to balancing a chemical reaction is balancing the number of atoms of each element on both sides of the equation. Only the coefficients in front of the reactants and products may be changed to accomplish this, not the subscripts in the molecules themselves. Try balancing the largest number of a type of atom first. Also, check if any odd numbers need to be changed to even. Always leave the uncombined elements to balance until the end.

Review Video: Balancing Chemical Equations
Visit mometrix.com/academy and enter code: 341228

Balance the Equation $KNO_3(s) \rightarrow KNO_2(s) + O_2(g)$.

First, determine the types and numbers of each type of atom on each side of the equation:

Element	Reactants	Products
K	1	1
N	1	1
O	3	4

"Oxygen" needs to be balanced. Add a coefficient of "2" to the left side to force "oxygen" to be even and update the counts:

Element	Reactants	Products
K	2	1
N	2	1
O	6	4

Now, balance the potassium and nitrogen by placing a coefficient of "2" in front of the KNO_2 and update the counts:

Element	Reactants	Products
K	2	2
N	2	2
O	6	6

The equation is now balanced: $2KNO_3(s) \rightarrow 2KNO_2(s) + O_2(g)$.

Balance the Equation $C_2H_2(g) + O_2(g) \rightarrow CO_2(g) + H_2O(g)$.

First, determine the types and numbers of each type of atom on each side of the equation:

Element	Reactants	Products
C	2	1
H	2	2
O	2	3

Oxygen needs to be balanced, but remember to leave the uncombined oxygen reactant until the end. Carbon also needs to be balanced. Add a coefficient of "4" to the CO_2 on the right side and a coefficient of "2" in front of the C_2H_2 and update the counts:

Element	Reactants	Products
C	4	4
H	4	4
O	2	9

Balance the hydrogen by adding a "2" in front of the H_2O and update the counts:

Element	Reactants	Products
C	4	4
H	4	4
O	2	10

Finally, balance the oxygen by adding a "5" in front of the O_2 on the left.

The equation is now balanced: $2C_2H_2(g) + 5O_2(g) \rightarrow 4CO_2(g) + 2H_2O(g)$.

Element	Reactants	Products
K	4	4
N	4	4
O	10	10

Chemical Equation Balancing Practice

Given the Following Equation at Standard Temperature and Pressure (STP): $4Fe(s) + 3O_2(g) \rightarrow 2Fe_2O_3(s)$, Determine the Volume of $O_2(g)$ Needed to Produce 10.0 mol of $Fe_2O_3(s)$.

One method to determine the volume of $O_2(g)$ needed to produce 10.0 mol of $Fe_2O_3(s)$ is to use dimensional analysis with the mole ratio for the balanced chemical equation. Because 3 mol of $O_2(g)$ produce 2 mol of $Fe_2O_3(s)$, the needed mole ratio is $\left(\frac{3 \text{ mol } O_2}{2 \text{ mol } Fe_2O_3}\right)$. Also, at STP, one mole of a gas has a volume of 22.4 L. This can be written as a conversion factor of $\left(\frac{22.4 \text{ L}}{1 \text{ mol } O_2}\right)$. Using dimensional analysis:

$$(10.0 \text{ mol } Fe_2O_3)\left(\frac{3 \text{ mol } O_2}{2 \text{ mol } Fe_2O_3}\right)\left(\frac{22.4 \text{ L}}{1 \text{ mol } O_2}\right) = 336 \text{ L}$$

Given the Following Equation at STP: $C_3H_8(l) + 5O_2(g) \rightarrow 3CO_2(g) + 4H_2O(g)$, Determine the Volume of $O_2(g)$ Needed to Burn 1.00 kg of $C_3H_8(l)$.

One method to determine the volume of $O_2(g)$ needed to burn 1.0 kg of $C_3H_8(l)$ is to use dimensional analysis with conversion factors for the molar mass, number of moles, and liters of gas at STP. The conversion factor for the molar mass of C_3H_8 can be written as $\left(\frac{1 \text{ mol } C_3H_8}{44.1 \text{ grams } C_3H_8}\right)$. Because 1 mol of $C_3H_8(l)$ requires 5 mol of $O_2(g)$, the needed mole ratio is $\left(\frac{5 \text{ mol } O_2}{1 \text{ mol } C_3H_8}\right)$.

Also, at STP, one mole of a gas has a volume of 22.4 L. This can be written as the conversion factor $\left(\frac{22.4 \text{ L}}{1 \text{ mol } O_2}\right)$. Using dimensional analysis:

$$(1.0 \text{ kg } C_3H_8)\left(\frac{1000 \text{ g}}{1 \text{ kg}}\right)\left(\frac{1 \text{ mol } C_3H_8}{44.1 \text{ g } C_3H_8}\right)\left(\frac{5 \text{ mol } O_2}{1 \text{ mol } C_3H_8}\right)\left(\frac{22.4 \text{ L } O_2}{1 \text{ mol } O_2}\right) = 2.54 \times 10^3 \text{ L } O_2$$

Given the Following Equation: $2Na(s) + Cl_2(g) \rightarrow 2NaCl(s)$, Determine the Amount in Grams of $Na(s)$ Needed to Produce 500.0 g of $NaCl(s)$.

One method to determine the amount in grams of Na(s) needed to produce 500.0 g of NaCl(s) is to use dimensional analysis with conversion factors for the molar mass and number of moles. The conversion factor for the molar mass of NaCl can be written as $\left(\frac{1 \text{ mol NaCl}}{58.44 \text{ g NaCl}}\right)$. Because 2 mol of Na(s) produce 2 mol of NaCl(s), the needed mole ratio is $\left(\frac{2 \text{ mol Na}}{2 \text{ mol NaCl}}\right)$. The conversion factor for the molar mass of Na(s) can be written as $\left(\frac{22.99 \text{ g Na}}{1 \text{ mol Na}}\right)$. Using dimensional analysis:

$$(500.0 \text{ g NaCl})\left(\frac{1 \text{ mol NaCl}}{58.44 \text{ g NaCl}}\right)\left(\frac{2 \text{ mol Na}}{2 \text{ mol NaCl}}\right)\left(\frac{22.99 \text{ g Na}}{1 \text{ mol Na}}\right) = 196.7 \text{ g Na(s)}$$

Given the Following Equation at STP: $2Na(s) + Cl_2(g) \rightarrow 2NaCl(s)$, Determine the Volume in whole Liters of $Cl_2(g)$ Needed to Produce 1.00 kg of $NaCl(s)$.

One method to determine the volume of $Cl_2(g)$ needed to produce 1.00 kg of NaCl(s) is to use dimensional analysis with conversion factors for the molar mass, number of moles, and liters of gas at STP. The conversion factor for the molar mass of NaCl can be written as $\left(\frac{1 \text{ mol NaCl}}{58.44 \text{ g NaCl}}\right)$. Because 1 mol of $Cl_2(g)$ produces 2 mol of NaCl(s), the needed mole ratio is $\left(\frac{1\text{ mol Cl}_2}{2\text{ mol NaCl}}\right)$. Also, at STP, one mole of a gas has a volume of 22.4 L. This can be written as a conversion factor $\left(\frac{22.4\text{ L}}{1\text{ mol Cl}_2}\right)$. Using dimensional analysis:

$$(1.00\text{ kg NaCl})\left(\frac{1000\text{ g}}{1\text{ kg}}\right)\left(\frac{1\text{ mol NaCl}}{58.44\text{ g NaCl}}\right)\left(\frac{1\text{ mol Cl}_2}{2\text{ mol NaCl}}\right)\left(\frac{22.4\text{ L O}_2}{1\text{ mol O}_2}\right) = 191.65\text{ L Cl}_2$$

This rounds up to 192 L because 191 L will not be enough.

Given that 100.0 g of $H_2(g)$ React with 350.0 g of $O_2(g)$, Determine the Limiting Reactant and the Amount of Excess Reactant That Remains $2H_2(g) + O_2(g) \rightarrow 2H_2O(g)$.

To determine the limiting reactant, first determine the amount of H_2O that can be produced from each of the reactants:

$$(100.0\text{ g H}_2)\left(\frac{1\text{ mol H}_2}{2.016\text{ g H}_2}\right)\left(\frac{2\text{ mol H}_2\text{O}}{2\text{ mol H}_2}\right)\left(\frac{18.016\text{ g H}_2\text{O}}{1\text{ mol H}_2\text{O}}\right) = 893.7\text{ g H}_2\text{O}$$

$$(350.0\text{ g O}_2)\left(\frac{1\text{ mol O}_2}{32.00\text{ g O}_2}\right)\left(\frac{2\text{ mol H}_2\text{O}}{1\text{ mol O}_2}\right)\left(\frac{18.016\text{ g H}_2\text{O}}{1\text{ mol H}_2\text{O}}\right) = 394.1\text{ g H}_2\text{O}$$

Because O_2 produces the least amount of H_2O, O_2 is the limiting reagent. Therefore, H_2 is the reactant that is in excess. Calculating the amount of H_2 consumed in this reaction:

$$(350.0\text{ g O}_2)\left(\frac{1\text{ mol O}_2}{32.00\text{ g O}_2}\right)\left(\frac{2\text{ mol H}_2}{1\text{ mol O}_2}\right)\left(\frac{2.016\text{ g H}_2}{1\text{ mol H}_2}\right) = 44.10\text{ g H}_2\ (\textit{consumed})$$

Subtracting this amount from the original amount yields the excess amount

$$100.0\text{ g H}_2 - 44.10\text{ g H}_2 = 55.91\text{ g H}_2\ (\textit{excess})$$

Find the Percent Yield in the Following Reaction if 200.0 g of Solid $KClO_3$. Produced 100.0 g of Solid KCl: $2KClO_3(s) \rightarrow 2KCl(s) + 3O_2(g)$.

To calculate the percent yield if 200.0 g of solid $KClO_3$ produced 100.0 g of solid KCl, first calculate the theoretical yield of KCl or the maximum amount of KCl that can be produced.

Theoretical yield:

$$(200.0\text{ g KClO}_3)\left(\frac{1\text{ mol KClO}_3}{122.6\text{ g KClO}_3}\right)\left(\frac{2\text{ mol KCl}}{2\text{ mol KClO}_3}\right)\left(\frac{74.55\text{ g KCl}}{1\text{ mol KCl}}\right) = 121.6\text{ g KCl}$$

The formula to calculate percent yield is $\frac{\text{actual yield}}{\text{theoretical yield}} \times 100\%$. Substituting in the 100.0 g of KCl for the actual yield and the 121.6 g of KCl for the theoretical yield:

$$\text{Percent yield} = \frac{100.0\text{ g}}{121.6\text{ g}} \times 100\% = 82.24\%$$

Review Video: How to Calculate Percent Yield
Visit mometrix.com/academy and enter code: 565738

Write a Balanced Equation for the Combustion of Methane.

The molecular formula for methane is CH_4. For a combustion equation, the reactants are methane (CH_4) and oxygen gas (O_2). The products of this combustion reaction are water vapor (H_2O) and carbon dioxide (CO_2). Setting up the equation yields the following reaction:

$$CH_4(g) + O_2(g) \rightarrow CO_2(g) + H_2O(g)$$

This equation must still be balanced. Finally, the combustion of methane is given by the following reaction:

$$CH_4(g) + 2O_2(g) \rightarrow CO_2(g) + 2H_2O(g)$$

Review Video: Combustion
Visit mometrix.com/academy and enter code: 592219

Write a Balanced Equation for the Neutralization of Hydrochloric Acid, HCl(aq), with Sodium Hydroxide, NaOH(aq).

In a neutralization reaction, an acid reacts with a base to form a salt and water. The salt forms from the cation of the base and the anion of the acid. The salt formed from these reactants is NaCl with the Na^+ from the base and the Cl^- from the acid. Water forms from the remaining H^+ and OH^- ions:

$$\text{acid} + \text{base} \rightarrow \text{salt} + \text{water}$$
$$HCl(aq) + NaOH(aq) \rightarrow NaCl(aq) + H_2O(l)$$

Write a Balanced Equation for the Decomposition Reaction of Solid Lithium Carbonate (Li_2CO_3).

The general form for a decomposition reaction is $AB \rightarrow A + B$. However, this metal oxide has three elements and may not seem to fit the general form at first. When many metal carbonates are heated, they form the metal oxide and carbon dioxide gas. In this case, the products will also be compounds. In this decomposition reaction, when heated, solid lithium oxide decomposes to form solid lithium oxide and gaseous carbon dioxide:

$$Li_2CO_3(s) \xrightarrow{\Delta} LiO(s) + CO_2(g)$$

Write a Balanced Equation for the Dehydration of Ethanol.

Ethanol (C_2H_5OH) can be dehydrated to produce ethene (C_2H_4). The gaseous ethanol is passed over a hot aluminum oxide catalyst to produce ethene and water.

$$\text{ethanol} \xrightarrow{\text{aluminum oxide}} \text{ethene} + \text{water}$$

$$C_2H_5OH(g) \xrightarrow{Al_2O_3} C_2H_4(g) + H_2O(l)$$

This can also be shown in the form of condensed structural formulas:

$$CH_3CH_2OH \xrightarrow{Al_2O_3} H_2C = CH_2 + H_2O$$

Balancing a Chemical Equation Involving Simple Oxidation-Reduction Reactions

One method to balance simple oxidation-reduction reactions is to split the reaction into half-reactions. First, write the oxidation half-reaction and the reduction half-reaction. Remember the phrase *"LEO the lion says GER,"* which is a reminder that the Loss of Electrons is Oxidation (LEO), and the Gain of Electrons is Reduction (GER). Next, balance the electrons by multiplying the equation(s) by the necessary factor(s). Finally, cancel the electron(s) and combine the balanced oxidation and reduction half-reactions into a balanced net chemical equation.

Balance the Following Chemical Equation Involving an Oxidation-Reduction Reaction: $Na + O_2 \rightarrow Na^+ + O^{2-}$.

In order to balance the equation $Na + O_2 \rightarrow Na^+ + O^{2-}$, first, write the individual half-reactions:

$$\text{oxidation: } Na \rightarrow Na^+ + e^-$$

$$\text{reduction: } O_2 + 4e^- \rightarrow 2O^{2-}$$

Next, balance the number of electrons by multiplying the oxidation half-reaction by 4:

$$\text{oxidation: } 4Na \rightarrow 4Na^+ + 4e^-$$

$$\text{reduction: } O_2 + 4e^- \rightarrow 2O^{2-}$$

Finally, cancel the electrons and combine the half-reactions into the net reaction:

$$4Na + O_2 \rightarrow 4Na^+ + 2O^{2-}$$

Write a Balanced Equation for the Oxidation-Reduction Reaction of Metallic Zinc Powder and Aqueous Copper(II) Sulfate.

According to the activity series, zinc is more reactive than copper. Therefore, the zinc is oxidized, and the copper is reduced. Write the half-reactions:

$$\text{oxidation: } Zn \rightarrow Zn^{2+} + 2e^-$$

$$\text{reduction: } Cu^{2+} + 2e^- \rightarrow Cu$$

Cancel the electrons and combine the two half-reactions into the net equation:

$$Zn + Cu^{2+} \rightarrow Zn^{2+} + Cu$$

Finally, add the symbols to indicate the state of each reactant and product:

$$Zn(s) + Cu^{2+}(aq) \rightarrow Zn^{2+}(aq) + Cu(s)$$

Interestingly, this equation can also be written as the following single-displacement reaction:

$$Zn(s) + CuSO_4(aq) \rightarrow ZnSO_4(aq) + Cu(s)$$

This single-displacement reaction has the same net ionic equation after canceling out the spectator ions.

Write a Balanced Equation for the Oxidation-Reduction Reaction of a Piece of Solid Copper Wire Immersed in an Aqueous Solution of Silver Nitrate.

According to the activity series, copper is more reactive than silver. Therefore, the copper is oxidized, and the silver is reduced. Write the half-reactions:

$$\text{oxidation: } Cu \rightarrow Cu^{2+} + 2e^-$$

$$\text{reduction: } Ag^+ + e^- \rightarrow Ag$$

Multiply the reduction half-reaction by 2 to balance the number of electrons:

$$\text{oxidation: } Cu \rightarrow Cu^{2+} + 2e^-$$

$$\text{reduction: } 2Ag^+ + 2e^- \rightarrow 2Ag$$

Cancel the electrons and combine the two half-reactions into the net equation:

$$Cu + 2Ag^+ \rightarrow Cu^{2+} + 2Ag$$

Finally, add the symbols to indicate the state of each reactant and product:

$$Cu(s) + 2Ag^+(aq) \rightarrow Cu^{2+}(aq) + 2Ag(s)$$

Note that this equation is also classified as a single-displacement reaction:

$$Cu(s) + 2AgNO_3(aq) \rightarrow Cu(NO_3)_2(aq) + 2Ag(s)$$

This single-displacement reaction has the same net ionic equation after canceling out the spectator ions.

Chemical Equations Involving Oxidation-Reduction

Determining the Oxidation State of an Element in a Molecule or Ion

In order to determine the **oxidation state** of an element in a molecule or ion, apply these general rules: Hydrogen is usually assigned an oxidation state of +1 except for metal hydrides. Oxygen is usually assigned an oxidation state of –2 except for peroxides. Halogens are usually assigned oxidation states of –1 unless they are combined to a more electronegative element. Alkali metals are always assigned oxidation states of +1. Alkaline earth metals are always assigned oxidation states of +2. Finally, the **sum of the oxidation states** must equal the charge of the molecule or ion.

Determining Oxidation States Examples

$$H_2O$$

Oxygen is usually assigned an oxidation state of –2, and hydrogen is usually assigned an oxidation state of +1. Check: $2(+1) + (-2) = 0$. Therefore, the oxidation states are as follows: hydrogen +1 and oxygen –2.

$$MgF_2$$

Halogens are usually assigned an oxidation state of –1, and alkaline earth metals are always assigned an oxidation state of +2. Check: $(+2) + 2(-1) = 0$. Therefore, the oxidation states are as follows: magnesium +2 and fluorine –1.

$$Ca(NO_3)_2$$

Oxygen is usually assigned an oxidation number of –2, and alkaline earth metals are always assigned an oxidation state of +2. The oxidation state of nitrogen may be found by balancing the charges of the NO_3^-. Let x represent the charge of the nitrogen atom: $x + 3(-2) = -1$. Solving for x yields $x = +5$. Checking: $(+2) + 2[(+5) + 3(-2)] = 0$. Therefore, the oxidation states are as follows: calcium +2, nitrogen +5, and oxygen –2.

Determining if a Reaction is an Oxidation-Reduction Reaction

To determine if a reaction is an **oxidation-reduction reaction**, try to determine if one reactant is **oxidized** and the other reactant is **reduced**. First, assign oxidation states to each atom in the reaction. Remember that atoms of elements in their uncombined state are always assigned oxidation states of 0. Alkali metals are assigned +1, and alkaline earth metals are assigned +2. Oxygen is usually assigned –2, hydrogen is usually +1, and halogens are usually assigned –1. Write the half-reactions for each atom in the reactants, and determine if any are oxidized and reduced. If an oxidation reaction and a reduction reaction are present, the reaction is an oxidation-reduction reaction.

Review Video: Oxidation-Reduction Reactions
Visit mometrix.com/academy and enter code: 317289

Determining Oxidation-Reduction Reaction Examples

$$2Mg(s) + O_2(g) \rightarrow 2MgO(s)$$

Assign oxidation states to each atom in the reaction. Atoms of an element in its uncombined state are always assigned 0. Therefore, both uncombined reactants are assigned 0. Oxygen is usually assigned –2, and magnesium is always assigned +2. Write the half-reactions:

- $Mg \rightarrow Mg^{2+} + 2e^-$ oxidation state of magnesium: $0 \rightarrow +2$
- $O_2 + 2e^- \rightarrow O^{2-}$ oxidation state of oxygen: $0 \rightarrow -2$

Magnesium is oxidized. Oxygen is reduced. Therefore, this is an oxidation-reduction reaction.

$$Ca(s) + 2HCl(aq) \rightarrow CaCl_2(aq) + H_2(g)$$

The reactant Ca(s) and the product $H_2(g)$ are assigned 0. Halogens such as chlorine are usually assigned –1. Hydrogen is usually assigned +1. Alkaline earth metals such as calcium are always assigned +2. Write the half-reactions:

- $Ca \rightarrow Ca^{2+} + 2e^-$ oxidation state of calcium: $0 \rightarrow +2$
- $2Cl^- \rightarrow 2Cl^-$ oxidation state of chlorine: $-1 \rightarrow -1$
- $2H^+ + 2e^- \rightarrow H_2$ oxidation state of hydrogen: $+1 \rightarrow 0$

Calcium is oxidized. Hydrogen is reduced. Therefore, this is an oxidation-reduction reaction.

Stoichiometry

Determining the Limiting Reagent in a Reaction

The **limiting reagent**, or **limiting reactant**, is the reactant that determines or "limits" the amount of product formed. The limiting reagent is **totally consumed** in the chemical reaction. The other reactants in the chemical reaction must be present in excess amounts than what is needed. The excess reactants will be left over after the limiting reactant is consumed. To determine the limiting reagent from the balanced chemical equation, select one of the products and calculate how much of that product can be produced from each reactant. The reactant that produces the least amount of that product is the limiting reactant or limiting reagent.

Calculating the Percent Yield for a Chemical Reaction

To calculate the **percent yield** for a chemical reaction, use the formula:

$$\frac{\text{actual yield}}{\text{theoretical yield}} \times 100\ \%$$

The actual yield should be stated in the problem or determined experimentally. The theoretical yield can be calculated from the balanced chemical equation with dimensional analysis using conversion factors for molar mass and number of moles. Divide the actual yield by the theoretical yield. This is a decimal that can be converted to a percentage by multiplying by 100 and adding the percent sign.

> **Review Video: Stoichiometry**
> Visit mometrix.com/academy and enter code: 801833

Reaction Types

Types of Reactions

One way to organize chemical reactions is to sort them into two categories: **oxidation/reduction reactions** (also called redox reactions) and **metathesis reactions** (which include acid/base reactions). Oxidation/reduction reactions can involve the transfer of one or more electrons, or they can occur as a result of the transfer of oxygen, hydrogen, or halogen atoms. The species that loses electrons (or increases its oxidation state) is oxidized and is referred to as the reducing agent. The species that gains electrons (or decreases its oxidation state) is reduced and is referred to as the oxidizing agent. **Single substitution reactions** are types of oxidation/reduction reactions. In a single substitution reaction, electrons are transferred from one chemical species to another. The transfer of electrons results in changes in the nature and charge of the species.

> **Review Video: Understanding Chemical Reactions**
> Visit mometrix.com/academy and enter code: 579876
>
> **Review Video: The Process of a Reaction**
> Visit mometrix.com/academy and enter code: 808039

Substitution Reactions

Single substitution, **displacement**, or **replacement reactions** are when one reactant is displaced by another to form the final product ($A + BC \rightarrow AB + C$). Single substitution reactions can be cationic or anionic. When a piece of copper (Cu) is placed into a solution of silver nitrate ($AgNO_3$), the solution turns blue. The copper appears to be replaced with a silvery white material. The equation is $2AgNO_3 + Cu \rightarrow Cu(NO_3)_2 + 2Ag$. When this reaction takes place, the copper dissolves and the silver in the silver nitrate solution precipitates (becomes a solid), resulting in copper nitrate and silver. Copper and silver have switched places in the nitrate.

Double substitution reactions, also called **double displacement**, **double replacement**, **metathesis**, or **ion exchange reactions**, are those where ions or bonds are exchanged by two compounds to form different compounds ($AC + BD \rightarrow AD + BC$). An example of this is that silver nitrate and sodium chloride form two different products (silver chloride and sodium nitrate) when they react. The formula for this reaction is $AgNO_3 + NaCl \rightarrow AgCl + NaNO_3$.

Review Video: Single-Replacement Reactions
Visit mometrix.com/academy and enter code: 442975

Combination and Decomposition Reactions

Combination, or **synthesis, reactions**: In a combination reaction, two or more reactants combine to form a single product (A + B → AB). These reactions are also called synthesis or **addition reactions**. An example is burning hydrogen in air to produce water. The equation is $2H_2(g) + O_2(g) \rightarrow 2H_2O(l)$. Another example is when water and sulfur trioxide react to form sulfuric acid. The equation is $H_2O + SO_3 \rightarrow H_2SO_4$.

Decomposition (or desynthesis, decombination, or deconstruction) reactions: In a decomposition reaction, a reactant is broken down into two or more products (AB → A + B). These reactions are also called analysis reactions. **Thermal decomposition** is caused by heat. **Electrolytic decomposition** is due to electricity. An example of this type of reaction is the decomposition of water into hydrogen and oxygen gas. The equation is $2H_2O \rightarrow 2H_2 + O_2$.

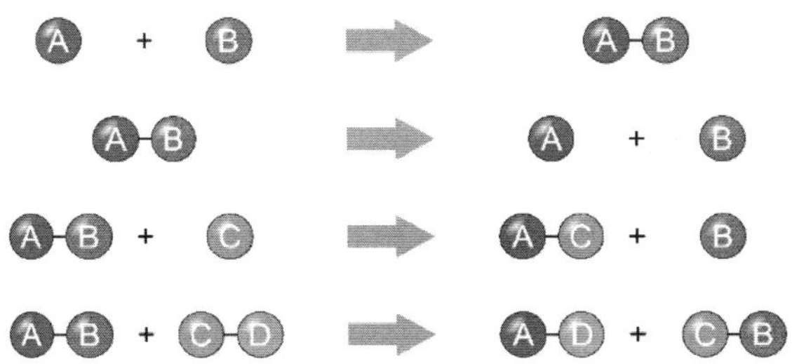

Acid/Base Reactions

In **acid/base reactions**, an **acid** is a compound that can donate a proton, while a **base** is a compound that can accept a proton. In these types of reactions, the acid and base react to form a salt and water. When the proton is donated, the base becomes water and the remaining ions form a salt. One method of determining whether a reaction is an oxidation/reduction or a metathesis reaction is that the oxidation number of atoms does not change during a metathesis reaction.

Isomerization and Neutralization Reactions

Isomerization, or **rearrangement**, is the process changing a compound to an isomer. Within a compound, bonds are reformed. The reactant and product have the same molecular formula, but different structural formulas and different properties (A → A'). For example, butane (C_4H_{10}) is a hydrocarbon consisting of four carbon atoms in a straight chain. Heating it to 100 °C or higher in the presence of a catalyst forms isobutane (methylpropane), which has a branched-chain structure. Boiling and freezing points are greatly different for butane and isobutane.

A **neutralization**, **acid-base**, or **proton transfer reaction** occurs when one compound acquires H^+ from another. These types of reactions are also usually double displacement reactions. The acid has an H^+ that is transferred to the base and the acid and base are neutralized in the form of a salt that, depending on the salt's solubility, may precipitate from the solution.

Chemical Kinetics

Chemical kinetics is the study of the **rates** of **chemical reactions** and the various factors that affect these rates. The rate of a reaction is the change in concentration of the reactants or products per unit of time. Another way to state this is that chemical kinetics is the study of the rate of change of the concentrations of the reactants and products and the factors that affect that rate of change. The study of catalysts is part of chemical kinetics. Catalysts are substances that speed up the rate of reactions without being consumed. Examples of reactions that occur at different rates include the explosion of trinitrotoluene (TNT), which occurs at a very fast rate, compared to the burning of a log, which occurs at a much slower rate.

Give the Rate Law for this General Reaction: $aA + bB + cC \rightarrow$ Products. Define Each Letter.

The rate of a chemical reaction can be defined as the following:

$$\text{rate} = \frac{\text{change in concentration}}{\text{change in time}}$$

This is usually represented by a rate law. The rate law for the general reaction $aA + bB + cC \rightarrow$ Products is given by rate $= k[A]^x[B]^y[C]^z$, where k is the rate constant; [A], [B], and [C] represent the concentrations of the reactants; and x, y, and z represent the reaction orders. The exponents x, y, and z must be experimentally determined. They do not necessarily equal the coefficients from the balanced chemical equation.

Activation Energy

Activation energy is the minimum amount of energy that must be possessed by reactant atoms or molecules in order to react. This is due to the fact that it takes a certain amount of energy to break bonds or form bonds between atoms. Reactants lacking the activation energy required will not be able to perform the necessary breaking or forming of bonds regardless of how often they collide. Catalysts lower the activation energy of a reaction and therefore increase the rate of reaction.

Reaction Mechanism

Often, when studying specific reactions, only the net reactions are given. Realistically, reactions take place in a series of steps or elementary reactions as shown in the reaction mechanism. **Reaction mechanisms** show how a reaction proceeds in a **series of steps**. Some steps are slow, and some are fast. Each step has its own reaction mechanism. The slowest step in the reaction mechanism coincides with the step with the greatest activation energy. This step is known as the rate-determining step.

Catalyst

A **catalyst** is a chemical that **accelerates** or speeds up a chemical reaction without being consumed or used up in the reaction. Although catalysts are not consumed or permanently changed during the process of the reaction, catalysts do participate in the elementary reaction of the reaction mechanisms. Catalysts lower the **activation energy** meaning more of the reactant molecules will have sufficient energy to react.

Review Video: Catalysts
Visit mometrix.com/academy and enter code: 288189

Factors That Affect Reaction Rate

Factors that affect reaction rate include concentration, surface area, and temperature. Increasing the **concentration** of the reactants increases the number of collisions between those reactants and therefore increases the reaction rate. Increasing the **surface area of contact** between the reactants also increases the number of collisions and therefore increases the reaction rate. Finally, increasing the **temperature** of the reactants increases the number of collisions but more significantly also increases the kinetic energy of the reactants, which in turn increases the fraction of molecules meeting the activation energy requirement. With more molecules at the activation energy, more of the reactants are capable of completing the reaction.

Chemical Reaction Equilibrium

Chemical Equilibrium

A **chemical equilibrium** occurs when a reaction is reversible and the rate of the forward reaction equals the rate of the reverse reaction. The forward and reverse reactions are continually occurring, but the individual concentration of the reaction and the products do not change. The concentration of the reactants and products are not necessarily equal to each other. For this to occur, the reaction must take place in a closed system in which none of the reactants or products can escape and in which no heat is added or lost.

Explain How to Write an Equilibrium Constant Expression from the Following Equilibrium Equation: $a\text{A} + b\text{B} \leftrightarrow c\text{C} + d\text{D}$.

Given the following **equilibrium reaction**: $a\text{A} + b\text{B} \leftrightarrow c\text{C} + d\text{D}$, the equilibrium constant is calculated by the expression $k = \frac{[\text{C}]^c[\text{D}]^d}{[\text{A}]^a[\text{B}]^b}$. The brackets indicate "the concentration of" each individual reactant and product. The coefficients from the balanced chemical equation are used for the exponents in the equilibrium constant expression. Pure liquids and pure solids are not represented in the equilibrium constants. The concentration of gases and the concentration of solutes do appear in the expressions for equilibrium constants. Note that the concentrations of the products are in the numerator and the concentrations of the reactant are in the denominator.

Explain How to Write Equilibrium Constant Expressions for Each of the Following Equilibriums:

2SO_2 (g) + O_2 (g) ↔ 2SO_3 (g)

All of the reactants and products are gases and need to be represented in the equilibrium constant. The concentration of the product is placed in the numerator, and the concentrations of the reactants are placed in the denominator. The coefficients from the balanced chemical equation are the exponents:

$$k = \frac{[\text{SO}_3]^2}{[\text{SO}_2]^2[\text{O}_2]}$$

$\text{CaCO}_3(\text{s}) \leftrightarrow \text{CaO}(\text{s}) + \text{CO}_2(\text{g})$

The solid reactant CaCO_3 and the solid product CaO are not part of the equilibrium constant. The concentration of the gaseous product CO_2 is represented in the numerator.

$$k = [\text{CO}_2]$$

$CaH_2(s) + 2H_2O(l) \leftrightarrow Ca(OH)_2(aq) + 2H_2(g)$

The solid reactant CaH_2 and the liquid reactant H_2O are not part of the equilibrium constant. Both products should be represented. The "2" coefficient of the gaseous hydrogen is the exponent on the concentration of the gaseous H_2.

$$k = [Ca(OH)_2][H_2]^2$$

$H^+(aq) + OH^-(aq) \leftrightarrow H_2O(l)$

Pure liquids are not represented in the equilibrium constant. Aqueous solutions are included in the equilibrium constant.

$$k = \frac{1}{[H^+][OH^-]}$$

Le Châtelier's Principle

Le Châtelier's principle states that when a stressor is applied to a system in equilibrium, the system will respond in such a way to at least partially offset the stressor. Stressors include increasing or decreasing the temperature, increasing or decreasing the concentration of a reactant or product, and increasing or decreasing the pressure. Systems can be described as "shifting left" or "shifting right" when a stressor is applied. For example, if the temperature is increased in an equilibrium in which the forward reaction is endothermic, the system will "shift right" in order to "use up" the heat that was applied. Increasing or decreasing the pressure of an equilibrium will only cause the equilibrium to "shift" if the number of moles of gases of the reactants differs from the number of moles of gases of the products. If there are no gases in the equilibrium or if the number of moles of gases of the reactants and products is equal, the change in pressure will have no effect on the equilibrium.

Review Video: Le Châtelier's Principle
Visit mometrix.com/academy and enter code: 360187

Oxidation-Reduction Reactions and Oxidation States

Oxidation-Reduction Reactions

An **oxidation-reduction reaction (redox reaction**)is a reaction in which one of the reactants either loses one or more electrons or increases its oxidation state and the other reactant either gains one or more electrons or decreases in oxidation state. Oxidation cannot take place without reduction, and reduction cannot take place without oxidation. Redox reactions can be classified as either electron-transfer or atom-transfer reactions.

For **electron-transfer redox reactions**, the reactant that loses the electrons undergoes oxidation. The reactant that gains the electrons undergoes reduction. A common phrase to help remember this is *LEO the lion says GER*, where *LEO* represents *loss of electrons is oxidation* and *GER* represents *gain of electrons is reduction.*

Atom-transfer redox reactions typically involve organic compounds and the transfer of oxygen, hydrogen, or halogen atoms. While these reactions are associated with more complicated reactions, the core principle of oxidation state changes remains the same: increasing oxidation state means oxidation and decreasing oxidation state means reduction.

Review Video: Oxidation-Reduction Reactions
Visit mometrix.com/academy and enter code: 317289

OXIDATION, REDUCTION, OXIDIZING AGENT, REDUCING AGENT, OXIDATION STATES

- **Oxidation** can be defined as any process involving either the loss of one or more electrons or the increase of oxidation state.
- **Reduction** can be defined as any process involving either a gain of one or more electrons or the decrease of oxidation state.
- **Oxidizing agent** can be defined as the reactant in an oxidation-reduction reaction that causes oxidation. The *oxidizing agent* is reduced.
- **Reducing agent** can be defined as the reactant in an oxidation-reduction reaction that causes reduction. The *reducing agent* is oxidized.
- **Oxidation states**, also known as oxidation numbers, represent the charge that an atom has in a molecule or ion.

Biochemical Compounds

The four major classes of biochemical compounds are carbohydrates, lipids, proteins, and nucleic acids. Examples of **carbohydrates** include monosaccharides such as glucose, fructose, and ribose; disaccharides such as sucrose and lactose; and polysaccharides such as starch, cellulose, and glycogen. Examples of **lipids** include fatty acids, triglycerides, oils, lard, fat-soluble vitamins, waxes, and steroids such as cholesterol. Examples of **proteins** include enzymes, collagen, hemoglobin, histones, many hormones, and antibodies. Examples of **nucleic acids** include deoxyribonucleic acid (DNA) and ribonucleic acid (RNA).

CARBOHYDRATES

Carbohydrates are organic compounds that produce energy. The empirical formula for most carbohydrates is CH_2O, which indicates that the ratio of carbon, hydrogen, and oxygen is always 1:2:1.The structure generally consists of aldehydes and ketones containing many hydroxyl groups. In general, carbohydrates are sugars and starches. Carbohydrates can be grouped as simple sugars or complex carbohydrates. The simple sugars include monosaccharides such as glucose and ribose and disaccharides such as sucrose and lactose. Complex carbohydrates are polymers of monosaccharides and include polysaccharides such as cellulose, starch, and glycogen.

Review Video: Carbohydrates
Visit mometrix.com/academy and enter code: 601714

MONOSACCHARIDES, DISACCHARIDES, AND POLYSACCHARIDES

Monosaccharides, disaccharides, and polysaccharides are specific types of carbohydrates. The term *saccharide* comes from the Greek word for sugar, *sákkharon*, and is synonymous with carbohydrate. **Monosaccharides** are the simplest carbohydrates. Examples of monosaccharides are glucose, fructose (fruit sugar), ribose, and galactose. **Disaccharides** consist of two monosaccharides joined together. Examples of disaccharides include sucrose (table sugar, which is a compound of glucose and fructose) and lactose (milk sugar, which is a compound of glucose and galactose). **Polysaccharides** are polymers of monosaccharides. Examples of polysaccharides include cellulose, starch, and glycogen.

Lipids

Lipids have many functions. The main function of lipids is storing energy. One type of lipid is **triglycerides**, which include fats and oils. Lipids known as **phospholipids** also form the cell membranes of all plant and animal cells. Lipids can relay messages among cells in the nervous system and in the immune system. Some lipids are **steroids**, which serve many functions. For example, cholesterol helps make cell membranes pliable, and some steroids make up hormones such as testosterone and estrogen. Fat-soluble vitamins are also steroids.

Review Video: Lipids
Visit mometrix.com/academy and enter code: 269746

Proteins

Proteins are polymers of **amino acids**. The amino acids are joined together by peptide bonds. The two major groups of proteins are fibrous proteins and globular proteins. **Fibrous proteins** provide structure in cells, bone tissue, connective tissue and line cartilage, tendons, and epidermal tissue. Examples of fibrous proteins include collage, elastin, and keratin. **Globular proteins** are folded molecules that include enzymes, hemoglobin, and some hormones. Antibodies are globular proteins that help defend the body from antigens. Some proteins such as actin and myosin are involved in muscle contraction. Some proteins act as storage containers for amino acids. Other proteins such as hemoglobin help transport materials throughout the body.

DNA

DNA, or deoxyribonucleic acid, is a two-stranded molecule in the shape of a double helix. DNA nucleotides consist of a deoxyribose (sugar), a phosphate, and a base. The bases are guanine, thymine, cytosine and adenine. Guanine always pairs with cytosine, and thymine always pairs with adenine. If the double helix is compared to a twisted ladder, the legs of the ladder are the sugars and phosphates while the rungs of the ladder consist of the bases. The bases that make up the rungs of the ladder are bound together with hydrogen bonds.

DNA Vs. RNA

Deoxyribonucleic acid (DNA) and ribonucleic acid (RNA) are both nucleic acids composed of **nucleotides**, which have three of their four bases in common: guanine, adenine, and cytosine. The sugar in DNA nucleotides is deoxyribose, whereas the sugar in RNA nucleotides is ribose. DNA contains the base thymine, but RNA replaces thymine with uracil. DNA is double-stranded, and RNA is single-stranded. DNA has the shape of a double helix, whereas RNA is complexly folded. DNA stores the genetic information of the cell, while RNA has several forms. For example, mRNA, or messenger RNA, is a working copy of DNA, and tRNA, or transfer RNA, collects the needed amino acids for the ribosomes during the assembling of proteins.

Review Video: DNA Vs. RNA
Visit mometrix.com/academy and enter code: 184871

Net Equation for Photosynthesis

Photosynthesis is the food-making process in green plants. Photosynthesis occurs in the chloroplasts of cells in the presence of light and chlorophyll. The reactants are **carbon dioxide** and

water. The energy from the sunlight is absorbed and stored in the glucose molecules. The net equation for photosynthesis can be represented by the following equations:

$$\text{carbon dioxide} + \text{water} + \text{light} \xrightarrow{\text{chlorophyll}} \text{glucose} + \text{oxygen}$$

$$6CO_2 + 6H_2O + \text{light} \xrightarrow{\text{chlorophyll}} C_6H_{12}O_6 + 6O_2$$

The products of photosynthesis are glucose and oxygen gas.

Respiration

Cellular respiration is the process in which energy is released from glucose in the form of adenosine triphosphate (ATP). **Cellular respiration** is the reverse process of photosynthesis. In cellular respiration, glucose is burned or combined with oxygen as shown in the following equations:

$$\text{glucose} + \text{oxygen} \rightarrow \text{carbon dioxide} + \text{water} + \text{ATP}$$

$$C_6H_{12}O_6 + 6O_2 \rightarrow 6CO_2 + 6H_2O$$

The products of cellular respiration are carbon dioxide and water. Energy is released from glucose in the form of ATP.

Common Organic Compounds

Organic Compounds

Organic compounds are compounds that contain carbon and hydrogen. Carbon has only four valence electrons and will form four covalent bonds with hydrogen and other atoms or groups of atoms in order to satisfy the octet rule. Carbon readily forms single, double, or triple bonds with other carbon atoms or with other elements. Organic compounds can form long chains, branched chains, and single- or multiple-ring structures. **Hydrocarbons** are organic compounds that contain only carbon and hydrogen. **Substituted hydrocarbons** are hydrocarbons that have a carbon backbone, but one (or more) of the hydrogen atoms has been substituted with a different atom or group of atoms called a functional group. **Functional groups** may be single atoms, such as in halocarbons where a halogen such as chlorine or fluorine is substituted for a hydrogen atom. Some functional groups consist of more than one atom; alcohols, for example, have the hydroxyl ($-OH$) functional group.

Chapter Quiz

Ready to see how well you retained what you just read? Scan the QR code to go directly to the chapter quiz interface for this study guide. If you're using a computer, simply visit the online resources page at mometrix.com/resources719/gacechemistry and click the Chapter Quizzes link.

Solutions and Solubility and Acid-Base Chemistry

Terminology for Solutions and Solubility

Dilute and Concentrated

The terms *dilute* and *concentrated* have opposite meanings. In a **solution**, the **solute** is dissolved in the **solvent**. The more solute that is dissolved, the more **concentrated** is the solution. The less solute that is dissolved, the less concentrated and the more **dilute** is the solution. The terms are often associated with the preparation of a stock solution for a laboratory experiment. Stock solutions are typically acquired in a higly concentrated form. Typically, diluted forms of the solutions are used which must be prepared from the concentrated stock solutions. The desired dilutions are achieved by combining a specific amount of a solvent with a specific amount of stock solution.

Saturated, Unsaturated, and Supersaturated

Solutions can be categorized based on their saturation. In a **saturated** solution, the solute is added to the solvent until no more solute is able to dissolve. The undissolved solute will settle down to the bottom of the beaker. A solution is considered **unsaturated** as long as more solute is able to go into solution under ordinary conditions. The solubility of solids in liquids typically increases as temperature increases. If the temperature of a solution is increased as the solute is being added, more solute than is normally possible may go into solution, forming a **supersaturated** solution.

Mixture, Solution, and Colloid

A **mixture** is made of two or more substances that are combined in various proportions. The exact proportion of the constituents is the defining characteristic of any mixture. There are two types of mixtures: homogeneous and heterogeneous. **Homogeneous** means that the mixture's composition and properties are uniform throughout. Conversely, **heterogeneous** means that the mixture's composition and properties are not uniform throughout.

A **solution** is a homogeneous mixture of substances that cannot be separated by filtration or centrifugation. Solutions are made by dissolving one or more solutes into a solvent. For example, in an aqueous glucose solution, glucose is the solute and water is the solvent. If there is more than one liquid present in the solution, then the most prevalent liquid is considered the solvent. The exact mechanism of dissolving varies depending on the mixture, but the result is always individual solute ions or molecules surrounded by solvent molecules. The proportion of solute to solvent for a particular solution is its **concentration**.

A **colloid** is a heterogeneous mixture in which small particles (<1 micrometer) are suspended, but not dissolved, in a liquid. As such, they can be separated by centrifugation. A commonplace example of a colloid is milk.

Review Video: Solutions
Visit mometrix.com/academy and enter code: 995937

Calculating Molarity

Calculating Mole Fraction, Parts Per Million, Parts Per Billion, and Percent by Mass or Volume

There are applications and processes across many different fields that make use of concentration. As such, there are different methods of measuring concentration leading to many different units being used to communicate concentration. **Mole fraction** (χ) is calculated by dividing the number of moles of one component by the total number of moles of all of the components of the solution. **Parts per million** (ppm) is calculated by dividing the mass of the solute in grams by the mass of the solvent and solute in grams and then multiplying the quotient by 1,000,000 ppm. **Parts per billion** (ppb) is calculated similarly, except the quotient is multiplied by 1,000,000,000 ppb. **Percent concentration** can be calculated by mass or by volume by dividing the mass or volume of the solute by the mass or volume of the solution. This quotient is a decimal that can be converted to a percentage by multiplying by 100.

Calculating the Molarity and Molality of a Solution

Molarity and molality are measures of the concentration of a solution. **Molarity** (M) is the amount of solute in moles per the amount of solution in liters. A 1.0 M solution consists of 1.0 mol of solute for each 1.0 L of solution.

$$\text{Molarity (M)} = \frac{\text{moles of solute}}{\textbf{liters}\text{ of }\textbf{solution}} = \frac{\text{mol}}{\text{L}}$$

Molality (m) is the amount of solute in moles per the amount of solvent in kilograms. A 1.0 m solution consists of 1.0 mol of solute for each 1.0 kg of solvent.

$$\text{Molality (m)} = \frac{\text{moles of solute}}{\textbf{kilograms}\text{ of }\textbf{solvent}} = \frac{\text{mol}}{\text{kg}}$$

Often, when performing these calculations, the amount of solute is given in grams. To convert from grams of solute to moles of solute, multiply the grams of solute by the molar mass of the solute.

Calculating the Molarity of 100.0 g of $CaCl_2$ in 500.0 mL of Solution.

To use the formula molarity, you can make the necessary conversions from grams $CaCl_2$ to moles $CaCl_2$ and from 500.0 mL to liters using dimensional analysis. An alternate method of working this problem would be doing the conversions first and then substituting those values directly into the equation. Substituting the given information into the equation yields:

$$\frac{100.0\text{ grams } CaCl_2}{500.0\text{ mL of solution}}$$

Adding the necessary conversions using dimensional analysis yields:

$$\left(\frac{100.0\text{ g } CaCl_2}{500.0\text{ mL of solution}}\right)\left(\frac{\text{mol } CaCl_2}{110.98\text{ g}}\right)\left(\frac{1{,}000\text{ mL}}{\text{L}}\right) = 1.802\text{ M}$$

Preparing a Dilute Solution from a Stock Solution

In order to prepare a dilute solution from a stock solution, the molarity and the needed volume of the diluted solution as well as the molarity of the stock solution must be known. The volume of the stock solution to be diluted can be calculated using the formula $V_{stock}M_{stock} = V_{dilute}M_{dilute}$, where V_{stock} is the unknown variable, M_{stock} is the molarity of the stock solution, V_{dilute} is the needed volume of the dilute solution, and M_{dilute} is the needed molarity of the dilute solution. Solving this formula for V_{stock} yields $V_{stock} = \frac{V_{dilute}M_{dilute}}{M_{stock}}$. Then, dilute the calculated amount of stock solution to the total volume required of the diluted solution.

Factors Affecting Solubility

Temperature, Surface Area, Agitation, and Pressure on the Dissolution Rate

Temperature, surface area, agitation, and pressure affect the **dissolution rate**. Increasing the **temperature** increases the kinetic energy of the molecules, which increases the number of collisions with the solute particles. Increasing the **surface area** of contact by stirring **(agitation)** or crushing a solid solute also increases the dissolution rate and helps prevent recrystallization. Increasing the **pressure** will increase the dissolution rate for gas solutes in liquid solvents because the added pressure will make it more difficult for the gas to escape. Increasing the pressure will have virtually no effect on the dissolution rate for solid solutes in liquid solvents under normal conditions.

Effect of Temperature and Pressure on Solubility

Temperature and pressure affect **solubility**. For gas solutes in liquid solvents, increasing the **temperature** increases the kinetic energy, causing more gas particles to escape the surface of the liquid solvents and thereby decreasing the solubility of the solutes. For most solid solutes in liquid solvents, increasing the temperature increases the solubility, as shown in this solubility curve for selected salts. For gas solutes in liquid solvents, increasing the **pressure** increases the solubility. Increasing the pressure of liquid or solid solutes in liquid solvents has virtually no effect under normal conditions.

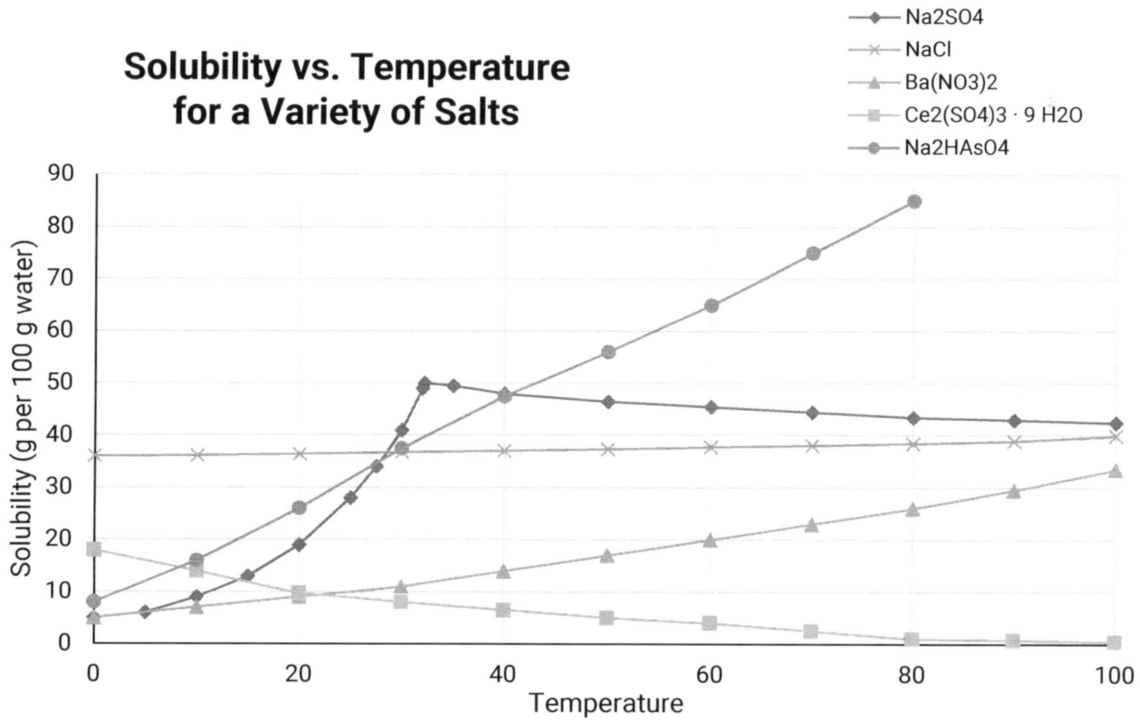

Colligative Properties of Solutions

FREEZING POINT DEPRESSION

Freezing point depression is a colligative property of solutions that depends only on the number of particles in the solution, not on the identity of those particles. Adding a nonvolatile solute to a solution will lower the freezing point of that solution. This decrease in temperature is known as **freezing point depression.** Basically, the particles of the nonvolatile solute occupy spaces near the surface and block or inhibit the solvent particles from escaping from the surface of the solution. As fewer particles escape, the vapor pressure lowers. This decrease in vapor pressure causes a decrease in the freezing point known as freezing point depression. The amount of depression can be calculated from the equation $\Delta T_{FP} = mk_f$, where m is the molality of the solution and k_f is the molal freezing point constant for that particular solvent.

BOILING POINT ELEVATION

Boiling point elevation is a colligative property of solutions that depends only on the number of particles in the solution, not on the identity of those particles. Adding a nonvolatile solute to a solution will raise the boiling point of that solution. This rise in temperature is known as **boiling point elevation**. Basically, the particles of the nonvolatile solute occupy spaces near the surface and block or inhibit the solvent particles from escaping from the surface of the solution. As fewer particles escape, the vapor pressure lowers. This decrease in vapor pressure causes an increase in the boiling point known as **boiling point elevation**. The amount of elevation can be calculated from the equation $\Delta T_{BP} = mk_b$, where m is the molality of the solution and k_b is the molal boiling point constant for that particular solvent.

VAPOR PRESSURE LOWERING

Vapor pressure lowering is a colligative property of solutions that depends only on the number of particles in the solution, not on the identity of those particles. Adding a nonvolatile solute to a solution will lower the vapor pressure of that solution. Basically, the particles of the nonvolatile solute occupy space near the surface and block or inhibit the solvent particles from escaping from the surface of the solution. As fewer particles escape, the vapor pressure lowers. This decrease in vapor pressure causes an increase in the boiling point and a decrease in the freezing point.

OSMOSIS

Osmosis can be defined as diffusion through a **semipermeable membrane**. Typically, small solvent particles can pass through, but larger solute particles are too large to pass through. This means that osmosis is the net flow of solvent from a solution with a lower concentration to a solution with a higher concentration until a state of equilibrium is reached. The pressure that must be applied to the semipermeable membrane to stop the flow of solvent to reach this equilibrium state is called **osmotic pressure**. Osmotic pressure is a colligative property that depends on the number of nonvolatile solute particles, not the identity.

Review Video: Passive Transport: Diffusion and Osmosis
Visit mometrix.com/academy and enter code: 642038

Applications of Equilibrium in Ionic Solutions

Solubility of Ions in Water

Some general guidelines regarding solubility include the following:

- All nitrates and acetates are soluble.
- All chlorides, bromides, and iodides are soluble except those of silver, mercury(I), and lead(II).
- All sulfates are soluble except those of strontium, barium, mercury(I), and lead(II).
- All sulfides are insoluble except those of ammonium, the alkali metal cations, calcium, strontium, and barium.
- All carbonates are insoluble except those of ammonium and the alkali metal cations.
- All phosphates are insoluble except those of ammonium and the alkali metal cations.
- All hydroxides are insoluble except those of the alkali metal cations and calcium, strontium, and barium.

Solubility of Ionic Compounds in Water

If an ionic compound is soluble in water, the cations and anions will separate from each other when combined with water. In general, the rule for solubility is "like dissolves like." However, some ionic compounds are not soluble in water because the forces joining the ions are stronger than the intermolecular forces between the ions and the water molecules.

Soluble Ionic Compounds		**Important Exceptions**
Compounds containing	NO_3^-	None
	$C_2H_3O_2^-$	None
	Cl^-	Compounds of Ag^+, Hg_2^{2+}, Pb^{2+}
	Br^-	Compounds of Ag^+, Hg_2^{2+}, Pb^{2+}
	I^-	Compounds of Ag^+, Hg_2^{2+}, Pb^{2+}
	SO_4^{2-}	Compounds of Sr^{2+}, Ba^{2+}, Hg_2^{2+}, Pb^{2+}

Insoluble Ionic Compounds		**Important Exceptions**
Compounds containing	S^{2-}	Compounds of NH_4^+, the alkali metal cations, and Ca^{2+}, Sr^{2+}, and Ba^{2+}
	CO_3^{2-}	Compounds of NH_4^+, the alkali metal cations
	PO_4^{3-}	Compounds of NH_4^+, the alkali metal cations
	OH^-	Compounds of the alkali metal cations, and Ca^{2+}, Sr^{2+}, and Ba^{2+}

Calculating K_{sp} and Percent Dissociation

The solubility product constant, K_{sp}, is the equilibrium constant for a solution equilibrium. The general chemical equation for an ionic solution equilibrium is given by:

$$\text{ionic compound(s)} \leftrightarrow \text{cation(aq)} + \text{anion(aq)}$$

For this, the solubility product constant is $K_{sp} = [\text{cation}][\text{anion}]$. The percent dissociation for each ion is calculated by the following formula: $\frac{\text{amount dissociated}}{\text{initial concentration}} \times 100\%$, where the amount dissociated is the molarity of the ion in solution and the initial concentration is the molarity of the original compound. In general, the more dilute a solution, the greater the percent dissociation.

Calculate the Solubility of AgBr if the Solubility Product Constant, K_{sp}, for AgBr is 4.9×10^{-13} at 25 °C.

The dissociation reaction for AgBr can be written as $AgBr(s) \leftrightarrow Ag^+(aq) + Br^-(aq)$. Because the dissociation of AgBr produces equal moles of Ag^+ and Br^- ions, the solubility is simply the concentration of the Ag^+ ions, $[Ag^+]$, or the concentration of the Br^- ions, $[Br^-]$. The solubility product constant for this reaction is given by $K_{sp} = [Ag^+][Br^-]$, but because $[Ag^+] = [Br^-]$, this can be written as $K_{sp} = [Ag^+]^2$. Substituting in the given value for K_{sp} yields $4.9 \times 10^{-13} = [Ag^+]^2$. Therefore, $[Ag^+] = 7.0 \times 10^{-7}$ M. Finally, the solubility of AgBr is 7.0×10^{-7} M.

Common Ion Effect

The common ion effect is the decrease in the solubility of a salt in an electrolyte when that electrolyte solution already has an ion in common with that salt. An example of the common ion effect is when sodium chloride, NaCl, is dissolved in an aqueous solution of hydrochloric acid, HCl. The ions of the NaCl are Na^+ and Cl^-, and the ions of the HCl solution are H^+ and Cl^-. Therefore, the solute NaCl and the aqueous solution HCl share a common Cl^- ion. The equilibrium of the aqueous HCl solution can be represented by the following equation:

$$HCl(g) + H_2O(l) \leftrightarrow H_3O^+(aq) + Cl^-(aq)$$

According to Le Châtelier's principle, when a stressor is applied to this equilibrium, the system will respond in such a way to at least partially offset the stressor. Adding the NaCl to this equilibrium increases the concentration of the Cl^- ions in solution, which would shift the equilibrium to the left. The overall effect is that less Cl^- goes into solution. Therefore, because the solute and the solution share a common ion, the common ion effect is shown as the decrease in the solubility of the Cl^- ions.

Review Video: Common Ion Effect
Visit mometrix.com/academy and enter code: 311611

Electrolytes and Nonelectrolytes

Electrolytes are substances that dissociate in solution to form ions. Strong electrolytes ionize essentially completely. Weak electrolytes only ionize partially and form only a few ions in solution. Nonelectrolytes do not dissociate or form ions in solution. Strong electrolytes such as salt water ($NaCl(aq)$) or hydrochloric acid ($HCl(aq)$) are good conductors of electricity. Weak electrolytes such as acetic acid ($HC_2H_2O_2(aq)$) and ammonia ($NH_3(aq)$) are poor conductors of electricity. **Nonelectrolytes** such as sugar water ($C_{12}H_{22}O_{11}(aq)$) and ethanol ($C_2H_5OH(aq)$) do not conduct electricity.

Overview of Acids and Bases

Differences Between Acids and Bases

There are several differences between acids and bases. While it is never a good idea to taste chemicals directly or feel chemicals without gloves, it has been done in the past and we now know that acidic solutions tend to taste sour, whereas basic solutions tend to taste bitter. Dilute bases tend to feel slippery, whereas dilute acids feel like water. Active metals such as magnesium and zinc react with acids to produce hydrogen gas, but active metals usually do not react with bases. Acids and bases form electrolytes in aqueous solutions and conduct electricity. Acids turn blue litmus red, but bases turn red litmus blue. Acidic solutions have a pH of less than 7, whereas basic solutions have a pH of greater than 7.

Review Video: Properties of Acids and Bases
Visit mometrix.com/academy and enter code: 645283

Arrhenius Acid and Base

Arrhenius acids are substances that produce hydrogen ions (H^+) when dissolved in water to form aqueous solutions. Arrhenius bases are substances that produce hydroxide ions (OH^-) when dissolved in water to form aqueous solutions. The **Arrhenius concept** is limited to acids and bases in aqueous solutions and cannot be applied to other solids, liquids, and gases. Examples of Arrhenius acids include hydrochloric acid (HCl) and sulfuric acid (H_2SO_4). Examples of Arrhenius bases include sodium hydroxide (NaOH) and magnesium hydroxide ($Mg(OH)_2$).

Brønsted–Lowry Acid and Base

The Brønsted–Lowry concept is based on the donation or the acceptance of a proton. According to the **Brønsted–Lowry concept**, an acid is a substance that donates one or more protons to another substance and a base is a substance that accepts a proton from another substance. The Brønsted–Lowry concept can be applied to substances other than aqueous solutions. This concept is much broader than the Arrhenius concept, which can only be applied to aqueous solutions. The Brønsted–Lowry concept states that a substance cannot act like an acid (donate its proton) unless another substance is available to act as a base (accept the donated proton). In this concept, water may act as either an acid or a base. Hydrochloric acid (HCl) is an example of a Brønsted–Lowry acid. Ammonia (NH_3) is an example of a Brønsted–Lowry base.

Lewis Acid and Base

A **Lewis acid** is any substance that can accept a pair of nonbonding electrons. A **Lewis base** is any substance that can donate a pair of nonbonding electrons. According to the **Lewis theory**, all cations such as Mg^{2+} and Cu^{2+} are Lewis acids. Trigonal planar molecules, which are exceptions to the octet rule such as BF_3, are Lewis acids. Molecules such as CO_2 that have multiple bonds between two atoms that differ in electronegativities are Lewis acids, also. According to the Lewis theory, all anions such as OH^- are Lewis bases. Other examples of Lewis bases include trigonal pyramidal molecules such as ammonia and nonmetal oxides such as carbon monoxide, CO. Some compounds, such as water, can act as either Lewis acids or bases depending on the context.

Neutralization Reaction

Neutralization is a reaction of an acid and a base that yields a salt and water. The general form of the reaction is:

$$\text{acid} + \text{base} \rightarrow \text{salt} + \text{water}$$

The salt is formed from the cation of the base and the anion of the acid. The water is formed from the cation of the acid and the anion of the base.

An example is the neutralization reaction of hydrochloric acid and sodium hydroxide to form sodium chloride and water:

$$HCl(aq) + NaOH(aq) \rightarrow NaCl(s) + H_2O(l)$$

Equivalence Point

The **equivalence point** is by definition the point in a titration at which the analyte is neutralized. When the acid–base indicator starts to change color, the equivalence point has been reached. At this point, equivalent amounts of acids and bases have reacted. Also, at this point the concentration of cations of hydrogen is equal to the concentration of hydroxide anions. On an acid–base titration curve, the slope of the curve increases dramatically at the equivalence point. For strong acids and bases, the equivalence point occurs at a pH of 7. The figures below show the equivalence points for a strong acid titrated with a strong base (a) and a strong base titrated with a strong acid (b).

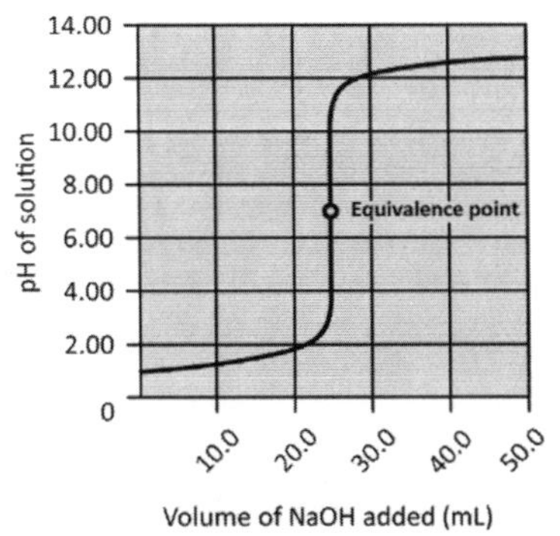

(a) Strong acid titrated with strong base

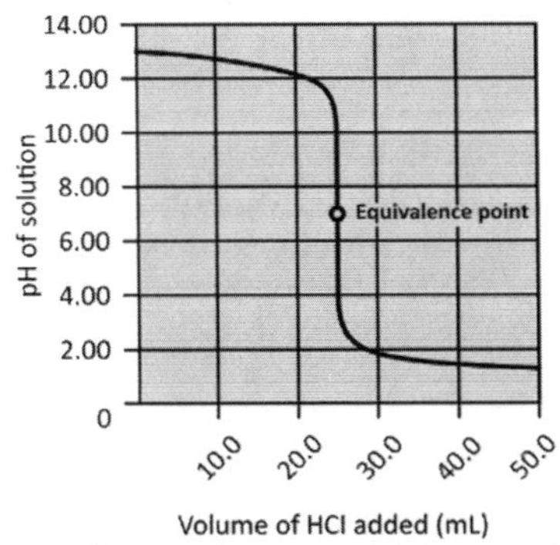

(b) Strong base titrated with strong acid

> **Review Video: Titration**
> Visit mometrix.com/academy and enter code: 550131

pH Scale and Calculations

Calculating pH, the Range of the pH Scale, and Acids and Bases on the pH Scale

The **pH scale** categorizes the **acidity** or **alkalinity** (basicity) of a solution. The pH value may be calculated by the formula $pH = -\log[H^+]$, where $[H^+]$ is the concentration of hydrogen ions. The pH scale ranges from 0 to 14 with pH values near 0 indicating the strongest acids and pH values near 14 indicating the strongest bases. With the pH scale, any solution with $pH < 7$ is considered an acid and any solution with $pH > 7$ is considered a base. Solutions with $pH = 7$ are considered to be neutral.

> **Review Video: Overview of pH Levels**
> Visit mometrix.com/academy and enter code: 187395

Relationship Between pH and pOH

The pH of a solution may be calculated using the formula $pH = -\log[H^+]$, where $[H^+]$ is the concentration of hydrogen ions. The pOH of a solution may be calculated using the similar formula $pOH = -\log[OH^-]$, where $[OH^-]$ is the concentration of hydroxide ions. The sum of the pH of a solution and the pOH of a solution is always 14. The pH of this HCl solution may be calculated using the formula $\text{pH} = -\log[0.0010\text{ M}] = 3$. The sum of the pH and pOH is always 14. Therefore, the pOH may be calculated by the formula $14 - 3 = 11$.

Calculate $[H^+]$ and $[OH^-]$ When Given the pH or pOH. Given a Solution with a pOH of 8.0, Explain How to Calculate pH, $[H^+]$, and $[OH^-]$.

Since $\text{pH} = -\log[H^+]$, $[H^+]$ may be calculated by $[H^+] = \text{antilog}(-\text{pH})$. Because $\text{pOH} = -\log[OH^-]$, $[OH^-]$ may be calculated by $[OH^-] = \text{antilog}(-\text{pOH})$. Also, because $\text{pH} + \text{pOH} = 14$, the pOH may be calculated by the formula $14 - \text{pH} = \text{pOH}$. For example, given a solution with a pOH of 8.0:

$$[OH^-] = \text{antilog}(-8.0) = 1.0 \times 10^{-8}$$

$$\text{pH} = 14 - 8.0 = 6.0$$

$$[H^+] = \text{antilog}(-6.0) = 1 \times 10^{-6}$$

K_w

Pure water dissociates to a very small extent and reaches this equilibrium:

$$H_2O(l) \leftrightarrow H_3O + (aq) + OH^-(aq)$$

The equilibrium constant for this equilibrium is called the ion product constant of water, or K_w. The constant K_w can be represented by $K_w = [H_3O^+][OH^-]$. The reactant H_2O is not represented in the equilibrium expression because it is essentially a pure liquid. The ion product constant of water K_w varies with temperature. As temperature increases, K_w increases and pH decreases. Therefore, this constant must be given at a specific temperature. At 25 °C, $[H_3O^+] = [OH^-] = 1 \times 10^{-7}$ M, which corresponds to pure water being neutral with a pH of 7.

Calculations Involving Acid-Base Titrations

Acid–Base Indicators

Acid–base indicators are one method to determine the range of the pH of a solution. **Acid–base indicators** change with the pH of the solution and are less precise than using a pH meter. However, acid–base indicators are used to indicate the completion of a titration to determine the concentration of an acidic or basic solution. Examples of acid–base indicators include methyl violet, litmus, and phenolphthalein. Methyl violet turns from yellow to blue with a pH range of 0.0–1.6. Litmus turns from red to blue with a pH range of 4.5–8.3. Phenolphthalein turns from colorless to reddish purple with a pH range of 8.3–10.0.

Determining the Endpoint in a Titration

During a **titration**, when the acid–base indicator has fully changed color, the **endpoint** has been reached. If the proper acid–base indicator with the correct pH range has been used, this should also correspond to the equivalence point. For example, if trying to determine the pH of an unknown base using phenolphthalein, the solution should change from colorless to pink at the equivalence point. If trying to determine the pH of an unknown acid using methyl violet, the solution should change from yellow to blue at the equivalence point. However, the endpoint and the equivalence point are not necessarily equal. Ideally, the equivalence point is the endpoint. If the solution is overtitrated, the endpoint will be past the equivalence point.

Calculating the Unknown Concentration of a Base from a Titration

The **unknown concentration of an acid or base** may be determined by a titration. To determine the unknown concentration of a base, titrate a known volume of the base with an acid of known molarity. Use an acid–base indicator such as phenolphthalein to indicate when the titration has reached the equivalence point. If the solution is not overtitrated, the equivalence point will also be the endpoint. Then, calculate the concentration of the base using the formula $V_b N_b = V_a N_a$, where V_b represents the volume of the base, N_b represents the normality of the base, V_a represents the volume of the acid used in the titration, and N_a represents the normality of the acid used in the titration.

During a Titration, 20.0 mL of 0.0100 M NaOH is Required to Neutralize a 50.0 mL Sample of HCl Solution. Explain How to Find the Molarity of the HCl.

To find the **concentration of the unknown acid**, use the formula $V_b N_b = V_a N_a$, where V_b represents the volume of the base, N_b represents the normality of the base, V_a represents the volume of the acid, and N_a represents the normality of the acid used in the titration. Solving the equation for the variable N_a yields $N_a = \frac{V_b N_b}{V_a}$. Because the molarity of the NaOH is 0.0100 M, the normality of the NaOH is 0.0100 N. Substituting in the appropriate values into the formula yields $N_a = \frac{(20.0\text{ mL})(0.0100\text{ N})}{50.0\text{ mL}} = 0.00400\text{ N}$. Because HCl is monoprotic, the molarity of HCl is 0.00400 M.

Equilibrium Relationships in Acid-Base Chemistry

Strong/Weak Acids and Bases

Acids or bases are categorized as strong or weak based on how completely they ionize in an aqueous solution. **Strong** acids and bases ionize essentially completely in an aqueous solution. **Weak** acids and bases ionize incompletely in an aqueous solution. Examples of strong acids include hydrochloric acid (HCl), sulfuric acid (H_2SO_4), and nitric acid (NO_3). Examples of weak acids are acetic acid ($HC_2H_3O_2$), hydrofluoric acid (HF), and carbonic acid (H_2CO_3). Examples of strong bases include sodium hydroxide (NaOH), potassium hydroxide (KOH), and calcium hydroxide ($Ca(OH)_2$). Ammonia (NH_3) is a common weak base.

Review Video: Strong and Weak Acids and Bases
Visit mometrix.com/academy and enter code: 268930

Monoprotic and Polyprotic Acids

Monoprotic acids are acids that have only one proton available to donate. **Polyprotic acids** have two or more protons available to donate. Typically, polyprotic acids donate their available protons in stages of one at a time. Specifically, diprotic acids can donate two protons, and triprotic acids can donate three protons. Common monoprotic acids include hydrochloric acid (HCl) and nitric acid (HNO_3). Common diprotic acids include sulfuric acid (H_2SO_4) and sulfurous acid (H_2SO_3). Phosphoric acid (H_3PO_4) is a common triprotic acid.

K_a of an Acid and the K_b of a Base

Given the general form $HA(aq) + H_2O(l) \leftrightarrow H_3O^+(aq) + A^-(aq)$ for the equilibrium of an acid in an aqueous solution, the equilibrium constant expression, called the **acid dissociation constant**, K_a, is:

$$K_a = \frac{[H_3O^+][A^-]}{[HA]}$$

Strong acids have high K_a values because strong acids ionize essentially completely in aqueous solution. Weak acids have low K_a values because weak acids do not ionize completely in aqueous solution.

Given the general form $B(aq) + H_2O(l) \leftrightarrow BH^+(aq) + OH^-(aq)$ for the equilibrium of a base in an aqueous solution, the equilibrium constant expression, called the **base dissociation constant**, K_b, is:

$$K_b = \frac{[BH^+][OH^-]}{[B]}$$

Strong bases have high K_b values because strong bases ionize essentially completely in aqueous solution. Weak bases have low K_b values because weak bases do not ionize completely in aqueous solution.

Hydrolysis

Hydrolysis is a chemical reaction between water and another reactant in which both compounds split apart. The water molecules split into hydrogen ions (H^+) and hydroxide ions (OH^-). The other compound splits into a cation and anion, too. Another way to state this is that hydrolysis is a decomposition reaction of a compound that is combined with water. The general form of a hydrolysis reaction is given by $X^-(aq) + H_2O(l) \leftrightarrow HX(aq) + OH^-(aq)$.

A salt hydrolysis reaction is the reverse process of a neutralization reaction. A neutralization reaction is given by the general form: acid + base → salt + water. In general, a salt hydrolysis reaction may be thought of as salt + water → acid + base.

Buffer Solution

A **buffer solution** is an aqueous solution that helps keep the pH constant. The addition of an acid or base to a buffer solution will not greatly affect the pH of that solution. A buffer consists of a weak acid and its conjugate base or a weak base and its conjugate acid. This combination of substances can remain in solution without the substances neutralizing each other. When acids or hydrogen ions (H^+) are added to a buffer solution, they are neutralized by the base in the buffer solution. When bases or hydroxide ions (OH^-) are added to a buffer solution, they are neutralized by the acid in the buffer solution.

Review Video: Buffer
Visit mometrix.com/academy and enter code: 389183

Chapter Quiz

Ready to see how well you retained what you just read? Scan the QR code to go directly to the chapter quiz interface for this study guide. If you're using a computer, simply visit the online resources page at **mometrix.com/resources719/gacechemistry** and click the Chapter Quizzes link.

GACE Practice Test

Want to take this practice test in an online interactive format?
Check out the online resources page, which includes interactive practice questions and much more: **mometrix.com/resources719/gacechemistry**

1. Which substance is most likely to be a solid at STP?

a. Kr
b. Na
c. NH_3
d. Xe

2. Which of the following actions would increase the freezing point of a solution?

I. Divide the solution into two separate containers.
II. Heat the solution to boil off some of the solvent.
III. Initiate a reaction that causes some of the solute to precipitate.

a. I and II
b. II
c. III
d. I and III

3. A gas at constant volume is cooled. Which statement about the gas must be true?

a. The kinetic energy of the gas molecules has decreased.
b. The gas has condensed to a liquid.
c. The weight of the gas has decreased.
d. The density of the gas has increased.

4. A weather balloon is filled with 1,000 mol of He gas at 25 °C and 101 kPa of pressure. What is the volume of the weather balloon?

a. 24,518 m^3
b. 24.5 m^3
c. 2 m^3
d. 245 m^3

5. One mole of oxygen gas and two moles of hydrogen are combined in a sealed container at STP. Which of the following statements is true?

a. The mass of hydrogen gas is greater than the mass of oxygen.
b. The volume of hydrogen is greater than the volume of oxygen.
c. The hydrogen and oxygen will react to produce two moles of water.
d. The partial pressure of hydrogen is greater than the partial pressure of oxygen.

6. Graham's law is best used to determine what relationship between two different materials?

a. Pressure and volume
b. Volume and temperature
c. Mass and diffusion rate
d. Diffusion rate and temperature

7. Which is the correct order of increasing attractive forces between particles?

a. Dipole – dipole < ionic < hydrogen bonding < London dispersion
b. Ionic < dipole – dipole < London dispersion < hydrogen bonding
c. Hydrogen bonding < London dispersion < ionic < dipole – dipole
d. London dispersion < dipole – dipole < hydrogen bonding < ionic

8. One mole of an ideal gas is compressed to 10 L and heated to 25 °C. What is the pressure of the gas?

a. 2.4 kPa
b. 2.4 atm
c. 0.2 atm
d. 0.2 kPa

9. A 10 L cylinder contains 4 moles of oxygen, 3 moles of nitrogen and 7 moles of neon. The temperature of the cylinder is increased from 20 °C to 40 °C. Determine the partial pressure of neon in the cylinder as a percentage of the whole.

a. 50%
b. 70%
c. 90%
d. 40%

10. Three liquids, X, Y and Z are placed in separate flasks, each of which is suspended in a water bath at 75 °C. The boiling points of each liquid are

X, 273 K
Y, 340 K
Z, 360 K

Which of the three liquids will begin to boil after warming to 75 °C?

a. X, Y, and Z
b. X and Z
c. X and Y
d. Y and Z

11. Which of the following statements about the physical properties of liquids and gases are true?

I. Liquids and gases are both compressible.
II. Liquids flow, but gases do not.
III. Liquids flow and gases are incompressible.
IV. Liquids flow and gases are compressible.
V. Gases flow and liquids are incompressible.

a. I and III
b. II and IV
c. III and V
d. IV and V

12. Which of the following statements generally describes the trend of electronegativity on the periodic table of elements?

a. Electronegativity increases going from left to right and from top to bottom
b. Electronegativity increases going from right to left and from bottom to top
c. Electronegativity increases going from left to right and from bottom to top
d. Electronegativity increases going from right to left and from top to bottom

13. Gas X is in a cylinder at 1 atm of pressure and has a volume of 10 L at 0 °C. Gas X spontaneously decomposes to gas Y, according to the equation

$$X \longrightarrow 3Y$$

The temperature in the cylinder remains the same during the reaction. What is the pressure in the cylinder now?

a. 1 atm
b. 3 atm
c. 4 atm
d. Cannot be determined

14. 1 mole of water and 1 mole of argon are in a cylinder at 110 °C and 1 atm of pressure. The temperature of the cylinder is reduced to –5 °C. Which statement about the contents of the cylinder is most accurate?

a. The pressure in the cylinder is decreased, and the partial pressure of argon is less than that of water.
b. The pressure in the cylinder is about the same, and the partial pressure of water is less than that of argon.
c. The pressure in the cylinder is decreased, and the partial pressure of water is much less than that of argon.
d. The pressure in the cylinder is decreased, and the partial pressure of water is the same as argon.

15. A solid is heated until it melts. Which of the following is true about the solid melting?

a. ΔH is positive, and ΔS is positive.
b. ΔH is negative and ΔS is positive.
c. ΔH is positive and ΔS is negative.
d. ΔH is negative and ΔS is negative.

16. A liquid is held at its freezing point and slowly allowed to solidify. Which of the following statements about this event is true?

a. During freezing, the temperature of the material decreases
b. While freezing, heat is given off by the material
c. During freezing, heat is absorbed by the material
d. During freezing, the temperature of the material increases

17. A liquid is heated from 50 °C to 80 °C. Which of the following statements is generally true about the solubility of solids and gases in the liquid?

a. The solubility of solids will increase, and the solubility of gases will decrease.
b. The solubility of solids will decrease, and the solubility of gases will increase.
c. The solubility of solids will increase, and the solubility of gases will increase.
d. The solubility of solids will decrease, and the solubility of gases will decrease.

18. 100 g of H_3PO_4 is dissolved in water, producing 400 mL of solution. What is the normality of the solution?

a. 2.55 N
b. 1.02 N
c. 7.65 N
d. 0.25 N

19. Silver nitrate ($AgNO_3$) is dissolved in water. One drop of an aqueous solution containing NaCl is added and almost instantly, a white milky precipitate forms. What is the precipitate?

a. NaCl
b. $NaNO_3$
c. $AgNO_3$
d. AgCl

20. 100 g of ethanol C_2H_6O is dissolved in 100 g of water. The final solution has a volume of 0.2 L. What is the density of the resulting solution?

a. 0.5 g/mL
b. 1 g/mL
c. 0.8 g/mL
d. 1.15 g/mL

21. 100 mL of a 0.1 M solution of NaOH is neutralized to pH 7 with H_2SO_4. How many grams of H_2SO_4 are required to achieve this neutralization?

a. 4.9 g
b. 0.98 g
c. 9.8 g
d. 0.49 g

22. Comparing pure water and a 1 M aqueous solution of NaCl, both at 1 atm of pressure, which of the following statements is most accurate?

a. The pure water will boil at a higher temperature and be less conductive.
b. The pure water will boil at a lower temperature and be less conductive.
c. The pure water will boil at a lower temperature and be more conductive.
d. The pure water will boil at the same temperature and be more conductive.

23. Place the following in the correct order of increasing acidity.

a. HCl < HF < HI < HBr
b. HCl < HBr < HI < HF
c. HI < HBr < HCl < HF
d. HF < HCl < HBr < HI

24. Place the following in the correct order of increasing solubility in water.

a. Butanol < ethanol < octane < NaCl
b. Ethanol < NaCl < octane < butanol
c. NaCl < octane < butanol < ethanol
d. Octane < butanol < ethanol < NaCl

25. 50 grams of acetic acid $C_2H_4O_2$ are dissolved in 200 g of water. Calculate the weight % and mole fraction of the acetic acid in the solution.

a. 20%; 0.069
b. 0.069%; 0.20
c. 25%; 0.075
d. 20%; 0.075

26. Ammonium Phosphate $(NH_4)_3PO_4$ is a strong electrolyte. What will be the concentration of all the ions in a 0.9 M solution of ammonium phosphate?

a. $[NH_4^+] = 0.9$ M, $[PO_4^{3-}] = 0.9$ M
b. $[NH_4^+] = 0.3$ M, $[PO_4^{3-}] = 0.9$ M
c. $[NH_4^+] = 2.7$ M, $[PO_4^{3-}] = 0.9$ M
d. $[NH_4^+] = 2.7$ M, $[PO_4^{3-}] = 2.7$ M

27. Which of the following represents the correct increasing order of acidity?

a. $CH_3COOH < CH_3OH < CH_3CH_3 < HCl$
b. $CH_3CH_3 < CH_3OH < CH_3COOH < HCl$
c. $CH_3CH_3 < CH_3COOH < CH_3OH < HCl$
d. $CH_3OH < CH_3CH_3 < HCl < CH_3COOH$

28. One liter of a 0.02 M solution of methanol in water is prepared. What is the mass of methanol in the solution, and what is the approximate molality of methanol?

a. 0.64 g, 0.02 m
b. 0.32 g, 0.01 m
c. 0.64 g, 0.03 m
d. 0.32 g, 0.02 m

29. A 1 M solution of NaCl (A) and a 0.5 M solution of NaCl (B) are joined together by a semi permeable membrane. What, if anything, is likely to happen between the two solutions?

a. No change will occur, as the solvents and solutes are the same in each.
b. Water will migrate from A to B.
c. NaCl will migrate from A to B and water will migrate from B to A.
d. Water will migrate from B to A.

30. Which of the following radioactive emissions results in an increase in atomic number?

a. Alpha
b. Negative Beta
c. Positive Beta
d. Gamma

31. A material has a half-life of 2 years. If you started with 1 kg of the material, how much would be left after 8 years?

a. 1 kg
b. 0.5 kg
c. 0.06 kg
d. 0.12 kg

32. The isotope carbon-14 has a half-life of 5,730 years. If you started with 1 mg of carbon-14 today, about how much would be left in 20,000 years?

a. 0.06 mg
b. 0.07 mg
c. 0.11 mg
d. 0.09 mg

33. The best way to separate isotopes of the same element is to exploit:

a. Differences in chemical reactivity
b. Differences in reduction potential
c. Differences in toxicity
d. Differences in mass

34. Nuclear chain reactions, such as the kind that is exploited in nuclear power plants, are propagated by what subatomic particle(s)?

a. Protons
b. Neutrons
c. Electrons
d. Neutrons and protons

35. Which of the following statements about radioactive decay is true?

a. The sum of the mass of the daughter particles is less than that of the parent nucleus.
b. The sum of the mass of the daughter particles is greater than that of the parent nucleus.
c. The sum of the mass of the daughter particles is equal to that of the parent nucleus.
d. The sum of the mass of the daughter particles cannot be accurately measured.

36. What are the numbers of neutrons, protons, and electrons in ^{238}U?

a. 238, 92, 238
b. 92, 146, 146
c. 146, 92, 92
d. 92, 92, 146

37. An alpha particle consists of:

a. Two electrons and two protons
b. Two electrons and two neutrons
c. Four neutrons
d. Two protons and two neutrons

38. Describe the correct outer shell electronic arrangement of phosphorous.

a. $4s^2 4p^3$
b. $3s^2 3p^3$
c. $2s^2 3p^3$
d. $2s^2 2p^3$

39. Hund's rule regarding electronic configuration states:

a. Electrons in the same orbital must have an opposite spin.
b. Electrons must fill lower energy orbitals before filling higher energy orbitals.
c. Electrons must populate empty orbitals of equal energy before filling occupied orbitals.
d. Electrons must have the same nuclear spin as the nucleus.

40. Arrange the following elements in order of increasing atomic radius:

a. $\mathrm{K} < \mathrm{Zn} < \mathrm{Fe} < \mathrm{As} < \mathrm{Kr}$
b. $\mathrm{K} < \mathrm{Fe} < \mathrm{Zn} < \mathrm{Kr} < \mathrm{As}$
c. $\mathrm{Kr} < \mathrm{As} < \mathrm{Fe} < \mathrm{K} < \mathrm{Zn}$
d. $\mathrm{Kr} < \mathrm{As} < \mathrm{Zn} < \mathrm{Fe} < \mathrm{K}$

41. When a solid is heated and transforms directly into the gaseous phases, this process is called:

a. Sublimation
b. Fusion
c. Diffusion
d. Condensation

42. Determine a possible set of oxidation states for the elements in $KMnO_4$:

a. $\mathrm{K}^{1+}, \mathrm{Mn}^{7+}, \mathrm{O}^{8-}$
b. $\mathrm{K}^{1-}, \mathrm{Mn}^{7+}, \mathrm{O}^{2-}$
c. $\mathrm{K}^{1+}, \mathrm{Mn}^{3+}, \mathrm{O}^{4-}$
d. $\mathrm{K}^{1+}, \mathrm{Mn}^{7+}, \mathrm{O}^{2-}$

43. Place the following elements in order of decreasing electronegativity:

N, As, Bi, P, Sb

a. $\mathrm{As} > \mathrm{Bi} > \mathrm{N} > \mathrm{P} > \mathrm{Sb}$
b. $\mathrm{N} > \mathrm{P} > \mathrm{As} > \mathrm{Sb} > \mathrm{Bi}$
c. $\mathrm{Bi} > \mathrm{Sb} > \mathrm{As} > \mathrm{P} > \mathrm{N}$
d. $\mathrm{P} > \mathrm{N} > \mathrm{As} > \mathrm{Sb} > \mathrm{Bi}$

44. Arrange the following compounds from most polar to least polar:

F_2, CH_3CH_2Cl, NaCl, CH_3OH

a. $NaCl > CH_3OH > CH_3CH_2Cl > F_2$
b. $F_2 > NaCl > CH_3OH > CH_3CH_2Cl$
c. $CH_3OH > NaCl > F_2 > CH_3CH_2Cl$
d. $NaCl > F_2 > CH_3OH > CH_3CH_2Cl$

45. Which of the following are incorrect Lewis structures?

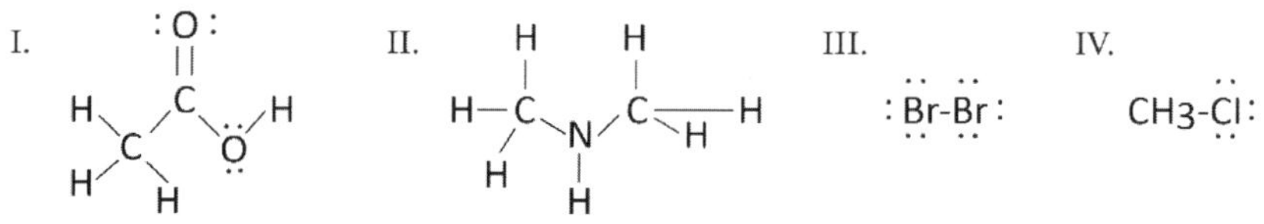

a. I and II
b. II and IV
c. I and III
d. III and IV

46. A bond involving which hybrid orbital is the shortest?

a. sp^2
b. sp^3
c. sp
d. sp^3d

47. Resonance structures can be defined as:

a. Two or more structures that have different atoms bound to different atoms
b. Two structures that have a similar structure but different formula
c. Two or more structures that have the same formula, but are different in shape
d. Two or more structures that differ only in the arrangement of electrons in the structures

48. Atoms that are sp^2 hybridized will have what sort of hybrid orbital geometry around them?

a. Tetrahedral
b. Trigonal planar
c. Linear
d. Angled

49. What is the chemical composition of ammonium sulfate?

a. N 21%, H 3%, S 24%, O 32%
b. N 10%, H 6%, S 24%, O 60%
c. N 10%, H 4%, S 12%, O 74%
d. N 21%, H 6%, S 24%, O 48%

50. What is the correct IUPAC name of the compound Fe_2O_3?

a. Iron (I) oxide
b. Iron (II) oxide
c. Iron (III) oxide
d. Iron (IV) oxide

51. Balance the following reaction between sulfuric acid and aluminum hydroxide by filling in the correct stoichiometric values for each chemical.

$$\_\,H_2SO_4 + \_\,Al(OH)_3 \rightarrow \_\,Al_2(SO_4)_3 + \_\,H_2O$$

a. 3, 2, 1, 6
b. 2, 3, 1, 3
c. 3, 3, 2, 6
d. 1, 2, 1, 4

52. Calculate the mass of water produced from the reaction of 1 kg of n-heptane with oxygen.

$$n\text{-heptane (1 kg)} + 11O_2 \rightarrow 7CO_2 + 8H_2O$$

a. 144 g
b. 8 kg
c. 800 g
d. 1.4 kg

53. Magnesium metal is reacted with hydrobromic acid according to the following equation:

$$Mg + 2HBr \rightarrow MgBr_2 + H_2$$

If 100 g of Mg is reacted with 100 g of HBr, which statement about the reaction is true?

a. Mg is the limiting reagent.
b. HBr is the excess reagent.
c. Mg is the excess reagent.
d. 100 g of $MgBr_2$ will be produced.

54. Methane gas is burned in pure oxygen at 200 °C and 1 atm of pressure to produce CO_2 and H_2O according to the equation:

$$CH_4 + 2O_2 \rightarrow CO_2 + 2H_2O$$

If 10 L of methane gas were burned, and the final temperature and pressure remained the same, how many liters of gaseous products are produced by the reaction?

a. 10 L
b. 20 L
c. 30 L
d. 40 L

55. The overall reaction A → D can be described by the following equation:

$$A \xrightarrow{\text{fast}} B \xrightarrow{\text{slow}} C \xrightarrow{\text{fast}} D$$

What would be the rate law for the overall reaction of A to D?

a. $\text{Rate} = \frac{k[D]}{[A]}$
b. $\text{Rate} = k[B]$
c. $\text{Rate} = [B]$
d. $\text{Rate} = \frac{k[C]}{[B]}$

56. How many electrons are in an uncharged atom of $^{45}_{20}Ca$?

a. 20
b. 45
c. 65
d. 25

57. For the reaction $CO_2(g) + H_2(g) \rightleftharpoons CO(g) + H_2O(l)$, which of the following will occur if the pressure of the reaction is increased?

a. The reaction order will increase.
b. The forward reaction rate will decrease.
c. The reaction equilibrium will shift to the right.
d. The reaction will stop.

58. For the gas phase reaction $CH_4 + 4Cl_2 \rightarrow CCl_4 + 4HCl$, what would be the equilibrium expression K_{eq} for this reaction?

a. $\frac{[CH_4][Cl_2]}{[CCl_4][4HCl]}$
b. $\frac{[CH_4][Cl_2]}{[CCl_4][HCl]^4}$
c. $\frac{[4Cl][CCl_4]}{[CH_4][4HCl]}$
d. $\frac{[CCl_4][HCl]^4}{[CH_4][Cl_2]^4}$

59. Adding a catalyst to a reaction will do which of the following?

a. Shift the reaction equilibrium towards the products
b. Increase the temperature of the reaction
c. Decrease the energy of activation for the reaction
d. Increase the purity of the reaction products

60. 10 g of salt XY ($MW = 100$ g/mol) is added to 1 liter of water with stirring. The salt dissociates into ions X^+ and Y^-. After equilibrium is established, the undissolved portion of the salt was removed by filtration, weighed, and found to be 9.5 g. What is the K_{sp} for this salt?

a. 5×10^{-2}
b. 5×10^{-3}
c. 1×10^{-2}
d. 2.5×10^{-5}

61. Which of the following are considered Lewis acids?

I. H_2SO_4
II. $AlCl_3$
III. PCl_3
IV. $FeCl_3$

a. II and IV
b. II and III
c. I and IV
d. I and II

62. Place the following in the correct order of increasing acidity:

H_3PO_4, HF, HCl, H_2O, NH_3

a. $H_3PO_4 < H_2O < NH_3 < HF < HCl$
b. $NH_3 < H_2O < HF < H_3PO_4 < HCl$
c. $H_2O < NH_3 < HF < H_3PO_4 < HCl$
d. $NH_3 < H_2O < HF < HCl < H_3PO_4$

63. The pK_a for ethanol (CH_3CH_2OH) is approximately 16. The pK_a for acetic acid (CH_3COOH) is about 4. The difference can be explained by:

a. Resonance stabilization
b. Electronegativity differences
c. Molecular weight differences
d. Molecular size differences

64. What will be the pH of 2 L of a 0.1 M aqueous solution of HCl?

a. 2
b. −1
c. 1
d. 0.05

65. What is the pH of a buffer containing 0.2 M NaOAc and 0.1 M AcOH? The pK_a of acetic acid is 4.75.

a. 4
b. 5
c. 6
d. 7

66. 50 mL of 1 M H_2SO_4 is added to an aqueous solution containing 4 g of NaOH. What will the final pH of the resulting solution be?

a. 5
b. 6
c. 7
d. 9

67. To make a good buffering system in the pH range of 5-9, which acid/base combinations would likely work the best?

a. HCl/NaOH
b. $HNO_3/NaNO_3$
c. $H_2SO_4/NaHSO_4$
d. NaH_2PO_4/Na_2HPO_4

68. For the conversion of water into steam, which of the following is true?

a. $\Delta T = 0, \Delta S > 0$
b. $\Delta T > 0, \Delta S = 0$
c. $\Delta T = 0, \Delta S < 0$
d. $\Delta T > 0, \Delta S > 0$

69. 100 g of NH_3 are cooled from 100 °C to 25 °C. What is the heat change for this transition? The heat capacity of ammonia gas is $35.1\ J/(mol \cdot K)$.

a. -263 kJ
b. 15.5 kJ
c. -15.5 kJ
d. 263 kJ

70. Determine the heat of combustion for the following reaction:

$$\text{Propane} + 5O_2 \rightarrow 3CO_2 + 4H_2O$$

The standard heats of formation for propane, CO_2 and water are -103.8 KJ/mol, -393.5 KJ/mol, and -285.8 KJ/mol respectively.

a. −2,220 KJ/mol
b. −2,323.7 KJ/mol
c. 2,220 KJ/mol
d. 2,323.7 KJ/mol

71. Which of the following reactions produces products with higher entropy than the starting materials?

I. Glucose(s) + water → glucose(aq)
II. $4Al(s) + 3O_2(g) \rightarrow 2Al_2O_3(s)$
III. Br_2 + light → 2Br
IV. Ice → water vapor

a. II, III
b. I, II
c. I, III
d. I, III, IV

72. Three 1-kg blocks—one made of iron, one of lead, one of nickel—are heated from 20 °C to 30 °C. Which of the following statements about the blocks is true?

a. The lead heats faster than the iron and the nickel.
b. The iron requires more heat to reach 30 °C than the nickel or lead.
c. All three blocks require a different amount of heat to reach 30 °C.
d. The iron requires more time to reach 30 °C than the nickel or the lead.

73. In the reaction $Pb + H_2SO_4 \rightarrow PbSO_4 + H_2$:

a. Lead is reduced, and hydrogen is oxidized.
b. Lead is oxidized, and hydrogen is oxidized.
c. Lead is reduced, and sulfate is oxidized.
d. Lead is oxidized, and hydrogen is reduced.

74. Which of the following elements would likely be a good reducing agent?

a. Br_2
b. N_2
c. Na
d. Ne

75. Molten magnesium chloride is electrolyzed. The products formed from this reaction are:

a. Mg at the anode and Cl^- at the cathode
b. Mg^{2+} at the anode and Cl^- at the cathode
c. Mg at the cathode and Cl_2 at the anode
d. Mg at the anode and Cl_2 at the cathode

76. The transformation of diamond to graphite has a $-\Delta G$. Which of the following is true?

a. The reaction is spontaneous and occurs rapidly at room temperature.
b. The reaction is not spontaneous and occurs slowly at room temperature.
c. The reaction is not spontaneous and does not occur at room temperature.
d. The reaction is spontaneous and occurs slowly at room temperature.

77. What would be the correct IUPAC name for the following compound?

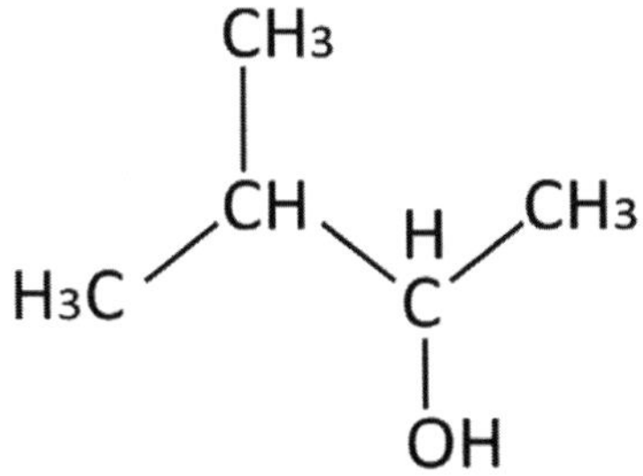

a. 3-methyl-2-butanol
b. 2-methyl-3-butanol
c. 3,3-dimethyl-2-propanol
d. 2-Hydroxy-3-methyl butane

78. Which of the following molecules is an alkene?

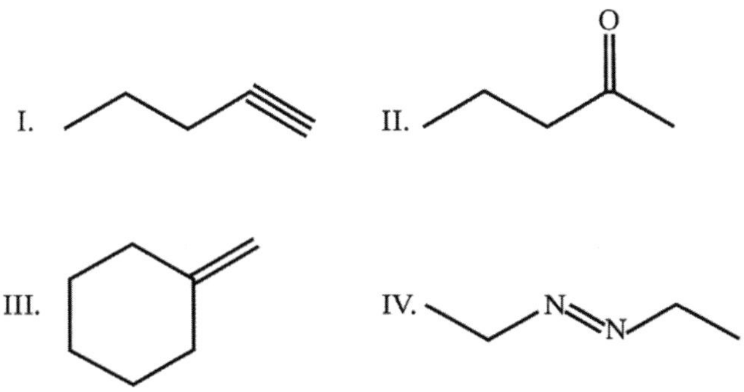

a. I
b. II
c. III
d. IV

79. What is the oxidation state of the carbon atom in a carboxylic acid functional group?

a. 4+
b. 3+
c. 2−
d. 3−

80. Which of the following molecules is named correctly?

a. 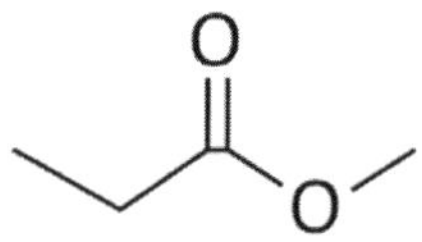

methyl propionoate

b. 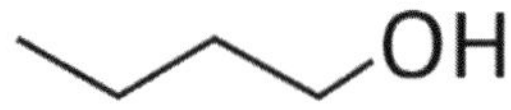

1-propanol

c. 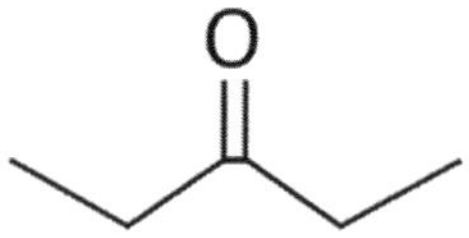

3-propanoic acid

d. 
3-butene

81. Which scientist was responsible for developing the format of the modern periodic table?

a. Faraday
b. Einstein
c. Hess
d. Mendeleev

82. Two different molecules can be isomers of each other if:

a. They have the same functional groups
b. They have the same oxidation state
c. They have the same molecular weight
d. They have the same chemical formula

83. Which of the following molecules are cis alkenes?

I. 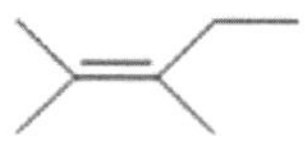

II. 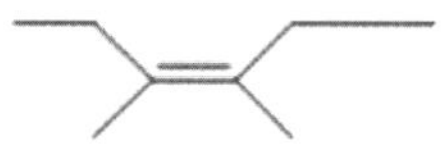

III. 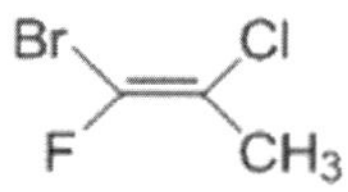

IV. 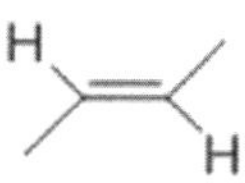

a. I, II
b. II, III
c. III, IV
d. I, IV

84. What would be the best analytical tool for determining the chemical structure of an organic compound?

a. NMR
b. HPLC
c. IR
d. Mass spec

85. Proteins are made up of repeating subunits of which of the following?

a. Sugars
b. Triglycerides
c. Amino acids
d. Nucleic acids

86. The precision of a number of data points refers to:

a. How accurate the data is
b. How many errors the data contains
c. How close the data points are to each other
d. How close the actual data is to the predicted result

87. The density of a material refers to:

a. Mass per volume
b. Mass per mole
c. Molecular weight per volume
d. Moles per volume

88. Which of the following types of chemicals are considered generally unsafe to store together?

I. Liquids and solids
II. Acids and bases
III. Reducing agents and oxidizing agents
IV. Metals and salts

a. I, II
b. II, III
c. III, IV
d. I, IV

89. Which statement about the impact of chemistry on society is NOT true?

a. The fluoridation of water has had no effect on the rate of cavities as compared to unfluoridated water.
b. Chemical fertilizers have tremendously increased food production per acre in the US.
c. Chemistry played a central role in the development of nuclear weapons.
d. The use of catalytic converters in automobiles has greatly reduced exhaust products that contribute to acid rain.

90. Methylmercury is a toxin produced indirectly from what energy source?

a. Oil
b. Natural gas
c. Wood
d. Coal

Answer Key and Explanations

1. B: Na (sodium) is a solid at standard temperature and pressure, which is 0 °C (273.15 K) and 100 kPa (0.987 atm), according to IUPAC. The stronger the intermolecular forces, the greater the likelihood of the material being a solid. Kr and Xe are noble gases and have negligible intermolecular attraction. NH_3 has some hydrogen bonding but is still a gas at STP. Sodium is an alkali metal whose atoms are bonded by metallic bonding and is therefore a solid at STP.

2. C: The freezing point of a solution is inversely correlated to the concentration of solute in the solution. Dividing the solution will have no impact on its properties. Driving off some of the solvent by heating will effectively increase the concentration and thus lower the freezing point. Precipitating out some of the solute will lower the concentration and increase the freezing point.

3. A: The kinetic energy of the gas molecules is directly proportional to the temperature. If the temperature decreases, so does the molecular motion. A decrease in temperature will not necessarily mean a gas condenses to a liquid. Neither the mass nor the density is impacted, as no material was added or removed, and the volume remained the same.

4. B: The ideal gas law $PV = nRT$ is rearranged to solve for V, and we get $V = \frac{nRT}{P}$. R is the gas constant, $\frac{0.08206 \text{ L atm}}{\text{mol K}}$, and the Celsius temperature must be converted to Kelvin, by adding 273 to 25 °C to obtain 298 K. The pressure must be converted to atmospheres, which 101 kPa is essentially 1 atm (0.9967 atm). Plugging the numbers into the equation, we get $V = 1{,}000 \text{ mol} \times \frac{\left(\frac{0.08206 \text{ L atm}}{\text{mol K}}\right)(298 \text{ K})}{1 \text{ atm}}$, which gives $V = 24{,}453$ L. A liter is a cubic decimeter (dm^3), and when converted, this gives $V = 24.5 \text{ m}^3$.

5. D: Since there are twice as many molecules of hydrogen as molecules of oxygen, the partial pressure of hydrogen will be greater. The mass of hydrogen will not be greater than the mass of oxygen present even though there are more moles of hydrogen, due to oxygen having a higher molecular weight. Each gas will occupy the same volume. Hydrogen and oxygen gas can coexist in the container without reacting to produce water. There is no indication given that a chemical reaction has occurred.

6. C: Graham's law of diffusion allows one to calculate the relative diffusion rate between two different gases based on their masses.

7. D: London dispersion forces are the weakest interparticle forces. These interactions occur in all molecules due to unequal electron density around the nucleus, which results in a momentary dipole. Dipole-dipole interactions are those between two polar molecules. The more positive portion of one molecule is attracted to the negative portion of a different molecule. Hydrogen bonding is a stronger type of dipole-dipole interaction which occurs between a hydrogen in one molecule and a nitrogen, oxygen or fluorine atom in another molecule. Hydrogen bonding only occurs between molecules containing H-F, H-O, or H-N bonds. Ionic bonds are the strongest interparticle forces. In ionic compounds, a positive ion is attracted to a negative ion. NaCl is entirely ionic with full charge separation, and the ions are tightly bound to each other in an organized crystalline network.

8. B: Plugging the data into the ideal gas law using the correct units gives the correct answer in atmospheres, which in this case is 2.4 atm. The equation is $P = \frac{nRT}{V}$. So we have P =

$\frac{1\,mol\left(\frac{0.08206\,L\,atm}{mol\,K}\right)(298\,K)}{10\,L}$. The R value is $\frac{0.08206\,L\,atm}{mol\,K}$ when using L as the volume unit, and delivers the pressure in atm.

9. A: Since there are 7 moles of neon out of a total of 14 moles of gas in the cylinder, the partial pressure of neon will always be 50% of the total pressure, regardless of the temperature.

10. C: To convert from degrees Celsius to Kelvin, add 273. 75 °C is equivalent to 348 K. Both X and Y have lower boiling points, which means that they will each boil in the water bath. Z will never become warm enough to boil.

11. D: Both liquids and gases are fluids and therefore flow, but only gases are compressible. The molecules that make up a gas are very far apart, allowing the gas to be compressed into a smaller volume.

12. C: The most electronegative atoms are found near the top right of the periodic table. Fluorine has a high electronegativity, while Cesium, located near the bottom left of the table, has a low electronegativity.

13. B: Since both the volume and the temperature remain fixed, the only variable that changes is the number of moles of particles. Because there are now 3 times the number of particles as there were originally, the pressure must increase proportionately and so the pressure must be 3 atm.

14. C: As the temperature drops to –5 °C, the water vapor condenses to a liquid, and then to a solid. The partial pressure of a solid is much less than that of the corresponding gas. The argon is still a gas at –5 °C, so almost all the pressure in the cylinder is due to argon. Since the partial pressure of the water decreases as it turns to a solid, the totally pressure in the cylinder also decreases.

15. A: Heat is absorbed by the solid during melting; therefore, ΔH is positive. Going from a solid to a liquid greatly increases the freedom of the particles, which increases the entropy, so ΔS is also positive.

16. B: Freezing is an exothermic event; therefore, heat must be given off. The temperature of the material remains unchanged at the freezing point during the process.

17. A: The higher the temperature of the liquid, the greater the solubility of the solid, while the higher the temperature, the lower the solubility of the gas.

18. C: Normality refers to the concentration of acid equivalents (H^+ ions), not the concentration of the solute. 100 g of phosphoric acid has a MW of 98 g/mol. So, 100g/98 g/mol = 1.02 moles of phosphoric acid are in solution. The total volume of the solution is 0.4 L, so the molarity of the solution is 1.02 mol/0.4 L = 2.55 M. Since there are three acid equivalents for every mole of phosphoric acid, the normality is 3 × 2.55 = 7.65 N.

19. D: $AgNO_3$, $NaNO_3$, and NaCl are all highly water soluble and would not precipitate under these conditions. All nitrate compounds and compounds containing Group I metals are soluble in water. AgCl is essentially insoluble in water, and this is the precipitate observed.

20. B: Density is determined by dividing the mass of the solution by its volume. The mass is 200 g, and the total volume is 0.2 L, or 200 mL. So, 200 g/200 mL = 1 g/mL.

21. D: 100 mL of a 0.1 M solution of NaOH contains 0.01 moles of NaOH. That means 0.01 moles of acid are required to completely neutralize the solution. The MW of sulfuric acid is 98, so 0.98 g of sulfuric acid is 0.01 mole. But since sulfuric acid has two equivalents of acid per mole, only 0.005 mole of the acid is required or 0.49 g.

22. B: Pure water boils at 100 °C. Water that has salts dissolved in it will boil at a slightly higher temperature and will conduct electricity much better than pure water.

23. D: Acidity increases as we travel down the periodic table with regard to the halogens. Even though fluorine is the most electronegative element and would be expected to stabilize a negative charge well, it is such a small atom that it is poorly able to stabilize the negative charge and therefore will have a stronger bond to the hydrogen. As the atoms get larger, moving from fluorine to iodine, the ability to stabilize a negative charge becomes greater and the bond with the hydrogen is weaker. A stronger bond with the between the halogen and the hydrogen will result in less acidity, since fewer hydrogen ions will be produced.

24. D: Octane is a nonpolar hydrocarbon with little or no water solubility. Butanol is an alcohol with a small amount of solubility due to its polar $-OH$ group. Ethanol is a smaller, more polar alcohol that is very soluble in water. NaCl is an ionic salt that is highly soluble in water.

25. A: The weight % of the acetic acid is the mass of acetic acid divided by the mass of the acetic acid plus the water. So, $\frac{50\text{ g}}{(50\text{ g}+200\text{ g})} = 0.2$, or 20%. The mole fraction is the moles of acetic acid divided by the total number of moles of the solution. So, 50 g of acetic acid (MW $=$ 60) is $\frac{50\text{ g}}{\frac{60\text{ g}}{\text{mol}}} =$ 0.83 moles. 200 g of water $=$ 11.11 moles. Therefore, $\frac{0.83\text{ mol}}{(0.83\text{ mol}+11.11\text{ mol})} = 0.069$.

26. C: Since there are three moles of NH_4^+ per mole of salt and 1 mole of PO_4^{3-} per mole of salt, the total ionic concentrations must be 2.7 M of NH_4^+, and 0.9 M of PO_4^{3-}.

27. B: Ethane is an alkane and only very weakly acidic. Methanol, an alcohol, has a slightly acidic proton attached to the oxygen. Acetic acid is much more acidic than methanol with the acidic proton attached to the carboxyl group. Hydrochloric acid is highly acidic and completely dissociates in water.

28. A: Since we have 1 liter of the solution, then 0.02 M represents 0.02 moles of methanol. The mass of methanol can then be found by 0.02 mol $\times$ MW of $CH_3OH(32) = 0.64$ g. Molality is the moles of solute (methanol) divided by the number of kilograms of solvent; in this case, it is essentially 1 kg. This is assumed since the solvent is water and the density of water is 1 g/mL. So, 0.02 mol/1 kg $=$ 0.02 m.

29. D: During osmosis, solvent flows from the lowest to the highest concentration of solute, in this case B to A. The membrane is semi-permeable and only allows the solvent to move, not the solute.

30. B: Negative beta emission represents the spontaneous decay of a neutron into a proton with the release of an electron. Therefore, the resulting nucleus will have one more proton than it did before the reaction, and protons represent the atomic number of an atom. Alpha decay results in the emission of a helium nucleus. The resulting nucleus of an alpha decay would lose two protons and two neutrons, causing a decrease in both the atomic number and the mass number. In contrast, positive beta (beta-plus) emission converts a proton into a neutron and thus decreases the atomic number by 1. Gamma decay does not affect the numbers of protons or neutrons in the nucleus. It is an emission of a photon, or packet of energy.

31. C: Since each half-life is 2 years, 8 years would be 4 half-lives. So the mass of material is halved 4 times. Therefore, if we start with 1 kg, after 2 years we would have 0.5 kg, after 4 years we would have 0.25 kg, after 6 years we would have 0.12 kg, and after 8 years we would have 0.06 kg.

32. D: This problem is best solved using the decay formula, $\text{remaining} = \text{initial}(0.5)^{\left(\frac{t}{t_{\text{half-life}}}\right)}$.

$$1\text{ mg}(0.5)^{\left(\frac{20,000}{5,730}\right)} \approx 0.09\text{ mg}$$

However, if a student is careful in their reasoning, this problem can be solved without the formula. Since after 3 half-lives $\frac{1}{8}$ would remain, after 4 half-lives $\frac{1}{16}$ would remain, and 3.5 is right in the middle, the amount remaining should be close to the average of the values:

$$\left(\frac{1}{8}+\frac{1}{16}\right) \div 2 = \frac{3}{32} = 0.09375$$

This makes 0.09 mg the best option for material remaining after 3.5 half-lives.

33. D: Isotopes of the same element must have the same chemical behavior, and (A), (B), and (C) all represent, in one form or another, chemical behavior. Isotopes differ in mass, and this can be used to separate them by some appropriate physical property.

34. B: In a nuclear chain reaction, free neutrons released from nuclear fission cause a nucleus to split and release more neutrons.

35. A: Radioactive decay converts mass into energy ($E = mc^2$). The mass of products is always less than that of the starting materials since some mass is now energy.

36. C: The mass number is the number of protons and the number of neutrons added together. The number of protons is also known as the atomic number and can be found on the periodic table; therefore, the number of neutrons is the mass number (238) less the number of protons (92), which equals 146 neutrons. The number of electrons always equals the number of protons in a neutral atom, so C is the correct answer.

37. D: An alpha particle is a helium nucleus, which contains two protons and two neutrons.

38. B: Phosphorus is in the third period, so the outermost levels must be $3s$, $3p$. Phosphorus is in Group 5A, which indicates that it has 5 valence electrons. To fill the $3s$ and $3p$, 2 electrons first fill the s orbital, and then the remaining 3 electrons enter the p orbitals, making $3s^2 3p^3$.

39. C: Hund's rule states that electrons must populate empty orbitals of similar energy before pairing up. The Aufbau principle states that electrons must fill lower energy orbitals before filling higher energy orbitals. The Pauli Exclusion Principle states that no two electrons in the same atom can have the same four quantum numbers, and, therefore, two electrons in the same orbital will have opposite spins.

40. D: All of the elements belong to the same row in the periodic table. Atomic radii increase going from right to left in any row of the periodic table. Although these elements belonged to the same row, it is important to also know that atomic radii increase from top to bottom in the groups of the periodic table.

41. A: Sublimation is the process of a solid changing directly into a gas without entering the liquid phase. Fusion refers to melting a solid into a liquid. Diffusion is the process of a material dispersing throughout another. Condensation is generally a gas turning into a liquid.

42. D: Each oxygen has an oxidation state of –2. Potassium (K) only exists in compounds as +1. Therefore, for the molecule to have a neutral charge, the Mn must be in a +7 oxidation state.

$$4(-2) + 1 + 7 = 0$$

None of the other options would result in a neutral molecule.

43. B: The trend within any column of the periodic table is that electronegativity decreases going down the column.

44. A: NaCl is an ionic salt, which is the most polar. F_2 is nonpolar since the two atoms share the electrons in an equal and symmetrical manner. CH_3OH is an alcohol with a very polar O-H bond. CH_3CH_2Cl is also a polar molecule due to the unequal sharing of electrons in the C-Cl bond.

45. B: The nitrogen is missing its lone pair of electrons, and should have two dots above it. A correct Lewis structure shows how the atoms are connected to each other as well as all of the valence electrons in the compound, so the abbreviated methyl group is also incorrect.

46. C: The more s character the bond has, the shorter it will be. A triple bond is stronger and shorter than a double bond, which is stronger and shorter than a single bond. An sp orbital is found in a triple bond. An sp^2 orbital is found in a double bond and sp^3 orbitals are found in single bonds.

47. D: Resonance structures have the same atoms connected to the same atoms, but differ only in electronic structure amongst the atoms. Isomers are molecules that have the same formula but differ in structure. Structural isomers differ in how the atoms are bonded to each other. Stereoisomers are isomers that have the same bonding structure but different arrangements, for example, cis- and trans- isomers.

48. B: Hybrid orbitals arrange themselves to be as far from each other as possible. An sp^2 atom has three hybrid orbitals, so they arrange themselves to be trigonal planar, with 120° between the bonds.

49. D: The correct structure of ammonium sulfate is $(NH_4)_2SO_4$. Its molecular weight is 132. The masses of the elements in the compound are nitrogen 28 (2 × 14), hydrogen 8 (1 × 8), sulfur 32 (32 × 1), and oxygen 64 (16 × 4). To find the percentage composition of each element, divide the element mass by the molecular weight of the compound and multiply by 100. So, nitrogen is $\left(\frac{28}{132}\right) \times 100 = 21\%$, hydrogen is $\left(\frac{8}{132}\right) \times 100 = 6\%$, sulfur is $\left(\frac{32}{132}\right) \times 100 = 24\%$ and oxygen is $\left(\frac{64}{132}\right) \times 100 = 48\%$.

50. C: Three oxygen are equal to a total charge of –6. Therefore, the two iron atoms must equal that with a positive charge, or +6. So, each iron atom must be +3, and the compound is iron (III) oxide.

51. A: By comparing the products to the reactants, there must be at least two Al atoms in the starting material, and at least three sulfate groups. Therefore, a coefficient of 2 must be placed in front of $Al(OH)_3$ and a coefficient of 3 must be placed in front of H_2SO_4. To make the number of hydrogen and oxygen atoms equal on both sides of the equation, a coefficient of 6 must be placed in front of H_2O.

52. D: 1 kg of heptane (MW 100) is equal to 10 moles of heptane. Since 8 moles of water is produced for every mole of heptane reacted, 80 moles of water must be produced. 80 moles of water (MW 18) equals 1,440 g, or 1.4 kg.

53. C: 100 g of HBr equals 1.23 moles, and 100 g of Mg equals 4.11 moles. From the coefficients of the balanced equation, the ratio of HBr to Mg is 2 : 1. This means that to react 1.23 moles of HBr, 2.46 moles of Mg would be required. Since 4.11 moles of Mg are present, Mg is in excess.

54. C: The equation shows that for every liter of methane reacted, one liter of CO_2 and 2 liters of water vapor will be produced. So, a total of three liters of gaseous products will be formed for every liter of methane burned. Because the temperature of the reaction products is 200 °C, the water produced will be in vapor (gas) form and not in liquid form. Since 10L of methane were burned, 30 L of gaseous products were formed.

55. B: Since the conversion of B to C is the slow step, this is the only one that determines the reaction rate law. Therefore, the rate law will be based on B since it is the only reactant in producing C.

56. A: Since the atomic number is 20, which represents the number of protons in the atom, there must be an equal number of electrons in a neutral atom. Protons have a positive charge and electrons are negative. Equal numbers of protons and electrons will result in a neutral atom, or zero charge.

57. C: Because there are 2 moles of gas on the reactant side and 1 mole of gas on the product side, a pressure increase will increase the forward reaction rate force the reaction to go further to the right. This, in turn, lowers gas pressure to restore equilibrium. Reaction order is not affected by environment changes.

58. D: For a general reaction, $aA + bB \rightarrow cC + dD$, the equilibrium equation would take the form:

$$\mathrm{K_{eq}} = \frac{[C]^c[D]^d}{[A]^a[B]^b}$$

where a, b, c, and d are the coefficients from the balanced chemical reaction. Pure liquids and solids are excluded from the equation. Since all reactants and products in the problem are gaseous, the equilibrium equation for the reaction would be:

$$\mathrm{K_{eq}} = \frac{[\mathrm{CCl_4}][\mathrm{HCl}]^4}{[\mathrm{CH_4}][\mathrm{Cl_2}]^4}$$

59. C: Catalysts lower the energy barrier between products and reactants and thus increase the reaction rate. Catalysts do not change the thermodynamic position of equilibrium, reaction temperature, or product purity on their own.

60. D: 0.5 g of the salt dissolved, which is 0.005 mol of the salt. Since the volume is 1 L, the molarity of the salt is 0.005 M. This means that both species X and Y are present at 0.005 M concentration. The $K_{sp} = [X][Y]$, or $[0.005][0.005]$ which equals 2.5×10^{-5}.

61. A: Lewis acids are compounds capable of accepting a lone pair of electrons. $AlCl_3$ is a very strong Lewis acid and can readily accept a pair of electrons due to Al only having 6 electrons instead of 8 in its outer shell. $FeCl_3$ is also a strong Lewis acid, though milder than $AlCl_3$. While sulfuric acid is a source for protons, which are considered Lewis acids, in its undissolved state,

H_2SO_4 is not able to accept electrons. PCl_3 is a Lewis base since the P can donate its lone pair of electrons to another species.

62. B: NH_3 is ammonia, which is a base. H_2O is amphoteric, meaning that it can act as either a weak acid or a weak base. HF is actually a weak acid, despite fluorine being the most electronegative atom. The small size of the F results in a stronger bond between the H and F, which reduces acidity since this bond will be harder to break. H_3PO_4, phosphoric acid, is high in acidity and HCl is a very strong acid, meaning it completely dissociates.

63. A: First, one must understand that pK_a is the acidity dissociation number. The larger the number, the less acidic. Acetic acid is a carboxylic acid. When H^+ is given off, a negative charge results on the O. Because there is a second equivalent oxygen bonded to the same carbon, this negative charge can be shared between both oxygen atoms. This is known as resonance stabilization and this conjugate base will be more stable and more of the acid molecules will remain dissociated resulting in higher acidity. For ethanol, when the O-H bond breaks, the negative charge resides completely on the O. It cannot be stabilized by other atoms and therefore reforms the methanol rapidly. This results in very low acidity, since very few protons will be released.

64. C: HCl is a strong acid that will completely dissociate. $pH = -\log_{10}[H^+]$, which for this problem is $pH = -\log_{10}(0.1) = 1$. The volume of the solution has no bearing on the pH since we know the concentration.

65. B: The K_a of acetic acid is determined from the pK_a, $K_a = 10^{-pK_a} = 1.7510^{-5}$. This is the equilibrium constant for the acetic acid dissociation, or $K_a = [H^+]\big[[CH_3COO^-]/[CH_3COOH]\big]$. Using this equilibrium equation to solve for the $[H^+]$, the pH of the buffer can then be found. Solving for the $[H^+]$ concentration, we get $[H^+] = K_a \times \big[[CH_3COOH]/[CH_3COO^-]\big]$, or $[H^+] = 1.75 \times 10^{-5} \times [0.1]/[0.2] = 8.75 \times 10^{-6}$. $pH = -\log[H^+] = 5.05$.

66. C: There are 0.05 mol of sulfuric acid being added, but a total of 0.10 mol of H^+ since sulfuric acid is diprotic (H_2SO_4). This is being added to 0.1 mol of NaOH. The moles of acid and base exactly cancel each other out; therefore, the pH of the resulting aqueous solution will be near 7.

67. D: To make a buffer, a weak acid and its conjugate base or a weak base and its conjugate acid are commonly used. Buffers work by using the common-ion effect and result in little change in the pH when an acid or a base is added. HCl/NaOH is a strong acid/strong base combination and will not result in a buffer solution. Although the $HNO_3/NaNO_3$ and $H_2SO_4/NaHSO_4$ mixtures are conjugate acid/base pairs, both HNO_3 and H_2SO_4 are strong acids, not weak acids. Neither of these solutions would result in a buffer. Only the NaH_2PO_4/Na_2HPO_4 mixture would result in a buffer as it is a combination of a weak acid and its conjugate base.

68. A: When liquid water changes to steam, the temperature is constant, as in all phase changes. The entropy increases due to the increase in disorder from a liquid to a gas.

69. C: The formula for heat change in a system is $Q = mc\Delta T$. Remember that Q is the heat change, m is for the amount of the substance (either in moles or mass depending on the units of the heat capacity), c is the specific heat of the substance, and ΔT is the temperature change of the substance. In this case, since the amount of substance given is a mass, it must be converted to moles to match the units of the heat capacity given. To begin, determine the molar mass of ammonia. Nitrogen is

14.01 g/mol and hydrogen is 1.01 g/mol, so ammonia is 17.04 g/mol. The 100 g of ammonia is equivalent to 5.9 moles. The ΔT is –75 °C, or –75 K. Now, substitute and find the heat change:

$$Q = mc\Delta T$$
$$Q = 5.9 \text{ mol} \times (35.1 \text{ J/(mol} \cdot \text{K)}) \times (-75 \text{ K})$$
$$Q = -15{,}531.8 \text{ J}$$
$$Q \approx -15.5 \text{ kJ}$$

70. A: The heat of combustion is determined by subtracting the heats of formation of the reactants from that of the products. So $3(-393.5) + 4(-285.8) - (-103.8) = -2{,}220$.

71. D: In I, dissolving a solid into a liquid breaks up the organized solid matrix, therefore increasing disorder. III converts single particles into two particles, and in IV, solid ice sublimes into a gas. Both of these processes also increase disorder and thus, entropy. II is a decrease in entropy, since 7 molecules, with 3 being gaseous, are reacted to form 2 solid molecules.

72. C: Because all unique materials have differing heat capacities, no two can heat up the same way. All require different amounts of heat to warm to the same temperature.

73. D: Lead (Pb) goes from a 0 oxidation state to a 2+ oxidation state and is therefore oxidized. Oxidation is the loss of electrons. Hydrogen goes from a 1+ oxidation state to a 0 oxidation state and is therefore reduced. Reduction is the gaining of electrons.

74. C: Reducing agents give up electrons to another chemical species, which cause that species to gain an electron and become reduced. Oxidizing agents cause another species to be oxidized, or to lose an electron, and are themselves reduced as they gain that electron. Bromine is very electronegative and is almost always an oxidizing agent. N_2 is nearly inert, or unreactive. Neon is an inert noble gas and would not be a reducing agent. Sodium (Na) is very reactive and eager to give up an electron, making it a good reducing agent in a wide variety of reactions.

75. C: Reduction takes place at the cathode and oxidation takes place at the anode. Mg^{2+} of the salt will be reduced to Mg at the cathode, and Cl^- will be oxidized to Cl_2 at the anode.

76. D: The fact that ΔG for the reaction is negative indicates the reaction is spontaneous. This does not mean the reaction will be faster or slow. Diamonds, as we all know, do not rapidly convert to graphite, and in fact do so only very slowly, over millions of years, thank goodness.

77. A: The longest straight chain of carbons is four, so the parent name is butane. The alcohol takes number precedence, so it is in the -2- position, placing the methyl in the -3- position. The suffix becomes –ol since it is an alcohol, so the name is 3-methyl-2-butanol.

78. C: The first is an alkyne, which contains a triple bond between carbon atoms. The second is a ketone and contains a carbon-oxygen double bond. The third is an alkene, which has a double bond between two carbon atoms. The fourth is an imide, which contains a double bond between two nitrogen atoms.

79. B: The carbon of a carboxylic acid has three bonds to oxygen atoms and one to a carbon atom. The carbon bonded to the carboxylic carbon will have an oxidation state of zero. Each oxygen atom will have an oxidation number of –2. However, one oxygen is bonded to a hydrogen, which will have an oxidation number of +1. This results in a total oxidation state of –3 for both oxygens and the hydrogen bonded to them. Therefore, since the carbon must balance the oxidation states of the oxygens (–3) and the carbon (0), the oxidation state of the carbon must be +3. The three bonds to oxygen give a +3, and the bond to carbon is 0.

80. A: B is 1-butanol, since its longest chain of carbons is 4, not 3. C is 3-pentanone, since there are 5 carbons in the chain and it is a ketone, rather than a carboxylic acid. D is 1-butene, not 3-butene. The name should be assigned by giving the double bond the lowest number.

81. D: Mendeleev was able to connect the trends of the different elements' behaviors and develop a table that showed the periodicity of the elements and their relationship to each other.

82. D: Different molecules must have the same chemical formula to be isomers. They differ only in which atoms are bound to which. Having the same molecular weight does not necessarily mean two molecules have the same formula.

83. B: Cis isomers have substituent groups that are on the same side of the molecule across the double bond. Trans isomers are those with substituent groups that are on opposite sides of the molecule across the double bond. I is neither cis nor trans, since both substituents on the same carbon are identical. IV is trans because the two methyl groups are on opposite sides of the molecule. II is cis due to both ethyl groups being on the same side of the molecule. III is also considered cis, although each substituent is different. The higher-priority groups on each end of the double bond must be on the same side of the double bond to be cis.

84. A: NMR, or nuclear magnetic resonance, allows one to determine the connectivity of atoms in an organic molecule, by "reading" the resonance signals from the attached hydrogen atoms. IR, or infrared spectroscopy, can help to identify the functional groups that are present, but does not give much information about its position in the molecule. Mass spectrometry breaks apart a large molecule and analyzes the masses of the fragments. It can be useful in analyzing protein structure. HPLC, or high-performance liquid chromatography, is a method used to separate a mixture into its components.

85. C: Proteins are large polypeptides, composed of many amino acids linked together by an amide bond. DNA and RNA are nucleic acids made up of repeating nucleotides. Carbohydrates are long chains of sugars. Triglycerides are fats and are composed of a glycerol molecule and three fatty acids.

86. C: The closer the data points are to each other, the more precise the data. This does not mean the data is accurate, but that the results are very reproducible.

87. A: Density is mass per volume, typically expressed in units such as g/cm^3, or kg/m^3.

88. B: Acids and bases will react violently if accidentally mixed, as will reducing and oxidizing agents. Both reactions can be highly exothermic and uncontrollable.

89. A: Communities around the world who drink fluoridated water have shown dramatic decreases in the number of dental cavities formed per citizen versus those communities that do not drink fluoridated water.

90. D: Combustion of coal releases significant amounts of Hg into the atmosphere. When the Hg settles into the water, it becomes methylated and concentrates in fish, making them toxic to eat.

How to Overcome Test Anxiety

Just the thought of taking a test is enough to make most people a little nervous. A test is an important event that can have a long-term impact on your future, so it's important to take it seriously and it's natural to feel anxious about performing well. But just because anxiety is normal, that doesn't mean that it's helpful in test taking, or that you should simply accept it as part of your life. Anxiety can have a variety of effects. These effects can be mild, like making you feel slightly nervous, or severe, like blocking your ability to focus or remember even a simple detail.

If you experience test anxiety—whether severe or mild—it's important to know how to beat it. To discover this, first you need to understand what causes test anxiety.

Causes of Test Anxiety

While we often think of anxiety as an uncontrollable emotional state, it can actually be caused by simple, practical things. One of the most common causes of test anxiety is that a person does not feel adequately prepared for their test. This feeling can be the result of many different issues such as poor study habits or lack of organization, but the most common culprit is time management. Starting to study too late, failing to organize your study time to cover all of the material, or being distracted while you study will mean that you're not well prepared for the test. This may lead to cramming the night before, which will cause you to be physically and mentally exhausted for the test. Poor time management also contributes to feelings of stress, fear, and hopelessness as you realize you are not well prepared but don't know what to do about it.

Other times, test anxiety is not related to your preparation for the test but comes from unresolved fear. This may be a past failure on a test, or poor performance on tests in general. It may come from comparing yourself to others who seem to be performing better or from the stress of living up to expectations. Anxiety may be driven by fears of the future—how failure on this test would affect your educational and career goals. These fears are often completely irrational, but they can still negatively impact your test performance.

Elements of Test Anxiety

As mentioned earlier, test anxiety is considered to be an emotional state, but it has physical and mental components as well. Sometimes you may not even realize that you are suffering from test anxiety until you notice the physical symptoms. These can include trembling hands, rapid heartbeat, sweating, nausea, and tense muscles. Extreme anxiety may lead to fainting or vomiting. Obviously, any of these symptoms can have a negative impact on testing. It is important to recognize them as soon as they begin to occur so that you can address the problem before it damages your performance.

The mental components of test anxiety include trouble focusing and inability to remember learned information. During a test, your mind is on high alert, which can help you recall information and stay focused for an extended period of time. However, anxiety interferes with your mind's natural processes, causing you to blank out, even on the questions you know well. The strain of testing during anxiety makes it difficult to stay focused, especially on a test that may take several hours. Extreme anxiety can take a huge mental toll, making it difficult not only to recall test information but even to understand the test questions or pull your thoughts together.

Effects of Test Anxiety

Test anxiety is like a disease—if left untreated, it will get progressively worse. Anxiety leads to poor performance, and this reinforces the feelings of fear and failure, which in turn lead to poor performances on subsequent tests. It can grow from a mild nervousness to a crippling condition. If allowed to progress, test anxiety can have a big impact on your schooling, and consequently on your future.

Test anxiety can spread to other parts of your life. Anxiety on tests can become anxiety in any stressful situation, and blanking on a test can turn into panicking in a job situation. But fortunately, you don't have to let anxiety rule your testing and determine your grades. There are a number of relatively simple steps you can take to move past anxiety and function normally on a test and in the rest of life.

Physical Steps for Beating Test Anxiety

While test anxiety is a serious problem, the good news is that it can be overcome. It doesn't have to control your ability to think and remember information. While it may take time, you can begin taking steps today to beat anxiety.

Just as your first hint that you may be struggling with anxiety comes from the physical symptoms, the first step to treating it is also physical. Rest is crucial for having a clear, strong mind. If you are tired, it is much easier to give in to anxiety. But if you establish good sleep habits, your body and mind will be ready to perform optimally, without the strain of exhaustion. Additionally, sleeping well helps you to retain information better, so you're more likely to recall the answers when you see the test questions.

Getting good sleep means more than going to bed on time. It's important to allow your brain time to relax. Take study breaks from time to time so it doesn't get overworked, and don't study right before bed. Take time to rest your mind before trying to rest your body, or you may find it difficult to fall asleep.

Along with sleep, other aspects of physical health are important in preparing for a test. Good nutrition is vital for good brain function. Sugary foods and drinks may give a burst of energy but this burst is followed by a crash, both physically and emotionally. Instead, fuel your body with protein and vitamin-rich foods.

Also, drink plenty of water. Dehydration can lead to headaches and exhaustion, especially if your brain is already under stress from the rigors of the test. Particularly if your test is a long one, drink water during the breaks. And if possible, take an energy-boosting snack to eat between sections.

Along with sleep and diet, a third important part of physical health is exercise. Maintaining a steady workout schedule is helpful, but even taking 5-minute study breaks to walk can help get your blood pumping faster and clear your head. Exercise also releases endorphins, which contribute to a positive feeling and can help combat test anxiety.

When you nurture your physical health, you are also contributing to your mental health. If your body is healthy, your mind is much more likely to be healthy as well. So take time to rest, nourish your body with healthy food and water, and get moving as much as possible. Taking these physical steps will make you stronger and more able to take the mental steps necessary to overcome test anxiety.

Mental Steps for Beating Test Anxiety

Working on the mental side of test anxiety can be more challenging, but as with the physical side, there are clear steps you can take to overcome it. As mentioned earlier, test anxiety often stems from lack of preparation, so the obvious solution is to prepare for the test. Effective studying may be the most important weapon you have for beating test anxiety, but you can and should employ several other mental tools to combat fear.

First, boost your confidence by reminding yourself of past success—tests or projects that you aced. If you're putting as much effort into preparing for this test as you did for those, there's no reason you should expect to fail here. Work hard to prepare; then trust your preparation.

Second, surround yourself with encouraging people. It can be helpful to find a study group, but be sure that the people you're around will encourage a positive attitude. If you spend time with others who are anxious or cynical, this will only contribute to your own anxiety. Look for others who are motivated to study hard from a desire to succeed, not from a fear of failure.

Third, reward yourself. A test is physically and mentally tiring, even without anxiety, and it can be helpful to have something to look forward to. Plan an activity following the test, regardless of the outcome, such as going to a movie or getting ice cream.

When you are taking the test, if you find yourself beginning to feel anxious, remind yourself that you know the material. Visualize successfully completing the test. Then take a few deep, relaxing breaths and return to it. Work through the questions carefully but with confidence, knowing that you are capable of succeeding.

Developing a healthy mental approach to test taking will also aid in other areas of life. Test anxiety affects more than just the actual test—it can be damaging to your mental health and even contribute to depression. It's important to beat test anxiety before it becomes a problem for more than testing.

Study Strategy

Being prepared for the test is necessary to combat anxiety, but what does being prepared look like? You may study for hours on end and still not feel prepared. What you need is a strategy for test prep. The next few pages outline our recommended steps to help you plan out and conquer the challenge of preparation.

Step 1: Scope Out the Test

Learn everything you can about the format (multiple choice, essay, etc.) and what will be on the test. Gather any study materials, course outlines, or sample exams that may be available. Not only will this help you to prepare, but knowing what to expect can help to alleviate test anxiety.

Step 2: Map Out the Material

Look through the textbook or study guide and make note of how many chapters or sections it has. Then divide these over the time you have. For example, if a book has 15 chapters and you have five days to study, you need to cover three chapters each day. Even better, if you have the time, leave an extra day at the end for overall review after you have gone through the material in depth.

If time is limited, you may need to prioritize the material. Look through it and make note of which sections you think you already have a good grasp on, and which need review. While you are studying, skim quickly through the familiar sections and take more time on the challenging parts.

Write out your plan so you don't get lost as you go. Having a written plan also helps you feel more in control of the study, so anxiety is less likely to arise from feeling overwhelmed at the amount to cover.

Step 3: Gather Your Tools

Decide what study method works best for you. Do you prefer to highlight in the book as you study and then go back over the highlighted portions? Or do you type out notes of the important information? Or is it helpful to make flashcards that you can carry with you? Assemble the pens, index cards, highlighters, post-it notes, and any other materials you may need so you won't be distracted by getting up to find things while you study.

If you're having a hard time retaining the information or organizing your notes, experiment with different methods. For example, try color-coding by subject with colored pens, highlighters, or post-it notes. If you learn better by hearing, try recording yourself reading your notes so you can listen while in the car, working out, or simply sitting at your desk. Ask a friend to quiz you from your flashcards, or try teaching someone the material to solidify it in your mind.

Step 4: Create Your Environment

It's important to avoid distractions while you study. This includes both the obvious distractions like visitors and the subtle distractions like an uncomfortable chair (or a too-comfortable couch that makes you want to fall asleep). Set up the best study environment possible: good lighting and a comfortable work area. If background music helps you focus, you may want to turn it on, but otherwise keep the room quiet. If you are using a computer to take notes, be sure you don't have any other windows open, especially applications like social media, games, or anything else that could distract you. Silence your phone and turn off notifications. Be sure to keep water close by so you stay hydrated while you study (but avoid unhealthy drinks and snacks).

Also, take into account the best time of day to study. Are you freshest first thing in the morning? Try to set aside some time then to work through the material. Is your mind clearer in the afternoon or evening? Schedule your study session then. Another method is to study at the same time of day that you will take the test, so that your brain gets used to working on the material at that time and will be ready to focus at test time.

Step 5: Study!

Once you have done all the study preparation, it's time to settle into the actual studying. Sit down, take a few moments to settle your mind so you can focus, and begin to follow your study plan. Don't give in to distractions or let yourself procrastinate. This is your time to prepare so you'll be ready to fearlessly approach the test. Make the most of the time and stay focused.

Of course, you don't want to burn out. If you study too long you may find that you're not retaining the information very well. Take regular study breaks. For example, taking five minutes out of every hour to walk briskly, breathing deeply and swinging your arms, can help your mind stay fresh.

As you get to the end of each chapter or section, it's a good idea to do a quick review. Remind yourself of what you learned and work on any difficult parts. When you feel that you've mastered the material, move on to the next part. At the end of your study session, briefly skim through your notes again.

But while review is helpful, cramming last minute is NOT. If at all possible, work ahead so that you won't need to fit all your study into the last day. Cramming overloads your brain with more information than it can process and retain, and your tired mind may struggle to recall even previously learned information when it is overwhelmed with last-minute study. Also, the urgent nature of cramming and the stress placed on your brain contribute to anxiety. You'll be more likely to go to the test feeling unprepared and having trouble thinking clearly.

So don't cram, and don't stay up late before the test, even just to review your notes at a leisurely pace. Your brain needs rest more than it needs to go over the information again. In fact, plan to finish your studies by noon or early afternoon the day before the test. Give your brain the rest of the day to relax or focus on other things, and get a good night's sleep. Then you will be fresh for the test and better able to recall what you've studied.

Step 6: Take a Practice Test

Many courses offer sample tests, either online or in the study materials. This is an excellent resource to check whether you have mastered the material, as well as to prepare for the test format and environment.

Check the test format ahead of time: the number of questions, the type (multiple choice, free response, etc.), and the time limit. Then create a plan for working through them. For example, if you have 30 minutes to take a 60-question test, your limit is 30 seconds per question. Spend less time on the questions you know well so that you can take more time on the difficult ones.

If you have time to take several practice tests, take the first one open book, with no time limit. Work through the questions at your own pace and make sure you fully understand them. Gradually work up to taking a test under test conditions: sit at a desk with all study materials put away and set a timer. Pace yourself to make sure you finish the test with time to spare and go back to check your answers if you have time.

After each test, check your answers. On the questions you missed, be sure you understand why you missed them. Did you misread the question (tests can use tricky wording)? Did you forget the information? Or was it something you hadn't learned? Go back and study any shaky areas that the practice tests reveal.

Taking these tests not only helps with your grade, but also aids in combating test anxiety. If you're already used to the test conditions, you're less likely to worry about it, and working through tests until you're scoring well gives you a confidence boost. Go through the practice tests until you feel comfortable, and then you can go into the test knowing that you're ready for it.

Test Tips

On test day, you should be confident, knowing that you've prepared well and are ready to answer the questions. But aside from preparation, there are several test day strategies you can employ to maximize your performance.

First, as stated before, get a good night's sleep the night before the test (and for several nights before that, if possible). Go into the test with a fresh, alert mind rather than staying up late to study.

Try not to change too much about your normal routine on the day of the test. It's important to eat a nutritious breakfast, but if you normally don't eat breakfast at all, consider eating just a protein bar. If you're a coffee drinker, go ahead and have your normal coffee. Just make sure you time it so that the caffeine doesn't wear off right in the middle of your test. Avoid sugary beverages, and drink enough water to stay hydrated but not so much that you need a restroom break 10 minutes into the test. If your test isn't first thing in the morning, consider going for a walk or doing a light workout before the test to get your blood flowing.

Allow yourself enough time to get ready, and leave for the test with plenty of time to spare so you won't have the anxiety of scrambling to arrive in time. Another reason to be early is to select a good seat. It's helpful to sit away from doors and windows, which can be distracting. Find a good seat, get out your supplies, and settle your mind before the test begins.

When the test begins, start by going over the instructions carefully, even if you already know what to expect. Make sure you avoid any careless mistakes by following the directions.

Then begin working through the questions, pacing yourself as you've practiced. If you're not sure on an answer, don't spend too much time on it, and don't let it shake your confidence. Either skip it and come back later, or eliminate as many wrong answers as possible and guess among the remaining ones. Don't dwell on these questions as you continue—put them out of your mind and focus on what lies ahead.

Be sure to read all of the answer choices, even if you're sure the first one is the right answer. Sometimes you'll find a better one if you keep reading. But don't second-guess yourself if you do immediately know the answer. Your gut instinct is usually right. Don't let test anxiety rob you of the information you know.

If you have time at the end of the test (and if the test format allows), go back and review your answers. Be cautious about changing any, since your first instinct tends to be correct, but make sure you didn't misread any of the questions or accidentally mark the wrong answer choice. Look over any you skipped and make an educated guess.

At the end, leave the test feeling confident. You've done your best, so don't waste time worrying about your performance or wishing you could change anything. Instead, celebrate the successful completion of this test. And finally, use this test to learn how to deal with anxiety even better next time.

Review Video: Test Anxiety
Visit mometrix.com/academy and enter code: 100340

Important Qualification

Not all anxiety is created equal. If your test anxiety is causing major issues in your life beyond the classroom or testing center, or if you are experiencing troubling physical symptoms related to your anxiety, it may be a sign of a serious physiological or psychological condition. If this sounds like your situation, we strongly encourage you to seek professional help.

Online Resources

Due to our efforts to try to keep this book to a manageable length, we've created a link that will give you access to all of your online resources:

mometrix.com/resources719/gacechemistry

It's Your Moment, Let's Celebrate It!

Share your story @mometrixtestpreparation